Uncommon People

Also by Miranda Sawyer

Park and Ride
Out of Time

Uncommon People

Britpop and Beyond in 20 Songs

Miranda Sawyer

JOHN MURRAY

First published in Great Britain in 2024 by John Murray (Publishers)

1

Copyright © Miranda Sawyer 2024

The right of Miranda Sawyer to be identified as the
Author of the Work has been asserted by her in accordance
with the Copyright, Designs and Patents Act 1988.

Chapter ornament © Delyrica/shutterstock.com

A CIP catalogue record for this title is available from the British Library

Hardback ISBN 9781399816892
Trade Paperback ISBN 9781399816908
ebook ISBN 9781399816922

Typeset in Minion Pro by Palimpsest Book Production Ltd,
Falkirk, Stirlingshire

Printed and bound in Great Britain by Clays Ltd, Elcograf S.p.A.

John Murray policy is to use papers that are natural, renewable and
recyclable products and made from wood grown in sustainable forests.
The logging and manufacturing processes are expected to conform to the
environmental regulations of the country of origin.

Carmelite House
50 Victoria Embankment
London EC4Y 0DZ

www.johnmurraypress.co.uk

John Murray Press, part of Hodder & Stoughton Limited
An Hachette UK company

The authorised representative in the EEA is Hachette Ireland, 8 Castlecour
Centre, Castleknock Road, Castleknock, Dublin 15, D15 YF6A, Ireland

You could strike sparks anywhere. There was a fantastic universal sense that whatever we were doing was right, that we were winning . . . We had all the momentum; we were riding the crest of a high and beautiful wave.

Hunter S. Thompson, *Fear and Loathing in Las Vegas*

Contents

Contents

Introduction

There are people who could spend all day arguing about Britpop: what it was, what it is, who invented it, when it started and ended, which bands are Britpop and which aren't. These people are journalists. Specifically, music journalists, who possess the pedantic instinct of all journalists to get the facts right, but also, because they write about pop music, have a competing desire to be romantic. To mythologise. To make people and events and songs and whole entire years seem more flamboyant, more life-changing and revolutionary than they actually were. The sort of people who, when 'Common People' is played in a bar, instead of dancing, or singing along, sit tight with a pint and physically pull your head closer to their mouth so you can hear them bang on about how they knew Pulp years before and what this song actually means, in case you didn't know. And – stop struggling – how all those bastards who say they know what was going on have got it wrong, because they were just patronising schmoozers or they weren't even there. (Full disclosure: I am a music journalist. But I also like to dance.)

The people who don't argue about it are the fans and the musicians. The fans, if they're of a certain age, remember a time when they felt like they were flying, when music meant everything to them because they were young and full of yearning and hope, and the songs were made by people who were young and hopeful and yearning too. That perfect era when the full-steam-ahead singers and the angst-driven guitarists and louche bassists and the madmen on the drums seemed like you, but cooler. They *were* you, distilled and made better-looking. Younger fans, if they're interested, tap into this without thinking about it. They just love the fantastic songs and, sometimes, how the bands looked at their peak.

The musicians don't argue about Britpop because they refuse to acknowledge it ever existed. Or at least, they refuse to acknowledge that they were part of it. No musician – no artist, really – ever wants to be lumped into a larger group of other bands whose music they might not like, or who they slagged off when they were drunk, or who they're a bit touchy about because they earnt more money than they did and played bigger venues. You can't say the B word around any '90s musician, because it will make them cross. It's the past, and artists are interested in what they're doing now, and believe that it's better – more interesting, less obvious – than the work they created when they were young. Sometimes they're right.

And this is all fine. Because we can believe that Britpop existed and we can believe it didn't, all at the same time.

Because there definitely were a few months in the mid-1990s when UK indie-pop bubbled up from its alternative, outsider origins to bound its way to actual Number Ones and shimmy into front-page mainstream culture. And it was genuinely thrilling, in the move-over-grandad-it's-our-time-now way of all youth-culture explosions. And there definitely was a time – a final, pre-internet time, music-biz hoorah – when boys in second-hand Crimplene trousers and girls in bovver boots somehow became worshipped rather than sneered at. When U2 had to step aside to let characters as unsettling as Brett Anderson and PJ Harvey and Thom Yorke take centre stage. When offbeat young people, by virtue of their enormous charm, excellent clothes sense, interesting reference points and brilliant tunes actually altered the country's everyday culture. That all happened.

And so Blur went to Walthamstow dog track to be interviewed and local kids shouted, 'I bet your mum cut your hair!' and, 'You look like my grandad. He has them glasses!' And Noel and Liam Gallagher argued in an *NME* interview and the recording of it was turned into a single on Fierce Panda. And Jarvis Cocker appeared on a TV show called *Pop Quiz*, with Des'ree and Chesney Hawkes, and, after a slow start, went on to bang through the quick-fire-round questions and pull his team to victory.

But that time, at the time, wasn't called anything. Everyone involved was too busy to give what was going on a name; plus, even then, no one in a band wanted to be pinned down to a collective label with other, rival bands.

And even when the term Britpop began to be bandied about, in late 1994, early 1995, by people other than the musicians – 'people' meaning journalists – it felt reductive. Surely what was going on was too diverse, too messy, too competitive, changeable and awkward to be categorised? This was because the scene, such as it was, was full of diverse, messy, competitive, changeable, awkward people, who were still quite young and unsure of how they might fit in or what their talent could mean or where it could take them. Were Underworld Britpop? Was Tricky? Or Garbage?

And what if you were Scottish, Welsh or Irish? You wouldn't be that happy with such a label. It was only the English (and Northern Irish Protestants) who wanted to be called British. For an awkward English person, calling yourself that meant you could somehow include all the cooler countries of the UK while also distancing yourself from St George's flag-waving racists. For everyone else, it was embarrassing.

I sometimes wonder if the bands who hate being called Britpop might be more inclined to have that name attached to them if it was, simply, a better word. A lot of punk bands don't mind being called punks; rave acts will acknowledge that, yes, they're partial to a rave; many grime artists accept that grime is a genre, even if they've moved on from it. But Britpop: nope. But there we were and here we are. Britpop is a word. And, like I said, there are grown men who argue about it. Who used it first?

It wasn't in Stuart Maconie's 1993 article about exciting new UK bands in *Select* magazine, which featured Brett from Suede looking foxy on the cover with a Union Jack behind him. (The flag was added after the photo session.) The cover line reads 'YANKS GO HOME', and Maconie's feature, which was funny and teasing, as well as sincere, argued that, although Nirvana were a great group, the American rock groups that came in Nirvana's wake were not, and surely it was time for some fantastic new British talent to get a look in. Aside from Maconie's overriding argument, there were interviews with Suede, Saint Etienne, The Auteurs, Denim and Pulp. (No Blur, because they'd been in the mag the month before.) It was in an article about Blur in *The Face* in August 1994, by Cliff Jones, where he wrote, 'If punk was the last English revolt into style, its legacy was a re-empowering of Brit pop.' And by the start of 1995, John Harris could dot 'Britpop' throughout an *NME* article entitled 'Modern Life Is . . . Brilliant!' and know that every reader understood what he meant. 'Think about the wonderment oozed by Suede and Oasis and Blur and Elastica,' he wrote, 'and allow yourself one smug thought: what a fantastic time to be young.'

Perhaps it was a feeling, then. A sensation of 'this is our time'. Youth culture waves tend to need a name, whether that's New Romantic or rave or shoegaze or emo, just so people outside that culture can understand a bit about what's going on. (Youth culture likes adult adult culture to disapprove of it, and a label helps.) And journalists, especially back then, delighted in creating those names. Before Britpop, there was a different tag for the loose collective of alternative indie bands that gathered at Syndrome, the small shiny indie music club on the south side of Oxford Street every Thursday between 1990 and '91, where Carl from Cud DJ'd. They were called 'The Scene That Celebrates Itself'. A bit long.

So if Britpop exists and doesn't, all at once, what does 'Britpop' mean now? Well, it's a search term. Music retailers like categories, as do bookshops, dating apps and Spotify recommendations. And Britpop signifies UK indie-pop music of the mid-'90s, in the same way as the late 1960s era of The Beatles and The Stones is called the Swingin' '60s, or early 2000s London UK hip-hop is usually described as grime, or grime kids. It's a sales shorthand. An if-you-like-this-why-not-try-these indicator. Are you browsing in the Britpop aisle? Buying a kilo of Elastica? Why not try this sample-size Supergrass?

All good – except that over the years, the label seems to have edited the music and the people that were around at that time. They've been flattened out, made boring. The Britpop label has become limited. Now, it appears to mean cheery, plodding, meat-and-potatoes, four-white-guys indie-rock with roots in '60s pop and '70s glam. But the music of that time, and the people that made it, were better than that. More interesting. More thrilling. Weirder.

Let's decide that the years between that April 1993 'Yanks Go Home' *Select* cover and August 1997, when Oasis released *Be Here Now*, are the years that we are discussing. In that time, a vast array, a fast affray of very different artists and bands such as Elastica, Manic Street Preachers, The Chemical Brothers, Garbage, Radiohead, Supergrass, Sleeper, Tricky, Underworld, PJ Harvey, The Prodigy – as well as Oasis, Blur, Pulp and Suede* – all blossomed and came to the fore. (Look at that festival line-up! Every one a winner!) All excellent, all very different, all from the UK (well: one-quarter from the UK, with Garbage).

And if we extend out, just a little, from that time, then we can pull in artists and songs that helped create that unusually celebratory mid-'90s atmosphere, or who stretched the upbeat feeling on towards the end of the decade. The musicians that ran with the central Britpop idea of making pop tunes whilst not compromising

---

* Only room for twenty songs on this particular mixtape, sadly.

on invention or identity, that knew what they wanted to do and how they wanted to look while they were doing it, that made odd music, specific to themselves, that somehow ended up winning the hearts of thousands. We want the bangers, the big singalong-ers, and we want the weirdo outsiders who found their voice and their moment, who stepped centre-stage and showed us all who they were; and, thus, who we were.

That's what *Uncommon People* is about. Just how excellent, how wide and deep and tall the music was. How exceptional the musicians were, and are, who made those songs. And if we concentrate on the songs of these bands at that time, we can show how important they were, plug into the small – yet suddenly big – lives of the people who made those songs and the mad exhilaration of what it was like to hear them, fresh, for the first time. You might not like all of the bands in this book. But you'll love the mixtape.

In the mid-'90s, I was writing for *Select* and *The Face*. *Select* was a monthly music magazine that combined the *NME*'s in-depth indie music knowledge with *Smash Hits*' cheeky attitude and ace posters, and it's what I think of, when I think of Britpop. It's what I'm channelling for this book. At *Select* our music adoration was expansive: we loved The Prodigy as much as we loved Suede, Stereolab as much as the Peej or Blur or Underworld. We loved any band with their own unique idea – their own daft manifesto – as well as their own particular sound and way of dressing; and we loved the fun of pop, the joy of mouthy popstars and up-and-at-you tunes. No time for tedious worthiness, for hey-man-we-make-music-for-ourselves-and-if-anyone-else-likes-it-it's-a-bonus rock. No dullards allowed. In *Select*, or in this book.

I was the same age as most of the bands that were coming up, and I was sent to hang out with them in pubs or travel around with them for a few days on tour. This was easy, really, as most of the musicians were out at the places I was, or knew the same people, so I could sort of fit in. And if we didn't know each other, we could understand each other anyway, because our reference points were the same. *Top of the Pops. Quadrophenia.* Mike Leigh. *Get Carter. The Great Escape. À Bout de Souffle.*

It's exciting, if stressful, dropping in and out of a band's world. Weird, if you've met them before they'd hit it big, when they were playing smaller venues to a handful of people and falling off the speaker stack because they were drunk before they'd even got on stage. Those little gigs were fine, but they couldn't prepare you, really, for when things got crazy.

You can tell when a band is hitting the big time because to arrive as an interviewer is like you're hopping on to a speeding train. Someone opens the door for a second, you run as fast as you can, and jump in. And then you can only bear it for a couple of days. The energy at the gigs is like a tornado, yanking everyone into the air, smashing them down, throwing them around, and that energy stays, doesn't quite disperse, when the band drinks afterwards at the hotel bar, with all the new friends that arrive when you're the most exciting thing to happen to a town. There's a wildness, an edgy feeling. Things get messy.

And so protectors become necessary. The people who keep journalists away. It could be hard, sometimes, to get anyone in the band to talk to you at all, even if they'd agreed to, even if they liked you. The press officer would plead. The tour manager would negotiate. And you'd get forty-five minutes in a portacabin with the singer in those tense, limbic moments between soundcheck and the actual gig. Or half an hour the morning after, when everyone was still smashed.

And then, you left the tour, hopped off that train, to return home to sit in your room and transcribe your burbled drunken interview, to try and make sense of what you've just witnessed, encapsulate the madness into 3,000 words. The bands continued on, to play gigs, and get hammered and avoid talking to other journalists in Glasgow, in Berlin, in Tokyo. For them, their new success was relentless and unforgiving, as well as exhilarating.

There is no way that anyone who goes through what the bigger bands went through in the '90s won't go bananas. Especially the lead singer, the recognisable one. Success is a destruction of everything you thought you were, as well as a validation.

All artists think of themselves as outsiders. Anyone who's felt ignored because they're the wrong class, or out of place at a party, or angry at the old people who form the Establishment, and who uses their discomfort to create something to make themselves feel better in this world . . . those people are never going to feel as though they belong to any recognisable scene or identifiable group. When they're young, their outsider awkwardness and resentment is what fires them into action. So when people who don't know them give them attention, assess their work, talk about them, line up to tell them they're brilliant, it wrecks their very sense of themselves. Finally, you made it! Into the VIP area where you hate everyone you meet.

And to come out the other side, years on, to move into middle age intact (if you're lucky), with a continuing career, or a different one: that is a special heroism. Because the outsider feeling doesn't go away. So, of course, you will prickle if your music is called Britpop. But you might also be delighted when you realise that actually, what you created when you were alienated and resentful is now not only accepted, but celebrated. That, actually, lots of people care.

If you're not in a band, but just reporting on bands, it's a strange thing to realise that a certain time in your past, with all its drunken embarrassments and money regrets and appalling kick-flare trousers, forms part of a recognised era, or a 'scene'. That a particular part of your life, which seemed not so different from the times before and after, a time that merged with them, is considered to be more important than your life five years before, or five years later.

(There are upsides, of course, to having been part of a time deemed special. Those appalling trousers? You can put them onto a second-hand clothes website and label them "90s style' and someone much younger than you will snap them up in a trice. And be delighted to receive them.)

Britpop is like other youth cultures: it was a small, friendly, competitive, alternative music scene packed with talent, and with people who wrote about that talent, and all those elements made it successful. And good music has continued to be made since then, of course. But in the mid-1990s, the UK music ecosystem had a heft and power that it doesn't have now. The music business was making a lot of money, and musicians got some of that money in record deals, even if they made music deemed awkward or hard to get your ears around. The thriving music press – *Select*, *Q*, *Smash Hits*, *NME*, *Melody Maker*, *Mixmag*, *DJ*, *Jockey Slut*, *Mojo* – got some of that money, too, so us writers and photographers went on properly funded trips with pop stars, and press officers and stylists were paid well. The musicians and the journalists would argue and have a laugh. They were intertwined.

Things aren't the same today, because there isn't as much money in the music industry, due to social media, streaming, the death of music magazines and the way that '90s music almost worked too well. Before the '90s, music wasn't really covered seriously in newspapers. Now, papers are often the only place for musicians to be seen.

But still, the UK is good at pop music. The US is good at films, we're good at pop. It's our greatest export. We're the best at creating bands, whether chart-eating O2-headlining monsters or small, offbeat solo artists. Underground music scenes pop up and flourish constantly in our restless, combative, creative, competitive culture. Teenagers and people in their twenties are programmed to chuck over the older generation, to bitch and moan and hang out together and wear odd clothes and take whatever is obsessing their own generation and turn it into three-minute tunes. Only later will some of these teenage scenes be deemed important, and that will be for various reasons. One is because the people who loved those artists get older and become more powerful, and they decide that their youthful high time was the best there ever was, and we all need a few documentaries about it. The other is that a song is used in a film and younger people discover this old scene and find elements that ring true to them, or fashion that feels fresh.

My daughter asked me the other day if I'd ever heard of Blur. Which is sweet and also funny, because she'd found out about them on TikTok, so she'd heard their songs all speeded up, as though played by squeaky cartoon pigs. 'Parklife', a cartoon song with a comic-strip video, sounds even more cartoony and comic strip when played at 1.5x speed.

This book is for my daughter, and for anyone who found a '90s band via social media and wondered who they were. But it's also for those of us who were there and are old enough to remember, but don't, not really. My memory is a disgrace. I never kept a diary, because I never thought my life – inner or outer – was worth documenting. And I was always out, and I only wrote if someone I respected and was a bit scared of was shouting at me about deadlines. (This is still the case.) But by working my way through my old work, by reading magazines I wrote for and talking to people who were there, about what they were doing and feeling, I've remembered.

So, I hope to give you a flavour of my Britpop, of what that mythical time and place and music was like. The atmosphere that the songs were created in. Some of that was large scale – who was in government at the time. But some of it was small: little ventures that took off. Small record labels, one-person press companies, a couple of friends who decided to form a band and put an advert in *Melody Maker* to get a bass player. And then they turn up at a grotty cold room and play their instruments and try out lyrics and attempt to create something amazing together. And it doesn't work for a bit and then, suddenly, it does. A song becomes real. One that changes other people's lives, as well as their own.

Because the songs are the thing, really. We might like to label them as part of a scene, but the songs always break free. It's the songs that have lasted, that bring in new fans and fill stadiums with people that weren't even born when they were released. So why not look at that time through the songs, as well as the clothes, the arguments, the love affairs, the rivalries? Why not find our way around that time in them? Songs cut through lives, stretch the years, compress them, make us cry on the top floor of the bus when everything's OK really, it's just life, you know, its desperation, its joy. They're not only about what's gone, though they can be a short cut there. They live in the moment, and because they do, they make us young and old, alone and together, back in the past and completely of now, all at the same time.

So let's make a mixtape, shall we? Don't forget to dance.

Some Things Are More Important Than Ability

SUEDE

'The Wild Ones'

Break-ups are what pop music is about. A broken heart gives us the music with a crack in it, the songs that catch you unawares, that soar and fall, that conjure quiet tears while you're queuing in a shop, that express all the hurt you can't articulate.

With Suede, unusually, a break-up actually created the band itself. And then another sent it in a different direction.

Before the break-up, though, the love affair. Actually, the love affairs. There are a few to consider. Shall we start with the central one, the flame to the fire? OK, let's begin with Suede and the press. Not really. We'll get to that later, along with the intense love affair between Suede and their fans, the one between them and chemical excess, and the one between them and their specific idea of romance. Which was not pop's usual hearts and flowers, but something wilder, more doomed and passionate, more entwined with the city. A cheap, grimy, frenzied, vulnerable, potent desire.

But we'll start where you want us to start. With ordinary/extraordinary young love.

Brett Anderson and Justine Frischmann met at UCL in the late '80s. Brett had a bob haircut and earrings, and Justine wasn't sure if he was a boy or a girl. Justine wore big clompy boots and old T-shirts which 'just managed to make her look more elegant and moneyed', according to Brett. Actually, she was so posh that when Brett and she first had a conversation, and he heard her languid, educated drawl, he thought she had a speech impediment. When she found out his dad was a taxi driver, she said she thought that was romantic.

They were friends, and then boyfriend and girlfriend. Brett was living with Mat Osman, Suede's eventual bassist, in a multi-tenanted house in Finsbury Park, and then a similar place in North Kensington. Justine had a flat in Kensington, paid for by her dad. They learnt from each other: Brett taught Justine about music (The Fall, The Smiths, Happy Mondays, Felt), she introduced him to art (Ingres, Allen Jones, Walter Gropius). They went to posh tea shops and marvelled at the hair-lacquered ladies; tried out wafty rave club Whirl-Y-Gig; lounged around drinking tea in her flat. She had a futon, an open fire, a Dansette record player, cats.

After a while, Brett, Mat and Justine started playing music together: Neil Young, David Bowie, The Cure and a few of Brett's own compositions. They called themselves The Perfect. Though they weren't yet great, by any stretch, they had ambition, taste and looks. Important attributes for any band, and they knew this, though they didn't yet fully understand their true power. They did know they needed someone else on guitar, so, in October 1989, they put an advert in the *NME*'s Musicians Wanted. It referenced 'Smiths, Commotions, Bowie, PSB'. They also put 'No musos please' and 'Some things are more important than ability'. (Ambition, taste, looks.)

And, all of a sudden, a new love affair began. Nineteen-year-old Bernard Butler walked in and shook all three of them up. They were completely wowed by his exceptional talent, but also his understated self-belief. Bernard was technically brilliant, hard-working, confident, with fantastic hair (important) and a sense of a clock ticking (yes, that too). 'You'd better get on with it, then,' he said when he first met the others, because Brett and Mat were twenty-two and, he thought, getting too old for what they wanted to do, which was be in a successful band. Bernard kicked everyone out of their cosy fug.

This new love – for Bernard's guitar playing – utterly changed Suede's dynamic (the new band name was Brett's idea, he liked it partly for its graphic potential). Bernard kept coming up with music; so Brett had to find the words. Also, Brett realised that his own guitar talents weren't anywhere near as good as Bernard's, so he'd better stop, and, instead, step up and sing. 'I wasn't a very good lead guitar player,' he told me. 'But I think that singing is a fascinating thing, because to be a good singer, you don't really have to be able to sing.' Brett could sing, of course, with drama and onstage abandon, though it took him some time to, as he put it, 'embrace the violence, madness and the river of feeling' that he felt he needed to become a real frontman and singer.

Although later it would seem as though Suede arrived as an

entirely thought-through concept, a full and whole idea, from passionate songs to untamed live act to 'big girl's blouse' style, in truth, everything about them was hard-won, earnt, worked at. Suede progressed bit-by-bit; they inched towards the beautiful. Brett and Mat met in 1984 at Haywards Heath College when they were seventeen (Brett was in a motorbike and folk-music phase; Mat, politically minded, slightly gothy, asked Brett to join his band, Paint It Black). Justine arrived three years later; Bernard, a year after that; and – after some try-outs for a drummer including Justin Welch, who would join Elastica, and Mike Joyce, who'd been in The Smiths – they recruited Simon Gilbert in June 1991. And still, it took almost two more years.

After Bernard joined, for some time Suede had the ideas, but not the ability to bring them to life. They still looked wrong (a bit floppy, a bit post-Madchester: 'all the charisma and presence of toilet-roll holders', remembered Brett). And, in terms of playing: 'We were terrible,' Brett told me later. 'Such bad musicians – apart from Bernard, who was brilliant. We weren't even able to emulate the hit bands at the time. We couldn't even sound like My Jealous God, or Northern Uproar.' They bashed on, performing live when they could (they played to four people; once, at the Amersham Arms in New Cross, they played to one). They made demo tapes. Justine would put on a leather skirt and go and sit in the foyer of record companies, trying to find someone to listen to their cassette.

Gradually, they started to play gigs outside London. On 16 October 1990, Suede supported Blur at the Zap Club in Brighton. It was the day after Blur's first single, 'She's So High', was released.

Damon was rude to them (when Justine said she wanted a Blur poster, he told her to buy one), but was actually very taken with Justine. He got her number, called her up. 'He announced that I was the one, and we would be married and I had no choice in the matter,' Justine said. No one had told her that before. A little later, Brett made a casual comment along the lines of, when they finished college, Justine could get a job as an architect and he would stay in the flat, doing the hoovering and making dinner. 'I had this vision of me working,' said Justine, and Brett being at home with a pinny on, cooking vegetarian pizza – and I just thought, "I can't let this happen. This isn't working."' Something was ending for Justine and something else was starting. In February 1991, Justine agreed to go out with Damon. A couple of months later, she and Brett finished.

It was incredibly painful for Brett. But it was necessary. 'I was very happy, living with Justine,' he told me. 'We had a fantastic time together, and young love is amazing. But it's not conducive to creating interesting, tormented, passionate music. I needed some sort of motor to get myself off my arse and have something to write about.'

After Justine and Brett split (him moving out of her flat, finding somewhere else to live), there were some weird months when they weren't together, but she was still in the band. That time was, said Brett, 'really odd, sticky, strange'. She would talk about Blur, which didn't help, but also, she was asking questions about Suede, wanting them to be different. In the autumn of 1991, Brett kicked her out of the band.

The break-up. Once Justine left, everything changed. Suede had two types of songs: punky, short and clever; and expansive, love-and-poison, London-is-ours epics. With Justine gone, they could ditch the first and lean into Brett's vision of the dark romance of the city, its seedy underground beauty. The remaining four – Brett, Bernard, Mat, Simon – all locked together. It was 'like magnets', Brett told me. 'It wasn't the missing piece, it was the removal of the piece. Suddenly we just linked, and all four of us became a little bit telepathic. We didn't talk about it too much, we just did it. Me and Bernard started writing these songs, and it was, "Oh, this is what we're doing now."'

The rest of the band supported Brett through his heartache, in the way that inarticulate young musicians do: by making music together. And Brett, devastated, shocked out of his cosy coupledom, had his ambition sharpened by hurt. Now he had two real reasons to write: broken heart, cold revenge. (Actually, three: rent.) This break-up was the catalyst. Suede became Suede in November 1991.

'I remember seeing Suede at an early gig at the Forum [then the Town and Country Club] and pissing myself laughing,' said The Wonder Stuff's Miles Hunt. 'He was doing the moves, but it was like Leonard Rossiter on a bad day. I couldn't see the sex in it at all.'

Suede were now Suede; but there were still more dues to be paid. In 1991, the music press, along with most of the music business, were not looking for an outré, glam, sexually ambiguous pop band, with a singer who had a penchant for posing in beads, his shirt undone to the belly. The Stone Roses had caused a massive splash, but, after 'Fools Gold' in 1990, had gone quiet. In the gap they left behind nestled a few Madchester-type bands – Happy Mondays, obviously, but also Inspiral Carpets, Northern Uproar, London's Flowered Up. From America, there was hip-hop and grunge, though it was more difficult for British music papers to get access to those bands. And, coming up fast, hopping onto the inkie front pages like a pack of friendly puppies, was a selection of cheerful, rowdy, long-haired shorts-wearers from the Midlands. Grebo: as if the roadies were actually the band.

Back then, the weekly music press was obsessed with inventing new music scenes, with putting bands together and finding the link. Between 1988 and 1991 there had been genuinely culture-changing music movements – acid house, rave, Madchester – that had seemed to topple down on top of each other, they'd arrived so fast. And now the inkies wanted more. They were constantly connecting bands that shared a record label, or a haircut, or a drum-beat. And they loved making up new names for these so-called scenes.

Here are a few. Grebo. These were bands mostly from Stourbridge – Pop Will Eat Itself, The Wonder Stuff, Ned's Atomic Dustbin – who made forgettable jump-up-and-down chum-pop. Closely related was the slightly grungier fraggle: Carter the Unstoppable Sex Machine, Mega City Four and Senseless Things. Somewhere swirling around in there was shoegaze, which really existed (dreamy pop soundscapes made by Ride, Moose, Slowdive). Also The Scene That Celebrates Itself, which didn't (indie bands that went to get drunk at Syndrome). Running parallel, and mostly ignored by the weeklies, were rave acts like Altern8 and The Prodigy. At one point Suede were deemed part of a 'new glam' scene with The Verve,

Adorable and Sweet Jesus. As soon as that was mentioned, Suede immediately dropped out of a gig that put those bands together.

Suede were very definitely not part of a scene. They barely knew any other bands, they didn't hang around Camden, they were based in west London. More trickily, in early 1991, they'd been given a hugely dismissive stinker of a review that ensured that no other journalist really gave them the time of day for several months. They were separate, driven, getting better and better, determined – as new bands always are – to wipe the pop slate clean. They felt, as Brett said, 'honour-bound' to rid the pop world of the shorts-wearers.

By August 1991, they had 'The Drowners', 'Moving', 'Pantomime Horse', 'To the Birds', all excellent songs that would end up on their eponymous first album. They started booking too-small gigs so that there were always people trying to get in. In December, they played The Underworld in Camden, and Damon and Justine came to watch. Suede were great. Brett's emotional yowl and his physical abandon; Bernard's long hair swinging with his hips, his fluid guitar riffs; Mat like Bernard, but taller and keeping time; Simon, never tucked away but seen. Justine, a naturally generous character, was thrilled ('I was jumping around, going, "That was amazing – they're going to be the next Smiths'''). Damon was not thrilled at all.

'The Drowners': not so much a statement of intent as a statement of being. The Bowie and Smiths influences were clear (Brett's estuary twang, his conscious posing) but there was something else, too. Brett's close observations: 'I wanted to record the world I saw around me. The blue plastic bag caught in the branches of the tree, the clatter and rumble of the escalator, London in all its wonderful shitty detail.' (Something that ran through a lot of Britpop bands, in the end: the universal revealed through the personal.) The chorus had weight and drama – *you're taking me over* – a mix of drugs, sex, love and power. A world away from rave's democracy, or from dull, straightforward blokery. Arch, passionate, swooning, daring, dramatic, camp.

And now there are more love affairs. Between Suede and the music press, and Suede and their fans. It's time for other people to fall in love with Suede.

On 25 April 1992, Steve Sutherland, editor of *Melody Maker*, put Suede on the cover as 'the best new band in Britain'. They hadn't even put a record out.

In his article, Steve wrote this: 'Suede are only the most audacious, androgynous, mysterious, sexy, ironic, absurd, perverse, glamorous, hilarious, honest, cocky, melodramatic, mesmerising band you're ever likely to fall in love with.' He asked the band questions that supported his thesis, and they did pretty well with their quotes. 'The reason that our music is English, twisted and sexual,' said Bernard, 'is just because our lives are English, twisted and sexual.' 'I believe life can be fascinating, extraordinary and absurd,' said Mat. And, from Brett: 'We're talking about the used condom as opposed to the beautiful bed. At the moment, I feel as though we're this big striped beast, this lunging sexual animal. We're the only band on the whole planet that actually matters.' The Tom Sheehan pictures had the band swathed in fake fur.

Music papers will always turn their favourite bands into living cartoons, outlaw pets; tame them, shape them, present them. Sometimes they make a band sexier than they are; often, they make them more interesting. They take an element (bolshy attitude, working-class background, hard partying, punky guitars) and they turn it into a persona. There were other elements of Suede that could have been highlighted, the awkward alt-musical side rather than the lascivious '70s glam, but that wasn't what the music papers wanted. 'When you first start becoming successful, you're told what kind of band you are,' said Brett to me later. 'And you're like, really? Are we that sort of band? I didn't know that.' Though, of course, there's a kernel of truth in the cartoon. 'You're complicit in creating it,' he said. 'But there's also an element which is partly fabricated and out of your control.'

At the weekly music papers, the writers wrote as individuals, and promoted themselves as personalities. This was the opposite of what we did at *Select*, where we wrote as a magazine, rather than as separate people (no 'I's in our copy). The inkie writers argued between each other, took their disagreements onto their pages, and the readers joined in the shouting match. And there was huge rivalry between the papers themselves, an intense dislike, deeply felt, as tribal as that between football-team supporters. Suede's first cover was as much about *Melody Maker* trying to steal a march on the *NME* as it was about Suede, even though Steve truly loved the band.

A month after the *Maker* cover, the 'Drowners' EP was released. It only went to Number 48, but that didn't matter, really; from then until March 1993, when *Suede*, their first album, came out, Suede were written about, discussed, celebrated, torn apart. There was so much press about them. Nineteen cover pieces before they released their album. An *NME* front with the words 'god-like genius' underneath; another one with Brett dressed as Sid Vicious. They were everywhere and everyone wanted them. After all the years of being ignored, it felt, said Brett later, like being in a pram that was hurtling downhill.

Because, as well as the press, suddenly, Suede had groups of dedicated young people that followed them around, dressed like them, sang the songs back at them. 'Wonderful zealots', Brett called them. The band were still small enough to be close to the fans, and would let some of the regulars into their dressing rooms after the gigs, for wired, sincere, upbeat conversations, excited dissections of music.

There was real hysteria at their gigs. In the summer and autumn months of 1992, they toured the UK – places like Aldershot, Leicester, Southampton, Leeds, every gig a frenzy. At each one, Brett would launch himself into the first few rows of fans and emerge with his shirt in tatters, the fans having ripped it from his skinny torso. ('A joyous tactile ceremony' he called it.) He started buying a cheap second-hand blouse wherever they played, just to get it torn from him within the first few songs. 'It's not just girls who pack themselves at the front of the stage and try to rip Brett's clothes off – it's boys, and it's nothing to do with homosexuality . . . it's everybody, it's a mania,' said a fan to the *Independent*.

Brett's sexiness was interesting. It wasn't straightforward – it wasn't quite straight – and it was definitely dangerous. To the more conventional, his arse-slapping and blouse-wearing was fey and unmanly. But to see it, it was a mad release, a sexual adrenaline, an energy untethered to male or female. Around this time, he gave a quote to *Lime Lizard* that followed him around for years: 'I see myself as a bisexual man who's never had a homosexual experience.' An amazing quote, though not quite what he meant: he was talking about how he adopted different personas in his songwriting, searching out the non-masculine, the androgynous. Later, he wondered if this part of him was a search for the feminine: his sister moved out when he was fifteen; his mum moved out too, and then died when he was twenty-one. Justine left him when he wasn't ready for it. 'I genuinely wasn't trying to do some sort of titillating, 1970s homage thing,' he said later. 'It felt like a search for something I felt was lacking in my life.'

But, anyhow, a girlish boy is catnip to teenage fans, to the kids who don't fit in. The glamour of discarding dull masculinity, the sense of being too strange or too big for where you're from, the need for something more than the thin and shabby walls of your small room. Brett showed the fans a way through and out. He had skinny hips, he wasn't macho, but there was something else, too: an ungentleness, a defiance, an imperiousness. Dripping in the tatty sleaze of the late-night city, cheap thrills with huge ambition. The fans, in eyeliner and charity-shop glamour, absolutely loved it all.

A scene only works if it breaks out of the bubble of the music press. Suede's scene was already there, in the smaller towns and dank suburbs, where teenagers yearned for something, anything, to help them change. Suede brought them out of the house and into a life they had only imagined.

'We came from a world of these little subtribes, you know,' Brett told me, 'the late '70s, early '80s thing of punks and mods and rockers, the playgrounds being divided into groups. I always wanted Suede to be the kind of band that inspired extreme loyalty, and a lot of that is to do with me wanting to find a tribe. Suede was me manufacturing my own tribe.'

And here they were: the wild ones, the beautiful ones, the drowners. Suede's new tribe. In July 1992, Suede played a gig supporting Blur. When Blur came on, they were drunk and shambolic. Suede were fantastic. They blew them off the stage.

In February 1993, introduced as 'the already legendary Suede,' they opened the Brit Awards, and blazed out a filthy high-octane performance of the week-old single 'Animal Nitrate' that stunned the in-the-room audience and smashed the band out of the TV screen and into even more teenagers' hearts. Brett, in black lace blouse open to the waist, started the song by banging his mic several times on his teeny-tiny bum. You could hear the thud of it through the speakers.

In March 1993, *Suede* went straight to Number One, the fastest-selling LP since Frankie Goes to Hollywood's *Welcome to the Pleasuredome*. In April, *Select* magazine put a picture of Brett on the cover, exposing his tummy and with a Union flag dropped in behind him. This was *Select's* way of making a scene. We wanted to put lots of bands we loved in the magazine, but they weren't big enough to warrant individual features, so we clubbed them all together as a concept. Blur would have been in there, but they'd been written about in the previous month's edition. So Suede, Pulp, The Auteurs, Denim and Saint Etienne it was. The Britpop cover that never mentioned Britpop.

Suede smashed onto the front pages; they sold lots of records. They had the Britpop ingredients: art and ambition; an outsider attitude; songs that weren't mainstream but were full of hooks; a look that could get you beaten up; a lead singer who was erudite and controversial as well as a sucker for attention. And, most shockingly, most amazingly: genuine success, without compromise. They were the ones who made the others believe. Somehow, they created a scene that they had nothing to do with.

So now, we're all in love. But another break-up is coming. Two, in fact. The music papers – itchy, competitive, searching for the next trick – were always going to move on.

But there's something worse than that looming: the break-up between Bernard and the rest of the band. From October 1993 into early 1994, communication between Bernard and the rest of the band started to fray, then disintegrate. They won the Mercury Prize and went on an American tour soon after. Bernard's dad had died of cancer three days after the Mercury, but no one seemed to acknowledge this properly; they just delayed starting the tour by a week. Their tourmates were The Cranberries; Bernard took to travelling with them, rather than with Suede. The other three members were partying very hard. Later, Mat said: 'All that happened in the band's life, we just kept on going . . . we just played more and wrote more and we just didn't know that that wasn't the way round everything.'

They ended the tour early, and returned to the UK to create *Dog Man Star*, their second album. It was late 1993. Brett sequestered himself in Highgate, took a lot of cocaine and acid and ecstasy. Bernard created tortuous, epic songs that lasted for eight

minutes, twelve minutes, eighteen minutes. He also did an interview with a magazine where he slated Brett, got married without
asking any of the band to his wedding, and picked arguments with
Simon and the album producer Ed Buller. He wanted to produce
the album. He wanted everyone to make music his way. He wanted
to leave, really. So he did.

Dog Man Star, which Brett, Mat and Simon finished by themselves, is a tortured, ambitious, swashbuckling, overblown record
with more ideas in it than it can control. Bernard had left, and
nobody really knew what to do. Unsurprisingly, the interviews
around *Dog Man Star* are strange. There are big gaps in the conversations, the band won't be photographed together, because then
they'd look like a three-piece. Brett is sullenly defiant and grandiose
(read: cokey). 'I completely devote every single minute of my life
to my personality and I pour it into music,' he told David Cavanagh
at *Select*. 'I'm obsessed about reaching a point of brilliance. You
can make a record and be immortal with it . . . I'll sacrifice every
inch of my personal life just for music.' Just watch me do it, he
seemed to be saying.

The break-up with Bernard threw Suede off-track for a while.
It's a break-up that Brett still puzzles over, still regrets a little, still
wonders how he could have acted differently so that Bernard
wouldn't feel he had to leave. Still, we can look into the future and
know that Suede will survive, and actually thrive; that, astonishingly, they'll find Richard Oakes, a seventeen-year-old schoolboy,
to replace Bernard in just a matter of weeks, and, a little later, the
perfect-for-the-part Neil Codling to play keyboards, and that, in
1996, they will bring out *Coming Up*, their glam-stomp chart-eating

pop triumph. We know that, after that, they'll stutter and stall, mostly due to Brett's mad drug-taking slipping into dangerous addiction. And we know that, twenty years after the release of their first album, they'll return with some of the most affecting and successful records of their career.

In the future, *Dog Man Star* will be recognised as Suede's mad masterpiece. Back in 1994, though, *Dog Man Star* was almost impossible to promote and tour. Suede were bruised and sad; Blur released *Parklife* around the same time; Pulp were waiting in the wings; the music press were looking elsewhere for their quick kicks.

Still, the fans continued screaming. That love affair didn't end. And *Dog Man Star* has 'The Wild Ones' on there. 'The Wild Ones' swoops, it sweeps. It's Suede's greatest single, a huge and gorgeous Scott Walker-esque epic about what could be saved if a loved one didn't leave. If they changed their mind, if they turned around and came back. If the break-up didn't happen, and the romance – so doomed, so passionate, so flawed and beautiful – could continue forever.

Implicit in 'The Wild Ones' is the knowledge, of course, that the love won't last. It can't. It's too much for the singer and the lover to handle. But, then, that's the beauty of it. The break-up is what makes the romance perfect.

It Really Could Happen

BLUR

'Girls and Boys'

When I worked at *Smash Hits* in the late 1980s, we would drink in the pubs near our Carnaby Street office. And so would everyone at Food Records, the small independent record label then on Golden Square. By everyone at Food Records, I mean Andy Ross (who ran Food with Dave Balfe) and Polly Birkbeck (who was the assistant, which meant she did everything) and whichever bands they were working with, and some they weren't. We'd drink at the Old Coffee House on Beak Street and the White Horse on Newburgh Street, as well as places that aren't there any more: a pizzeria, some sort of brasserie. Sometimes we'd go to Syndrome. We'd all go to gigs. Anyway, it was in one of those places, in spring 1990, that us *Smash Hitters* got to know Food Records' new signing, a band once called Seymour, renamed as Blur. I recall Andy showing me the list of possible band names. Andy was a journalist, on *Sounds*, as well as running Food, so he knew how pop writers' minds worked. The list of potential new names came from thinking up descriptions that a music journo might use of a great band: shimmery, revving. Et voilà! Blur.

Anyhow, we soon discovered that Blur were excellent company; funny, handsome, clever, challenging, usually drunk. There was wry, friendly drummer, Dave Rowntree, who had a nice line in side-quips, and was bonkers and punchy when he was hammered, which was most of the time. But bonkers and punchy in a friendly manner, like: 'Let's play a punching game!' Then: bassist Alex James, also super-friendly and impossibly good-looking, with a fringe to die for, so tall and thin he had to stand in an S-shape. He laughed a bit like Muttley. He took very little seriously. Guitarist Graham Coxon, the best-dressed of the four, was more nervy and sensitive, always crinkling his brow, tugging on his hair like a small boy. He'd actually pout when things seemed to be going wrong, twist his body into strange shapes when he was sitting. And singer Damon Albarn. 'I don't own any records,' he said. 'Only books.' Damon had a bowl cut, and a string of beads around his neck, and, in between those, a jut-chinned blank stare, a challenge. It didn't really bother us, because it wasn't really aimed at us. It was directed further out, at the world, like, 'Notice me', and also like, 'Yeah, and what?' He, too, was fun, though more impatient, more easily bored; intense, motivated, bossy, charismatic, a show-off. He liked Bertold Brecht, Herman Hesse, Umberto Eco, classical music. He'd wanted to be an actor, and had gone to East 15 drama school for a little bit. He had opinions, which weren't always required (he once told me my then boyfriend was too lightweight, meaning not serious enough). He liked an argument. But then, so did we. All journalists do.

Blur were good with women (they each had one sister). They had girlfriends, sometimes, and their girlfriends were also clever, though usually slightly quieter and more mysterious. Outside music, Dave knew a lot about weird science. Alex did too and liked to talk about stars. They could all discuss art and books.

To us – perhaps not to journalists from more serious music magazines – Blur's records were secondary, really. You knew the records would come. They had all the other stuff that was needed: the looks, the togetherness, the charisma, the ambition, the ideas. When they played, even when they were terrible (which they sometimes were), they were mesmerising. Full of mad, often undirected, energy. Damon had a jump that lifted his knees around his ears and he was always climbing things: speaker stacks, ceiling pipes, the walls. Graham would often end up on his back, making screeching noises come out of his guitar. Alex, a fringe on a stick with a cigarette poking out, liked to turn around and waggle his bum at the girls. Dave – eyes like coals, focused on nothing, dripping in sweat – would play so hard he'd be sick afterwards.

You could tell Blur were going to do something – though I don't think anyone imagined they would become quite as big and as mainstream as they did – and we liked 'She's So High' and 'Sing' and 'There's No Other Way'. And, most importantly, we liked them.

Britpop wouldn't have happened without Blur, which can be a difficult thing for them to acknowledge. Still, it's the truth. It wouldn't have happened, not just because in 1993 they brought out their *Modern Life Is Rubbish* album, a deliberate step away from generic, baggy, post-Madchester grooves and sloppy imitation grunge, into sharp, spiky, Kinks-y art-pop; not just because they then upped the ante with '94's *Parklife*, sending third-person observation slap bang into the nation's heart, through singalong tunes; not just because, a year later, they were confident enough to move the release date of 'Country House', their first single from their fourth album, *The Great Escape*, to the same release date as Oasis's 'Roll With It'. All that was important, but fundamentally, Britpop wouldn't have happened without Blur because of *who they were*, especially Damon.

From the start, they were unashamed about wanting to make interesting music, but also wanting lots of people to like them. When they had their first hit – 1991's 'There's No Other Way', the first track they ever created together, on the first afternoon they ever played together – they were delighted, but also unsurprised. 'It's definitely what I want,' said Damon, around that time. 'I feel we've got the potential to be the first band in a long time to really cross over and stay noisy, mad and slightly dangerous.' That was Blur's aim: to go mainstream without compromise, to be both art school and heart-throb, big and clever, indie kids turned pop kings. Yes, they wanted the attention. Alex would quote Shelley: 'Poets' food is fame and love.' Damon could be even more straightforward: 'We always wanted to be stars. That's what made us pick up our instruments.' You did wonder if Graham felt that as strongly; all his ambitions were achieved, he told me, once Blur played *Top of the Pops*. But Damon was the leader. 'Me and Graham would still be picking our noses, retaking our final degree exams,' Alex said to me, 'if it wasn't for Damon having a firework up his arse.'

Anyway, because of this ambition – which was in all of them, but most obviously in Damon – they put the work in. They really tried with their music (which not all bands did, due to . . . distractions), and they did the same with all the other stuff, too. No demurring at appearing in *Smash Hits*, no worries about *Top of the Pops*, happy to be photographed, understanding of the press process. They'd review the singles, they'd guest-edit an issue, they'd turn up to awards ceremonies, they'd play the gigs. It was their job, and they were good at it, mostly because it didn't seem like a job when they were doing it. They were having fun. 'BUSTY GIRLS GO WILD FOR BOOZY BAND', said the *Daily Star*. They were out, all the time, and hugely sociable when they were. If you saw one of Blur when you were at a party, then you knew the night would be a laugh (their stamina for drink and drugs was unparalleled); though if it was Graham, you knew it might get weird. They charmed journalists, made friends with everyone. You'd bump into Damon and he'd be with Ray Winstone. Or you'd bump into him and he'd be with Dave Stewart. Or Mark from Ride.

Damon grew up around cultural analysis (his parents were artists; his dad ran an art college in Colchester – he was art school born and bred). This could make things tough for him creatively – 'I'm far more vulnerable to criticism than Graham because I respect criticism,' he told me (though Graham, too, was highly sensitive to what others thought of him); and, another time, 'I don't get too upset to take it seriously, but I do get upset' – because he listened to opinions, understood the associations, rather than just dismissing them as irrelevant. It made him self-conscious and self-aware. In his songs, his emotions were cloaked, hidden under other people's stories, tucked inside a tune. He found it hard to disengage his head, to write straight from the heart.

But it also meant that he understood the wider scope of what Blur could be, where they sat within British pop. In Blur's first interview with *Q*, he said that the reason why Blur would succeed was because they were relevant and of their moment. 'We're like The Jam, The Smiths and The Stone Roses were in place and time,' he said. Which is fine, and fairly standard band bluster. But then, he said: 'Next year, we'll have to recreate ourselves, and we'll either be clear enough to know what's going wrong to get it right or we'll be too detached.' There aren't so many bands that understand that. That's why all second albums attract the perennial adjective 'the difficult'.

Anyway, it turned out that Blur weren't too detached to recreate themselves, refine their talent and ideas into something new, something better. *Leisure*, their first LP, was a bit of a disappointment, especially if you'd seen them play live: the sound was sludgy and the lyrics were vague. They had to reinvent themselves. And their next incarnation – the one that set them on the path to success – was hard-won.

Leisure came out in August 1991. Between 28 October and 17 November 1991, Blur did a sixteen-date North American tour to promote it. It was tough. Nirvana had brought out *Nevermind* in September and it was an unstoppable force, selling 400,000 copies a week in the US by the end of the year. America was having a love affair with grunge and Blur did not fit in at all. They had a rough time. After coming home, a few months later, in April 1992, they went back to the US and Canada again, and played thirty-one gigs. Again, it was brutal.

Just before that second run, they'd played around the UK as

part of Rollercoaster, a sort of mini-Lollapalooza, which featured My Bloody Valentine, Dinosaur Jr. and The Jesus and Mary Chain, as well as Blur. Rollercoaster was a success. Blur were the naughty kids of the tour, and they'd invented a game that involved drinking and punching someone in the head. They took it to each of the other bands' dressing rooms, to varying degrees of welcome. With Rollercoaster, Blur played Brixton Academy for three nights in a row. America was a huge comedown after that, especially because, in truth, they were mostly there because they'd discovered they were £60,000 in debt and needed to pay some of it off.

Slogging across the US, playing to small, indifferent crowds, taking it out on each other (the punching became a regular inter-band emotional release), at some point Blur decided that their next album would be a reaction against everything they were witnessing. The USA was not who they were. So Damon used that experience, and a new-found obsession with The Kinks, and started to write better lyrics. Blur were convinced that grunge had no relevance to the UK, that there was something more specific to say, and to sound like, that would have more meaning for British kids. (It's the same argument that Noel Gallagher used as a reason to write 'Live Forever': that 'I Hate Myself and Want to Die' is no way for teenagers to think.) And the result, *Modern Life Is Rubbish*, though it only got to Number 15, was massively important for them. Partly because of the music, but also because of how hard the band had to fight – with Food and with their grunge-obsessed American record company – to be able to make it. At one point, the Americans wanted them to re-record the whole thing with Butch Vig.

*

Modern Life . . . was also important because of the two band photos that Blur issued to go with it. British Image No. 2 has, mostly, been forgotten: it's of the band with their hair slicked down, taking tea in stripy blazers. But British Image No. 1, of them in jeans, jackets and lace-up boots, Damon in a Fred Perry, holding the lead of a mastiff dog – that one got attention. Such a look was seen as a bit dangerous, with its suggestion of British nationalism. But it also drew on references that we liked: The Specials, *Quadrophenia*, rude-boy culture. Plus, that bovver-boy look was cheap. The Fred Perry/jeans/Dr. Martens boots uniform was adopted by boys and girls alike. The Britpop look was there before the hits.

There was, of course, another reason for Blur to get into bovver mode. While they were away on that second US tour, in April 1992, Suede had become the 'Best New Band in Britain', courtesy of *Melody Maker*. Blur had endured grunge, then fled home to land slap bang in Suede-mania. Another kick up the bum.

Because the main driver for Blur's inadvertent creation of Britpop was not so photogenic. Aside from everything else they had going for them, they – well, Damon – wanted to win. Damon was hugely competitive, driven by challenge. If someone chucked down the gauntlet, he couldn't kick it aside, whether they did it indirectly, as with Suede, who never acknowledged Blur as rivals (Brett still doesn't), or, later, directly, as with Oasis. The rest of the band weren't so bothered. They wanted to be big, but they had no particular desire to get aggy about it. But when Oasis got to Number One with 'Some Might Say', Damon went to their celebration party. Liam came up to him and said, NUMBER FUCKING ONE, right in Damon's face. And Damon took that on. Damon was about being Number One, in all ways. Years later, I asked him about his need to be the winner. This was around 2015, when he was established and feted as a one-man musical genius, able to move between genres and collaborators with unimpeachable credibility. And he said, yeah, he was madly competitive. He couldn't help himself. 'There's a lot of competition between men,' he said. 'I think it's always been about that.' Football, which Damon came to once he became famous – both playing and supporting – is a way to negotiate male competition, frustration and hurt, with useful rules. At the end of the match, you know who's won. If it wasn't you, there's another game next week.

The most difficult part of being in a band is finding the other people in the band. Alex told me that. Blur found each other through education, and gigs. Damon and Graham met at school, Stanway Comprehensive in Colchester. Damon was one year above Graham, more confident and middle class. He'd moved to a village just outside Colchester when he was around nine, from Leytonstone, east London. The move didn't suit him. In London, his house had paper cuts on the windows instead of curtains, and the sitting room was completely silver. His dad made clip-together bubble furniture in the garden, his parents were part of a mixed, artistic community. They had parties that took over the street.

Things were not the same in Colchester, where wide boys roamed the flat lands in packs. Damon didn't really care. The first time Graham ever saw him (before they spoke), Damon was singing 'Gee Officer Krupke' in a school production of *West Side Story*.

When they met, Damon was rude about Graham's shoes. They started hanging out in the music room.

Graham was working class, an army kid whose dad was an army musician and whose mum worked at Nestlé. As a teenager, Graham spent his free time working his way through the songs of The Jam and The Smiths; and painting. Graham's taste hasn't changed since then; he ploughs his own furrow in terms of sound, style and art. When Blur aren't being Blur, he's busy making music, sometimes painting. Like Damon; but more concentrated, less diffuse.

Dave was in various bands in Colchester; he saw Damon play in one, and thought he was great, 'much better than everyone else'. A few years older than the others, Dave's homelife was difficult (his parents had alcohol problems). He'd developed various ways of escaping: taking computers apart and putting them back together again, tinkering with radios, designing things. And making music. (When Blur went into hiatus after the early 2000s, he formed a small company and made animations for MTV, then became a defence solicitor and also a Labour councillor. Not a man to sit still, Dave.)

He joined a band with Damon and Graham and two others, a guitarist and a bassist. In 1989, the two others left, after Dave had an argument with them. Graham took over guitar and suggested that his new friend Alex might join. Graham was studying Fine Art at Goldsmiths; Alex was there doing French. He'd come from Bournemouth, with a happy middle-class family (dad a sales manager, mum a voluntary worker), where he'd decided to be in a band long before he had a guitar: 'it was an extension of my haircut'. When he met Graham, on the very first day he arrived at Goldsmiths, he knew he'd be a big part of his life.

When Graham asked Alex to join the band, all four went to the Beat Factory studios where Damon was working, having given up drama school. They walked into a rehearsal room, set up, and wrote 'There's No Other Way' on the spot.

In 1994, when *Parklife* was finished, Alex was living in a house in Covent Garden (very Alex). When the 12" single of 'Girls and Boys' arrived, he put his speakers on the window ledge, put the record on the player, turned up the volume, and blasted it out to the world. It felt like a lift-off. 'Girls and Boys' is, in a way, a vindication of Alex: it's his funky up and down disco bass that carries it (this after early producers insisted that his bass-playing wasn't good enough). It shows that Blur can be fun, and silly–sexy, as well as art. Graham's jerky, discordant guitar, when it comes in, does the opposite of what Alex is up to, as Graham was wont to do; he provides the jagged angst that slices through Alex's blitheness.

'Girls and Boys' is also, of course, a Damon record, meaning: observational and tuneful, but with a football chant chorus. It's about 18–30 holidays – a reminder of the Essex girls and boys of Damon's past – but you could also read it as commentating on Britpop. Girls who like boys who like boys to be girls; a summary of Britpop's asexual look, within a very (hetero)sexually driven environment. Such gender flip-flopping would soon make way for the more straightforwardly laddy Benny Hill dolly birds, in the video of 'Country House'. In 'Girls and Boys', the sex, and the sexes, are perfectly balanced. I remember getting a tape of it, and playing it over and over as I drove round London, banging out the 'one two three four . . . five fingers' with my hand on the steering wheel. So upbeat and optimistic. Funny.

And 'Girls and Boys' going to Number Five was enormous. Blur just didn't have hits like that. (They've had fewer Number One singles than you might think: just two – 'Country House' and 'Beetlebum'. 'Song 2' and 'Tender' got to Number Two.) They had a big launch party for *Parklife* at Walthamstow dog-racing track on 26 April 1994, and it felt exciting. They played at Mile End Stadium on 17 June, and it seemed absolutely seminal. They headlined the *NME* Stage on Sunday at Glastonbury, after Oasis, Pulp and Radiohead; the first time that their no-roof arm-wavers like 'To the End' and 'The Universal' had ever been played in that way, out into the sunset, everyone singing, up and away. It was all bigger than anyone could have imagined.

Blur's shift, from defiant, everyone's-against-us-but-we-know-we're-right outsiders to festival headliners and full-on popstars was abrupt and huge. Completely vindicating, utterly shattering. As *The List* put it, pre-*Parklife*, Blur were known for three things: 'Great laugh. Good press. Zilch success.' 'At least now,' said Damon, 'we've done something that lives up to my big mouth.' There was something that relaxed in Damon once Blur were famous; he became easier to be around. But the change for Blur was sudden: they'd leapt from making mannered, interesting scuzz pop for outsiders to making tunes that you heard playing from van windows, that were hollered at football matches, that made thousands of people jump up and down.

I once asked Damon what it was like to become well known, and he said: 'It's like having a passport that gets you into everywhere, parties with models as well as crack dens.' You turn up, you're let in. And with work, it's more than that. Though a star never quite knows this, everyone is always waiting for you, swaying on their feet like aimless *Sims* characters until they're activated by your arrival. Nothing starts, nothing happens, until the star is here.

What happened next? Well, you know. In August 1995, there was the Battle of Britpop™. This came about because Blur and Oasis had a sort of agreement that they wouldn't bring out a single on the same day. It was Blur's turn to bring their single out first, but Oasis moved the release date of 'Roll With It' to the week before 'Country House'. Andy Ross was astute enough to realise that the momentum behind Oasis would mean that their single would stay at Number One for more than a week, and Blur's single would stall at Number Two. So Food moved the 'Country House' release to the same day as 'Roll With It': made it a proper fight. And everything kicked off.

The battle was taken up by the mainstream press, the top item on the *News at Ten*. I talked to Matt Kelly, a *Mirror* journalist at that time, about Blur vs Oasis, and he said: 'We loved it. Tabloids don't care about music history, we didn't care about Blur's old records. We like events. Blur vs Oasis was an event.' (Similarly, Jarvis going on stage at the Brits was an event, too.) The *Mirror* wanted Oasis to win: they saw Oasis as their readers – working class, Northern, gobby.

It was a close call, but Blur won. Though their success felt short-lived. The impetus was with Oasis, and very soon Damon's popular caricature went from handsome, clever prince of indie pop to embarrassing try-hard Mockney art twat. People sang Oasis songs at him in the street when he was home, which wasn't often. Blur played over a hundred gigs in 1994, and around eighty in 1995, mostly arenas. They did 250 promo interviews in a single month. But (*What's The Story) Morning Glory?* was seen as a better album than *The Great Escape*; Oasis were regarded as more authentic. They had an even bigger fanbase than Blur, and they weren't backing down. 'It's like being back at school,' said Damon, tiredly. 'We're in two different gangs.' And: 'Our mistake was we assumed Oasis could see it as a quirky cultural event as opposed to a real battle. And the nation, in the end, sympathised with them.'

The noisy nation did. But not everyone. There were always those who wanted the offbeat, the weird, the odd new-wave-meets-disco of 'Girls and Boys', the 'did we make it? maybe not' love song of 'To the End', the strange seaside yearning of 'This Is a Low'. There is something pure about artists ploughing the same furrow, about knowing what they're good at and trying to refine it until it's perfect. But it's also exhilarating when a band changes, experiments, tries ideas out while bringing you along. Not revving on the spot, but travelling – lurching, spinning, stumbling – through life. Testing out new approaches, changing perspective, in the centre of the action but with an observer's eye, insider outsiders. Watching the Magaluf hordes, celebrating them while knowing you could never be the same, and then writing a song for them, and you, to dance to. Oasis sounded like early Beatles, but Blur had the Fab Four's weird experimental hearts.

*

There's a separate world within all bands; a place where they communicate without words, and that's the space where they make music. Outside of that, inter-band connections can be tense and difficult, but through much of the 1990s, Blur's connections, though tested, were strong. Alex and Dave had an understanding because the rhythm section always does, but also because they were both science and astronomy nerds (later, they were both involved in the *Beagle II* Mars mission). After a couple of years, they both got flying licences and sometimes flew planes to gigs. Aside from that, Dave and Graham often instinctively agreed on things, they would find themselves finishing each other's sentences. Alex and Graham had a Goldsmiths connection, an art thing, because of where they met. Towards the end of the '90s, Damon and Alex had Iceland in common for a time; Damon went there in 1996 and called up Alex, blissed out, to tell him about it. Damon, Graham and Dave all have Colchester in common.

But the most important relationship within Blur, the start of it, and the on–off romance all the way through, is the relationship between Damon and Graham. They overlapped and understood each other without trying, and when their relationship started to go wrong after *Parklife*, the group began to fracture.

Graham was finding it hard to cope. Alex's easy social nonchalance and celebration of the good times drove him mad, and Damon, a bit, too. Alex's roistering and Groucho life (hanging out with Keith Allen and Damien Hirst, climbing out of the top window of the Groucho, over the roof and down through another window, into a different drinking club) made Graham embarrassed. 'If Alex was down Groucho's, then I might as well have been down

Groucho's, because *Blur* were down at Groucho's,' he said. 'Alex's idea of glamour is my idea of death.' Graham couldn't handle the screaming at the gigs. He was unable to be light about the rivalry with Oasis. He wanted to be taken seriously.

But then, Graham's ability to have everyone worry about him, constantly check he was OK ('don't let him get drunk!') could get on the others' nerves. When he was drinking, he shouted at people, he'd tell journalists to fuck off, flip from insecure to mawkish to bolshy. He'd be found unconscious on the floor at 4 a.m. 'It totally wrecked our ability to get on with each other,' Damon said.

And Damon, entirely unexpectedly, started to have panic attacks. Heart palpitations, thinking about death 'virtually daily'. 'I was in a state of constant agitation for nearly two years,' he said. 'A real physical sense that the off button was going to be switched off very soon.' Going to Iceland helped. And football. Almost as self-protection, he moved towards laddishness with his football friends, away from what he thought of as art, though that jarred with Graham too. Graham and Dave had addiction problems, which they dealt with individually, and gradually.

Blur hadn't split up, but they weren't together. The turning point was when Graham wrote Damon a letter to say how he felt, saying he wanted to go back to what Blur were. 'I wrote that I wanted to scare people and I wanted to make music that's important, not just like a packet of sweets or something,' he said. That got them back in the studio.

After *The Great Escape*, they made *Blur*, with regular producer Stephen Street, a U-turn away from English observation into fuzzy slacker sounds. A more democratic album, less driven by Damon, that brought them their much-desired American hit in 'Song 2'. And then, in 1999, *13*, Damon's heartbreak LP, the band's blues album, with William Orbit. That was hard to make. Four years later, *Think Tank* was like a stepping stone out for them all. Graham left, Alex got together with his wife during the recording, Damon started to imagine a band where he couldn't be seen. Blur were done, for a time.

In 2023, Blur released a new album, *The Ballad of Darren* (which should have perhaps been called 'The Ballad of Damon', as that's who it was about). The band did some interviews around it.

Alex said: 'I think maybe singers and guitar players feel like they have to suffer, otherwise they haven't turned up. But to me, Blur has always been an effortless, joyous, weightless kind of experience.'

Graham said: 'The '90s, it was a very intense time. On the same sort of level as a relationship, or marriages. I think it's OK to say that time apart was taken up with other friendships and just sort of recuperating or doing other things.'

Dave said: 'The fact that we haven't always got on, that is one of the chemistry points that has led to us being able to make the music we do.'

And Alex, again: 'We love each other and we cannot stand each other, simultaneously, in the way that only family can.'

When Blur played at Mile End in 1994, I remember thinking, Who are all these people? Where did they come from? Somehow there was a disconnect in my head between journalists like me writing about bands, telling the world how great they are, and people actually going to buy the records. Hearing songs on the radio, and not truly understanding that thousands of others were listening too. We were used to bobbing along to Blur gigs, popping in to see friends, familiar faces. It wasn't like that any more.

It was the same when I went to see Blur at Wembley Stadium in 2023. There had been a shift in how they were seen when they played Glastonbury in 2009, and again when they played Hyde Park in 2015. Somehow Blur were no longer art school, but familiar and celebrated, acknowledged as one of the UK's pop music heavyweights, a legacy band, one to see before you get old. Alongside their hardcore fans, of which there are thousands, there are those who quite like a couple of tunes, who fancy a big night out and a singsong.

At Wembley, which holds 90,000 people, on the Sunday, there was a celebratory atmosphere. Entire families in a row, the mum losing her shit, the kids having to film the stage because she was too busy singing along. Oddly, plenty of people in the audience looked like a carbon copy of a '90s Oasis devotee: bucket hat, band T-shirt, jeans, Gazelles. Some were in Fred Perrys and boots. All now the uniform of the British middle-aged.

There was a lot of singing. It was emotional. Hearing songs yelled out by so many people, everyone joining in like they were popular hymns. 'Parklife' became a call-and-response football chant. 'To the End' was enormous, an everyone-together understanding of what it can take to become a grown-up, all that you go through, sometimes with others, sometimes not. 'Tender' felt like a folk song, one of those ones that someone starts and someone else joins in a line later and goes round and round, overlapping. Damon wrote 'Tender' when he was 'off my head, on my own, distraught' over the end of his relationship with Justine. It was an attempt to make sense of the then most terrible time in his life, a direct expression of devastation and heartbreak, that was taken up and supported by his friends, transformed into music. And then it was helped on by others, the producer, the engineer, the radio pluggers, the DJs, the journalists, and offered out into the world. Until years later, thousands of people – too many to think about or understand – stood in a stadium and sang along, turning that initial lonely broken distress into a communal sense of solidarity, a group insistence that love will prevail.

How do songs do that, I wonder? Blur, like every band, spent no time at all on some tracks ('Song 2' was a sort of warm-up), and, with others, took days experimenting, rewriting and starting again. 'My life', Dave once said to me, 'is I hit things, trying to get the sound in my head.' Graham expresses his emotions through the sound of his guitar when he hasn't got the words to say them out loud. 'It's a very, very precious thing we've got, all those years of playing together,' said Alex.

Precious to them, and to their fans. And, at Wembley, even Damon felt it. During the gig, he said to Graham: 'I met you when you were twelve and I was thirteen, and we're here now. That's mad, it really is.' When they finished 'Under the Westway', he burst into sobs, with his head on the piano. And afterwards, he said: 'I don't know, something happened, it was one of the most amazing things I've ever done. There was this guy, bless him . . . He was so overwhelmed, people around him were consoling him and he was in bits. I don't know whether it was sadness or joy or whatever. And it just got to me.'

49

'It was all of it,' said Damon. 'It's an emotional thing, being at this age. Our lives are not getting any longer. Younger people who were there can appreciate the event . . . But for us, it's like time travel in a way.'

Time travel. It's a kind of sadness, it's definitely a joy. It isn't quite nostalgia and it isn't only celebration. It swells, it takes over, it can overwhelm. The songs don't recapture a time, because how can they? They seem to pinpoint it, but it's moved. Blur made some of these songs a long time ago. They were of that moment, but they take on different meanings, they grow from their starting point, move into and around and through your life. I used to just listen to the bass and guitar in 'Girls and Boys', the strange blankness of the vocals. Now I notice the video-game sound of falling down a hole. Toppling into trouble. No going back. You have to laugh.

You Love Us

MANIC STREET PREACHERS
'A Design for Life'

You love us, sang Manic Street Preachers on their second ever proper single and, the thing was, they were right. The Manics, four working-class Welsh lads with shatter-sharp minds, shiny songs, glittering ambition, were adored by the music press from around 1991 onwards. Even those who couldn't get on with their music – rock with punk elements, nihilistic lyrics, no easy groove or singalong tune or love-me-cos-I-love-you lyrics to keep things sweet – were wild about the Manics themselves. Bassist Nicky Wire: tall with an unexpected burn-down-the-house grin, who skewered everything and everyone from Margaret Thatcher to Glastonbury festival with perfectly argued disdain; Richey Edwards, rhythm guitar: sensitive, well-read, provocative, equally scornful, with that particular self-immolation aura that outsider teenagers can sense at one hundred paces; lead singer and guitarist James Dean Bradfield: prickly, shy, physically tough, who wrote the music and came alive on stage. Sean Moore: ridiculously young-looking, classically trained musician-turned-drummer. They loved each other unself-consciously; they read books self-consciously. They were steeped in political theory and actual politics (they saw how the miners' strike affected their area). They were bored and pretty. They refused to hide their intelligence. And they hated with a beautiful intensity.

There was a huge amount of early Manics hyperbole. Those who loved them in the music press wrote things like 'nothing yet has been more furious, hilarious and dizzyingly perplexing' and 'a deadly and hugely welcome antidote to baggy culture' and 'quite simply, the most articulate, and the most politicised, and the most furious and the sexiest white rock band in the entire world'.

Of course, there were many writers who didn't like them, too. But even they seemed to like them really. 'When they're average, Manic Street Preachers are very poor,' wrote one *NME* writer in a feature that was one long argument between him and the group. But he followed it with: 'When they get it right, when the audience understands and responds accordingly, they're explosive, corrosive demons.'

They told us that their musical heroes were Public Enemy and Guns N' Roses: a headline-friendly mix that made sense when they explained. Public Enemy was about having something important to say, in lyrics and interviews, and using music to sell their message with as much confrontation and clarity as possible. And when it came to the irredeemably naff Guns N' Roses – well, with their black eyeliner, black back-combed hair, tight trousers and propensity for star jumps, Nicky and Richey had something of the spandex about them, and James, who also kept his trousers close to the bone, was fond of a tops-off full rock guitar riff. Heavy metal and glam metal were huge in the Welsh Valleys, where they were from. But the real reason was that, at the end of the 1980s, GN'R were the biggest rock band in the world. The Manics weren't interested in becoming the best band in their hometown, or in only appealing to the music press cognoscenti. They wanted to be massive.

Their ambition was stratospheric. The problem was, in 1991, they didn't yet have the sound to back up their ambitions. Their first few records sounded like dull punk. Still, everything else was perfect. They had a manifesto, which included tenets such as: no love songs, no drugs, no trip-out sounds, no encores. They had a plan: they were going to sell 25 million copies of their first album and then split up and/or set themselves on fire on *Top of the Pops*. They had intelligence, physical beauty, youth (they lied about how old Sean was, making him two or three years younger). They understood the power of imagery, worshipping beautiful icons like Marilyn Monroe and not just because they fancied her. They wore white jeans, black eyeliner, leopard-print fake fur, T-shirts with slogans they spray-painted on themselves: ENGLAND NEEDS REVOLUTION NOW, NO MORE STATE, CLASSIFIED MACHINE, CULTURE OF DESTRUCTION. They were insepar-able, a small gang. Importantly, they respected the power of the music press – they'd written letters to several inkie journalists asking them to listen to their single or come along to a gig. All they needed, in their first few years at least, was the records.

Simon Price wrote for *Melody Maker* at the time. He was enchanted by them.

'I was crying out for something exciting to happen at the begin-ning of the 90s,' he says. 'Shoegazing, grunge, Madchester, none of them spoke to me. I secretly wanted a band to be saying something, ruffling feathers, kicking over statues, to quote The Redskins. I'm the same age as them, I come from South Wales, we share sensibilities.

'They were working class, they wore make-up. They were like a guilty pleasure.'

Simon went on to write the excellent *Everything (A Book About Manic Street Preachers)* about their early records. He understands that, early on, the band weren't quite up to making the music in their heads – 'the first few songs sounded like Stiff Little Fingers, trebly and thrashy' – that James was still developing into a good enough guitarist to play how they wanted. And, even then, their sound was quite traditionally rock 'n' roll.

'They'd done the maths, they'd thought, Who's the biggest rock band in the world? and the answer was Guns N' Roses,' he says. 'But they got the timing wrong, corporate hair metal had peaked. They made an overproduced FM rock album just at the point when grunge was coming in. But through their mixture of charm and rhetoric, even though they were making a form of music that the world was leaving behind, they were still valued.'

Perhaps the oddest thing about the Manics was who was offered up to the press for interviews. Usually, with bands, it's the lead singer: the perceived leader of the group, the photo-centred show-off, the writer of the words and, often, the music. (Obviously, that's not always the case: Oasis had a lead singer who didn't write the music or the lyrics, and who wasn't seen as the band's boss.) But with the Manics, things were more complicated. The lead singer, James, and the drummer, Sean, wrote the music but didn't write the lyrics and neither, at first, did the interviews. It was Nicky and Richey who did the talking; they were referred to, slightly jokily, as the 'political wing' of the Manics, with James and Sean being the musical wing. Nicky and Richey wrote the lyrics, they sold the look, they were the best at articulating what the Manics were about, who they were for, what they stood for.

Richey seemed born to be a lead singer, but he couldn't sing or play. James played his guitar parts on the albums; he could barely retain the guitar chords that James taught him. The joke was that his guitar wasn't plugged in when they performed (it was, but turned down low). Richey was absolutely integral to the group . . . but he wasn't actually a musician. Which is about as punk rock as you can get.

The Manics grew up together in the working-class Welsh Valleys, in Blackwood (Richey), Oakdale (Nicky) and Pontllanfraith (Sean and James). 'If you were to build a museum out of Blackwood, all you'd be able to fill it with is rubble and shit,' said Richey. It was a mining area and, Nicky recalled later, the atmosphere when they grew up, during the miners' strikes, was 'militant and highly charged and morbidly angry'. It shaped them. 'We embody the destructive working-class thing,' he said, 'mixing stupendous intelligence with nihilistic destruction.' They knew they had to leave Wales to get where they wanted to be, but were sensitive to anyone who patronised them for being Welsh. (James, later: 'There was definite anti-Welsh bigotry from the music press. All they talked about were sheep shaggers and Tom Jones. Lazy, lazy bigotry.')

They all went to Oakdale comprehensive: Richey and Sean were in the same year; James and Nicky, the year below. But they'd known each other for ages before then, through playing football. Nicky and James met when they were five. Cousins Sean and James lived together from their early teens, after Sean's dad left and Sean moved into James's house; they shared a bedroom, slept in bunk beds. They were more like brothers than cousins.

In 1986, James, Sean and Nicky started Manic Street Preachers, with another friend, Flicker, after seeing a local band, Funeral In Berlin; the Manics played their first gig at the Railway Inn in Crumlin. Flicker lasted a couple of years as bassist until he left. Richey and Nicky got to know each other better from going to Swansea University. Richey saw the Manics play in 1988. He joined soon after. Their world was small and tight: they went round each others' houses, watched films (*Rumblefish* was a particular favourite), read books, played computer games. Around that time, they saw *So It Goes*, a music show hosted by Mancunian motor-mouth Tony Wilson and were introduced to The Clash, which excited them.

Actually, though they hid this for several years, because they knew it wasn't as compelling as their Public Enemy/Guns N' Roses idea, they listened to much of the same indie as everyone else: The The, The Cure, The Smiths, even some C86 bands. These were exorcised from their manifesto and CV as being too boring. Fair enough. But the Manics were, essentially, bored.

Richey: 'I think all great art is based on the politics of boredom. When there's nothing around, you've got nothing in your life, you can just solely concentrate on what you're trying to say and what you're trying to do, which is definitely what happened with us.'

For the band's first single, 1988's 'Suicide Alley', Richey took the photo and did the artwork. He played with the Manics first in

1989, at Swansea Uni, and very soon after that, they played in the Horse and Groom in London and were seen by Saint Etienne's Bob Stanley, then a writer for *Melody Maker*. Bob had received one of Richey's letters. Later, he remembered the audience stifling laughter, 'but only because it was so unexpected': the band were full of mad conviction. They made such an impact on Bob that he went on to form Saint Etienne, despite not being able to play an instrument. (Saint Etienne used the Manics' manifesto in their lyrics for 'Woodcabin'.)

Nicky: 'We had this evangelical desire to start the revolution and be absolutely fucking massive. It didn't just mean getting a record deal. It was all conquering, psycho, egotistical.'

By 1991 things were falling into place: Heavenly put out 'Motown Junk' in January, then 'You Love Us' in May. The band had landed a manager/PR agent in the well-respected Philip Hall and moved into his and his wife Terri's house in London, where the Manics diligently cleaned the house during the day and made tea for when Philip and Terri got home. Hall lent them money to live on until they got a record contract.

From the start, Richey's commitment and desire to be understood was more intense than most artists. Infamously, he used a razor blade to carve 4 REAL into his arm during an argumentative interview with the *NME*'s Steve Lamacq. Lamacq said later that the weirdest thing about it was how calm Richey seemed. He went to A&E but felt bad about wasting the NHS's time, and let others with accidental injuries be treated first. He ended up with seventeen stitches.

Ed Sirrs, the *NME* photographer, took a picture of Richey's arm.

The photograph is still shocking. It probably wouldn't be printed today, though no doubt the images would have leaked and gone viral. The *NME* decided to print it, but in black and white. It caused a huge sensation – in the music press.

Six days later, Manic Street Preachers were signed by Sony.

Over the next couple of years, along with every other music journalist, I interviewed the Manics a few times and enjoyed it. Once, James told me off for writing that he had a cauliflower chest. Which, in my defence, he did: pale and bumpy, because of his muscles. But he didn't like my description, which was fair enough, and he told me without being nasty about it.

Another time, I had to talk to them about porn, which was difficult, though no doubt an easier experience than it would have been with most other bands. Asking questions such as, 'What's the difference between porn and erotica?' and 'Are image and reality intertwined?' of most other rhythm guitarists would have been quite the journalistic assignment.

Anyway, at the time, *Select* was trying to compete with the lads' mags (*Loaded* was launched in 1994) and its executives felt that the new bands that we liked weren't appealing enough to sell magazines. Hence, the word PORN in big letters on the cover, over a shot of Richey and James lounging (Richey with his top off, James in cute sailor suit lying with his head on Richey's stomach) atop a selection of porn mags, both straight and gay. Plus – this is very Manics – some scattered books, including *The Story of O* and one by the Marquis de Sade. Inside, there was a picture of Nicky with his army trousers slung low and black make-up smeared all over his face. Ah, 1994.

I spoke to Richey and James. Richey was as brilliant as ever, but weirdly opaque; there but not there. Hard to grasp. I felt a bit like he was testing me and I was coming up short. Anyway, he spoke about Andrea Dworkin, Bret Easton Ellis (he liked both and thought *Mercy* and *American Psycho* shared similar violence and plots) and how he found J. G. Ballard's *Crash* sexy. 'I think people are becoming more machine-like and that's the imagery I like. Also sex and death are closely linked. Sado-masochistic imagery, bleeding . . .'

Is porn propaganda for a sexist society? I asked him (fun fun fun for the light-ent reader). Richey said yes, and, brilliantly, followed it with, 'but everything is propaganda for a sexist society'. 'I find Danny Baker rampaging into people's houses going, this washing powder is great, I find that really disturbing,' he said, referencing a Daz advert. 'You're allowing an unknown man into your house and then he dictates to you what you should think. That's propaganda for a sexist society.'

James, too, was great. He said he used porn – 'it's helped me through my fallow periods' – but was uncertain about it too. 'That Wonderbra advert . . . we'd be kidding ourselves if we didn't say that's a picture of a woman being subservient to a little sexual token, a bra . . .' he said. '*Penthouse* and *Playboy* try to diffuse their pornographic images by putting in features about cars or lifestyles of the rich and famous – that's just backing up an advertising industry. It's fusing pornography and product.' And he was supposedly the blokey one.

Teenage girls have a weird, all-knowing instinct about pop stars. They're psychic, almost. They see things that others don't; often that the bands themselves aren't fully aware of. The teenage girls could see Richey's beauty and sense his distress; some loved him because of it.

The Manics were an interesting band for young women to be into. They wrote about how hard girls' lives could be. They sang about abortion and prostitution. (The Manics had wanted Kylie Minogue to sing 'Little Baby Nothing'. There was no way she would ever have said yes. But you have to admire their chutzpah. In the end, they got porn star Traci Lords to sing the part instead.) Nicky wore dresses a lot and extolled the joys of housework (he had OCD symptoms and cleanliness was important to him). They appeared in teen magazines like *Just 17* and *Smash Hits*, which, at the time, many so-called credible bands refused to do. The Manics understood the power of a poster, they cavorted in videos, they celebrated doomy teenage desires in a pop way.

They respected their fans' intelligence, putting quotes on their records, from poets e.e. cummings, Sylvia Plath and Philip Larkin, from philosopher Nietzsche, from Valerie Solonas ('60s Society for Cutting Up Men feminist, who tried to assassinate Andy Warhol). Also from the Situationists and the Futurist movements. Here was Primo Levi on their second album *Gold Against the Soul*, Octave Mirbeau on their third, *The Holy Bible*. All designed to provoke Manics fans into investigating where the quotes were from. 'The Richey reading list', Simon Price calls it, and says that many of their early fans have gone on to work as educators: 'manic street teachers'.

A certain type of teenager will always be attracted to someone of Richey's intelligence and sensitivity, not despite but because it manifests in self-harm. Broadly, especially back then, feelings of anger and expressions of violence are directed outwards by young men, but inwards by young women. Richey was not a person that slotted easily into gendered stereotypes, and he couldn't bring himself to hurt anyone, so he turned difficult feelings on himself. Anorexia, which he had on and off from his teenage years, can be to do with control and a dislike of growing into adulthood, especially sexual adulthood. He wrote about it in '4st 7lb' on *The Holy Bible*, the third and darkest of the Manics' albums.

And Richey's cutting himself was so common that the band were used to it. 'The only people who are disturbed by Richey cutting himself are those who don't know him,' Sean said. 'They don't understand. We do know him, we do understand.' He'd done it without fanfare throughout the whole of the Manics' career, even while living at the Halls (he would cut himself while watching TV and did so until asked to stop). On tour in Thailand in 1993, he used knives sent to him by a fan to draw blood on his chest before he went on stage. He said to the *NME*'s Barbara Ellen, who was there: 'When I cut myself I feel so much better. All the little things that might have been annoying me suddenly seem so trivial because I'm concentrating on the pain. I'm not a person who can scream and shout so this is my only outlet. It's all done very logically.'

When I talked to him about porn, I asked him about the cutting. He said: 'I find it attractive. I find it sexual.' He asked the photographer if he should cut himself for the pictures. The photographer said no.

The black hole in the centre of the story of the Manics – in the 1990s and, still, now – is Richey's disappearance. When he went away, the band's history, their personas and presentation, just seemed to topple into the gap he left behind. For a time, it seemed as though the band might follow.

It's a story that's been told a lot; there are many books about what happened. On 1 February 1995, Richey and James were due to go to America to do some interviews. They were staying in a London hotel, but at some point during the night, Richey checked out and travelled home to Cardiff, where he left his passport in his flat and then went away. For two weeks, he seems to have been in and around Newport, possibly living in his car. His car was discovered near the Severn bridge around two weeks after he went missing. He left a letter and other items for an on–off girlfriend. Several people claim to have seen him since, but their accounts don't really add up. Many years later some CCTV footage of the bridge was examined. It was inconclusive.

1994 had been a tough time. Richey, like the rest of the band, had been devastated by the death of manager Philip Hall in December 1993. At the start of the year, he'd been drinking too much, self-harming and not eating. Though the band still loved each other, Nicky had got married, Sean was living with his girl-friend, James was out and about in London. Richey was alone in his Cardiff flat. He'd gone into hospital in the spring because he'd cut himself very badly and his weight had dropped to six stone, and from there, to the Priory, where he went through a 12-step programme and stopped drinking. The Manics played some festival gigs without him. At the end of August, *The Holy Bible* – bleak, black-eyed punk, with samples of interview dialogue including the mother of one of Peter Sutcliffe's victims and a report from the

Nuremberg trials, its horror-filled lyrics mostly written by Richey
– came out on the same week as Oasis's debut *Definitely Maybe*.
This wasn't a Blur vs Oasis battle. *The Holy Bible* went in at Number
Six. The band were defiant, as always.

A few days before he disappeared, Richey cut off his hair. He
was sad about his dog Snoopy dying. He was writing a lot, then
scribbling much of it out. In the last interview he did, a week
before disappearing, he talked about how hard intimate relationships were for him – he was hugely idealistic about love – but it
wasn't a downbeat conversation. 'The band is getting better and
better,' he said. 'The lyrics are too.'

It took a while for people to understand that Richey wasn't
there. The band weren't sure whether to continue. 'A Design for
Life', their astonishing anthem for the working class, was what
saved them. Nicky wrote the lyrics; James blended them with some
others, from 'Pure Motive', and created the tune in about ten
minutes. The song is an angry lament for the days when workers
had access to education and real jobs ('libraries gave us power'),
and a pinpoint description of small-minded assumptions about
working-class life, that everyone just gets pissed and understands
nothing.

'A Design for Life' swept aside the nay-sayers with its emotion
and its violins, its thunder down the scale into its enormous chorus:
'We don't talk about love/We only want to get drunk' with its
missing 'you think' before it. It went to Number Two. Its artwork
deliberately drew on New Order, with an embossed metallic grey
sleeve, designed by Mark Farrow, who'd worked with Factory
Records. (The Manics considered changing their name, as Joy

Division did after Ian Curtis killed himself, but didn't.) *Everything Must Go*, the successor to *The Holy Bible*, went to Number Two as well. It was still in the Top Five a year after it was released.

At the 1996 Brit Awards, Manic Street Preachers played 'A Design for Life', with images from the Poll Tax riots, Northern Ireland protests, Eton, and slogans like George Orwell's HOPE LIES IN THE PROLES flashing up behind them. They won best band and best album, and dedicated their awards to Philip Hall and to Richey. Nicky wore a T-shirt that said 'I Love Hoovering'.

'Richey has become set in the firmament, he will always be there, and troubled young people will always find Richey Edwards,' says Simon Price. 'But the iconography of that doesn't mean he wasn't a real person. He was.'

The emotional churn of your twenties is hard for anyone, everything shifts at speed. And if your mind is constantly reeling with interior chatter, if it moves quickly and makes constant connections and finds significance and has everything overlap and intertwine into a pattern that only you can see, then that is hard to live with. Both for the person whose head is like that, and for the people around them. Something meant as a joke – an aside, just a light sentence – can land heavily. Everything can be picked apart and found wanting. And success is almost impossible to deal with, because it's never how anyone expects it to be. It doesn't heal anything.

The Manics will never shed the devastation of Richey's disappearance. On *Everything Must Go*'s title track, they acknowledge this, and have done on every album since. They pay a quarter of their royalties to his family; they set up a microphone stand for him every time they play. The fall-out has been complicated and has affected the band and his family ever since. But they've lived thirty years now, they have families, they're successful, with a work ethic so strong that when they stopped making albums as a band for a short while, they brought out solo LPs instead.

If they'd continued along the Richey/*Holy Bible* route, they wouldn't have been the stadium-filling rock entity they are now. But without him, they would never have understood who they were, nor made the impression they did. Some of their fans don't know Richey existed. Some of them only follow the Manics because of him.

He was – is – their friend. What were the Manic Street Preachers supposed to do? You do what you can. And they can and do make music. So they do that.

Big for Your Boots

ELASTICA
'Connection'

Honestly? Elastica were everyone's favourite. We loved them. We loved their spiky, snarky, over-in-a-blink songs, we adored their boysy style, we thrilled to see snotty young women (girls, we called them then) – skinny-jeaned, leather-jacketed, bovver-booted – playing guitar and jumping up and down. They were smart, they were sexy, they sounded like Blondie and The Fall and the Buzzcocks and all your scuzzy junky-punk faves. No love-drippiness, no woe-is-me heartbreak, no angst in their lyrics. Instead, they sang about disappointing lovers, about having a lie-in, about silly groupies, about having sex in a car. Live, they were harder and jerkier than their records, and God, it was a thrill to see three women stepping forward, holding their guitars like weapons, bullet-proof. We all loved them; but women really, really loved Elastica. Why? Because – if you haven't guessed, if you want it spelt out – Elastica were cool.

Justine Frischmann was always cool. Way before Elastica, you'd spot her walking slowly across a backstage area in a sludgy man's suit, her dark fringe falling over her eyebrows, talking to her best friend Jane Oliver, or Jarvis, or a journalist, and you'd think, yup, that woman is cooool. She was clever (she could do the proper crossword in *The Times*, which always impressed); posh, but carried it; surprisingly friendly and fun; also slouchy and louche, unusual qualities in a woman. Guitarist Donna Matthews looked great too, in a saucer-eyed, urchin, pop-punk way, a forgotten Fagin's pick-pocket kid, a member of The Strokes before The Strokes had even been invented. Always moving, always on the edge of sticking out her tongue. On stage she was like those toys you got as a child, a small plastic character atop a single spring. You squashed the character down onto the plastic stand, licking it to make it stick, and after a few seconds, boingggg, it popped up and bounced around on the spot. That was Donna. Kohl-eyed bassist Annie Holland, who appeared to be made up of equal parts Chrissie Hynde and Keith Richards, was quieter, harder to read, less press-friendly, so mysterious that Donna (and Jane Oliver) wrote a song called Annie about her (it described going to Brighton, where Annie lived, and getting drunk). And behind them all, on drums, was the loopily talented skinny-boy Justin Welch, pretty and nuts, who'd mug for the camera and hit his head with his drumstick. Elastica's band look was: small leather bombers (not motorcycle jackets), black sleeveless T-shirts or men's shirts with several buttons undone, straight scruffy jeans maybe with a turn-up, hi-tops or Dr. Martens boots. See? Cool.

Of course, cool isn't a cure-all. It doesn't calm your turmoil, soothe your inner self. It can get you a few friends (but are they really?); it can pay some bills, though not the big ones. Really, being cool doesn't make your life that much better. But it's an armour. It attracts others but scares them into not coming too close, lets you cut through the world with a force field around you, makes people feel grateful when you're nice to them, rather than the other way around. For women, it can deaden a lot – but not all – of normalised sexism, simply by scaring away all the silly boys.

Within the lads-lads-lads noise of the mid-'90s, Elastica's cool came out of them not being girly. I interviewed Justine a few times, and in 1993 she said, 'I don't think we sound like we're making girl music. That's the unusual bit.' Girliness was anathema. All four of them had the same aesthetic: lean and crop-haired and tough and smart-mouthed, and all of them sexed and drugged and rock 'n' rolled without gender division. Not androgynous, but sexual in a bad-boy manner: off-hand, unfussed, the opposite of try-hard. Said Justine, in her airy way: 'The girl who looks boyish is the intelligent boy's choice.' A delight to hear for any young straight woman uncomfortable with the proffered option of getting your tits out for the lads.

Justine refused to discuss women in rock. She wanted Elastica's music to be fun, as opposed to earnest, which was how feminism was often regarded in the music press: a reaction to 1980s political correctness and some of the more po-faced aspects of riot grrrl. (Riot grrrl bands were small, noisy, punky, feminist, genuinely independent, no-sell-out noiseniks that included the UK's Huggy Bear and the US's Bikini Kill. Jo from Huggy Bear went out with Graham for a while in the mid-'90s.) 'A lot of the riot grrrl bands I've seen have made me feel ashamed to be a girl,' Justine said to *Select*. 'It seems stupid to me to be in a band if you've no actual talent or gift for it'. Her refusal to get into the weeds of feminism's third age was astute given that the woman in rock topic was more of a US music-media obsession. In the UK, Elastica had different press hurdles. There was journalistic cynicism around Justine's money and class (her father and grandfather were hugely successful civil engineering consultants, so well-off their company appeared in the *Sunday Times* Rich List), a few raised eyebrows about her love life, some questions as to whether Elastica were actually any good, or just fashionable.

But Elastica blew all that away. The cynicism was understandable, not because of the class or hype queries, but because what happened with Elastica was so completely unusual within indie music at that time. They made it all look so . . . easy.

Unlike Suede or Pulp or Sleeper, bands which laboured away unappreciated and ignored for years; unlike Blur, who aired their embarrassing growing pains in public; unlike Radiohead, who ended up having to claw their way into a future after being frozen to the spot by 'Creep' ; unlike almost any band at any time, Elastica didn't seem to have to try. They weren't old friends from a dead-end town. They didn't go through different personnel (that came post-Britpop), they didn't spend years wandering in and out of artistic cul-de-sacs, they didn't write letters to journalists or record companies, or hammer on doors trying to get music business attention. They just formed, wrote songs a bit like the bands they liked, rehearsed for a short while, and bang! they were successful. It was like a fairy-tale story; a ridiculous plot line for a stupid film. But it happened.

*

What everyone knows about Justine is that she went out with Brett from Suede and then Damon from Blur. But more important, really, was that she played guitar in Suede and then watched Blur play a lot.

Justine was a founder member of Suede with Brett and Mat Osman; Suede were a messy project, a chaotic slow-burn of a band, taking their time to arrive at their correct bedsit-sleaze-passion form. In 1991, when they'd created 'The Drowners' and had just come up with 'Metal Mickey', Justine left. She'd started seeing Damon, so that made things very difficult with Brett; and she didn't like the music they were making any more. 'I've never been a fan of Bernard's guitar playing,' she told me later. 'I always thought he was going to get simpler and he never did. He got a lot more twiddly.'

She did like how Blur's guitarist played, though. 'For years, I watched Graham play and thought, "You are God, I want to play guitar like that." Just being able to go down to the studio and listen to what they're doing was a really good thing for me.'

She and Damon had got it together a few months after a 1990 gig in Brighton when Suede had supported Blur. He was cute and clever, like her; they'd hang out at Syndrome, which was packed with music journalists and with bands, from Cud to Ride to Lush to Curve to Pulp to Slowdive to Five Thirty. 'It was a weekly snogfest', Justine said, 'where everyone got off with everyone and everyone was in a band.'

At first, post-Suede, Justine decided she would become an architect, and got a job at a good firm. But it was a disaster; after designing beautiful cliff-hanging glass sculptures at university, she was spending her time detailing access panels and car-park layouts. 'We weren't allowed to listen to Walkmans and we weren't allowed to smoke,' she said, 'and I had to get there at 9 a.m. I thought, "Fuck this."' A band seemed the logical alternative. Plus, almost as soon as she'd left, Suede had got a record deal, and by 1992, they were officially 'the best new band in Britain', according to *Melody Maker*. Though she was pleased for Brett ('He wanted to do it so much and he was so determined and I just thought, "I can't bear it if he's going to be playing to three people at the Falcon for the next five years"'), it was also a wake-up call: 'Obviously, it was a bit like, "Shiiiiiittt".'

For a little while, there were some weird rumours about Justine forming a band with Jane (Graham's girlfriend) and Other Justine (Alex's girlfriend), which seemed . . . odd. Blur's girlfriends turning themselves into a band? Just like that? But Justine had other ideas. She remembered Justin from Suede – he'd played with them for a few weeks – so she got in touch and they started rehearsing together. She met Annie, who lived in Brighton and made stained glass, through a friend. And Donna, mad guitar hedonist, up for anything, arrived via a *Melody Maker* advert. Justine nearly didn't bother seeing her because Donna lived in Newport and she thought, 'Great, one in Brighton, one in Newport, this will never work.' But Donna was the catalyst that fired the band into action. By October 1992, the band were in place.

Justine had observed Blur's difficulties around *Modern Life Is Rubbish*; the pressure from their labels to write a single, to alter lyrics, to change producer to someone deemed more current. She'd also learnt from Suede: she once sat in a record company's office for eight hours, waiting to meet a particular A&R person and give them their tape ('I was sent because I was the bird'). So, she was alive to the difficulties of being in an alternative band, how long everything could take, how many things could go wrong.

But, for Elastica, it all happened very quickly – like tumbling down a set of stairs – across a few months in 1993. The bit that Justine liked, which was rehearsing, creating songs, sitting on top of the gear in the back of a little van driving to gigs; all that was over and done in under a year. During that time they acquired a manager; landed a publishing deal, plus a small UK record deal with Defective, and a big one with Geffen in the US; got a PR, the hugely popular Polly Birkbeck, who'd moved from Food to Savage and Best, the press company for Suede, Pulp, Echobelly; played some gigs. They had to use a fake name, Onk, for their first live shows, because there was so much interest. Their first gig proper was in May, at the Old Trout in Windsor. They played for twenty-two minutes, because they only had twenty-two minutes of songs. Six months later, they were supporting Pulp on their Lipgloss tour.

In November 1993, Elastica brought out 'Stutter', a funny rant about a male lover underperforming in the bedroom. It only went to Number 80, but still, they were voted 1993's best new band by both *NME* and *Melody Maker* readers. On New Year's Day 1994, Justine was in the *Observer*; by February, Elastica had a mini-feature in *Vogue*, and Justine was on the front cover of *Select* – winking, smoking a cigar – under the coverline 'This Is the Future'. Elastica had released a grand total of two singles. 'It was lightning,' she said to me later. 'It felt like the time and the place, one of those weird moments where everything lines up for a bunch of people, and not just us.'

Not just them, no. Things started happening for Blur, too: in April 1994, they released *Parklife*, it went to Number One and Damon's life became utterly public. He started having panic attacks from the strangeness of achieving his dreams, but Justine couldn't help much; she was busy with her band now. The press were all over Elastica, not just the music press but other magazines: *The Face, i-D, Arena*. Polly, in her first ever formal PR job, had to manage the demand.

Control was really important to Justine. Control of image (their album's cover was shot by Juergen Teller in black and white, and they looked exactly as they wished), and control of songs, too, was vital. She had a template, which was no repeating of the bridge or the chorus to fade out, and no wig-out guitar solos, so most Elastica songs were over in under three minutes. Which meant they needed quite a few to make an album. That was OK: Justine wrote most of the songs and her avowed technique was listening to songs by bands she liked, and then working out what she could take from them. (This ended up with Wire and The Stranglers suing Elastica for plagiarism, though The Stranglers said they didn't approve of their lawyers doing it.) Elastica's influences weren't solely British, though Justine used an affectedly London accent to say lines like 'Make a cup of tea, put a record on'. There was English scuzz-pop in there; but also a good slice of late 1970s CBGBs punk. When Elastica first went to America, in early 1995, they played at the Mercury Lounge, and in the audience were Iggy Pop and Blondie's

Debbie Harry. Debbie danced throughout the whole of their set. (See? Cool.)

It was the press interest, really, that showed that Elastica might become something more than an indie band of the old variety – loved by fans but not destined for the Top Ten. Over 1994, they only released two singles, 'Line Up' (which got to Number 20) and 'Connection' (Number 17): hardly setting the charts ablaze. Still, they were statements. They both featured jagged guitars, a sort of *heurrrgh* puke sound, and Justine's wry, almost spoken delivery. 'Connection' was the better song, though; heavier, straight in, no messing, over and done with in under two-and-a-half minutes, the guitar riff a direct steal from Wire's 'Three Girl Rhumba' (three girl Elastica), the subject matter either love or fame. It inspires a straight jump-and-down pogo dance, rather than anything wafty.

Elastica were art-rock (as opposed to Pulp and Blur's art-pop), and in Justine's mind – and, really, in everyone else's – they were destined to be a hip underground act, like The Fall or, yes, Wire. Instead, when they put out *Elastica*, their first album, in March 1995 (on the same day as Radiohead put out *The Bends*), it was the fastest-selling debut LP since Oasis's *Definitely Maybe*, and went straight in at Number One.

Justine loved 1993 and 1994, though, like everyone else, she hated the Britpop label: 'The bands didn't all go together. But there was a core gang of people who had known each other for a long time, we'd dated, been flatmates, played gigs together.' Blur, Pulp and Elastica's social lives overlapped a lot: Jane Oliver, Justine's best friend, had gone out with Graham for many years and featured in the video for Pulp's 'Razzmatazz'; Steve Mackey, Pulp's bassist, and Elastica's Justin ended up sharing a flat. It was thrilling to see their gang be noticed, be appreciated, and the culmination, really, was 1995.

Everything was still pretty easy for Elastica. Perhaps because of the 1970s New York influence, even the US succumbed to their charms. Unlike the dismal travails of Blur, Oasis and what the Americans called 'London Suede', Elastica were greeted with, if not open arms, a friendly elbow crooked around the shoulder, a pat on the back, a ticket backstage to the best parties. They made an impression on the US alternative charts, and their record label put them on a heavy-duty tour around the country, and then, to other places in the world. They did almost a hundred gigs, hopped between the US, Spain and Japan, and joined Lollapalooza when Sinéad O'Connor dropped out.

The year started out fun. 'Waking Up' went to Number 13 and Elastica played on *Top of the Pops*, with Damon on keyboards, mugging like mad in silly specs, playing with one finger, in the background but wanting attention. (Blur played 'Jubilee' on the same episode.) Justine rode it out. She made a lot of things seem effortless, though they weren't. It was Justine's band, she was the leader, she did most of the interviews, had the talks with the manager, did the grown-up work. It wasn't always fun and it set her a little apart from the others in Elastica.

But she was also separated by being the only band member without a hard-drug habit. Annie and Donna, from the start, were wrapped up quite tightly with Class As, including heroin; Justin joined in too. And as certain drugs will, it made them secretive. Gradually, while they slogged around the USA, the other three cast Justine into the unlovely role of headteacher – they called her Führer behind her back – without her being aware of it. Her careful control was starting to curdle.

Still, there was a lot of fun and chaos to be had, especially around Donna and Justin: the *NME* came out to New York and noted down the larks. Donna was chucked out of a radio interview for belching, Donna and Annie blew smoke into a carrier bag on a plane, Justin got fleeced out of nearly $300 by a professional gambler, Justine hung off Brooklyn Bridge for the photos. But, busy as they were, silly as their fun was, other aspects were getting harder to plan and control. In March 1995, *Select* put Justine on the cover, with others, under the coverline 'Lust'. She was styled like Christine Keeler, with no top on, straddled across a turned-around chair. She didn't like those pictures much. And then, in the middle of 1995, for *Select*'s fifth birthday, the whole band were photographed as though they were at a swanky party: in black and red, all slick and sparkles. When the band saw the pictures, they hated them and refused to do the interview. It was so close to deadline that nothing else could replace it. *Select* put the picture on the cover anyway.

At Glastonbury in 1995, on Sunday, Elastica headlined the *NME* stage. They were the culmination of a weekend that had seemed like a shift to the new: Pulp had triumphed as last-minute Pyramid Stage headliner, after Orbital, who were also amazing; The Prodigy had become full Prodge, with Keith and his pink hair; Take That's Robbie Williams had appeared on stage with Oasis, like a clown; John Major had resigned. It was hot and it felt like we might be winning. Elastica were as blistering as the weather. During their last song, 'Vaseline', a man described later as 'a George Best look-alike' streaked around the stage. It was Anthony Genn, ex-Pulp bass player, Jarvis's old friend. If you wanted, you could see his moment of glory as like Damon on *Top of the Pops*: boys stealing attention from the women's special time. But, really, it was just a laugh.

Later, August would seem like the turning point. On the 7th, after playing T in the Park in Scotland on the 5th, and then the Féile festival in Ireland on the 6th, Annie left the band. Touring was breaking her, as were her habits. She hated being on the Lollapalooza bill; the big stages, the unfamiliar crew, the heat, the far-away crowds behind the VIP seats who didn't know who Elastica were. So she left, and the other three just carried on, fulfilling their contracts, with Abby Travis, who was also on Lollapalooza, playing in Beck's band, stepping in to play bass. Justin said later he couldn't quite believe it when Annie left. 'I remember getting on the plane and thinking, "What are we thinking? We're going back to the States without her. Our friend."' In October, Donna came to Justine saying she was worried she couldn't come off heroin, but Justine said she was sure she'd be OK. No one quite knew what they were doing.

Drugs and touring will always take their toll; they're traditional rock 'n' roll pitfalls that some cope with, some don't. But then, after Blur vs Oasis, came a new, weird challenge. The tabloids arrived, on Damon and Justine's doorstep. 'Photographers outside our house,' she said to me later. 'People going through our rubbish, people bothering my family, a lot of stuff written that wasn't true. I absolutely hated it, it ruined the whole thing for me.' A stalker poured petrol through their letterbox and set fire to it. They were followed everywhere by paparazzi, photographed going to the shop.

Even when they went on holiday, they couldn't find peace. 'We went on holiday to Spain and we just couldn't find anywhere to go where people didn't recognise him,' she said. 'We couldn't have a single meal without people coming up and taking pictures, we couldn't be on a beach, we'd get in the car and drive for three hours to the most remote place we could find and there'd be a bunch of Blur fans there.' During 1995, due to their bands' touring schedules, Damon and Justine were together for around three weeks.

After Elastica's tour finally ended, in February 1996 in Australia, they came home. Outside, pop culture had become glitzy. The Spice Girls popped up, Britpop turned into Cool Britannia, New Labour got in, everything went *TFI* and *FHM*. But for many of their friends, inside was darker. Heroin had worked its way into a lot of people's lives, now including Justine's too. Time got stretchy. Elastica knew they had to come up with another LP, but Donna and Justine weren't getting on, and narcotics meant nobody could come up with an idea and complete it. Justine went missing for weeks on end. Donna spent hours searching for the perfect note.

Everything dragged: in 1997, Justine and Damon finally finished, and Justine ended it with Donna, too, and sacked Polly, Elastica's PR. (Polly chucked all her front covers, all the features and pictures into a rubbish sack and binned the lot.) After a few months, Justine went through rehab; it took Donna a few years longer. In 2000, Elastica made another album, *The Menace*. Annie was back, along with some new members, but there was no Donna. *The Menace* got to Number 24.

After 1995, everything shifted, the kaleidoscope was shaken and the shards and sparkles landed in different combinations. Jane Oliver started going out with *Tank Girl* artist Jamie Hewlett. Jamie shared a flat with Damon, which didn't help Damon and Graham's relationship. Damon formed Gorillaz with Jamie in 1998. Elastica didn't have a deep and long-term history with each other; they'd come together so easily, but their ties weren't strong.

Perhaps Elastica should have done what Sleeper would go on to do in 1998: assess the situation with open eyes, and just stop. Justine says she regrets it now, that she wishes that they'd just made one album. So let's imagine that's what they did. (You can do this with lots of other bands. Oasis stopping after *Be Here Now* would be neater, at least.) Elastica formed, gave us one brilliant LP, played Reading and Glastonbury, conquered America, and, fin.

Justine moved to America in 2006. She had to leave England to feel normal, she told me, to be able to walk the street and be anonymous and take a breath. 'The whole thing took its toll on me mentally and spiritually,' she said. 'It took me some time to readjust.'

I used to want Elastica to reform, to play again, because so many other bands from the '90s were doing just that, and I loved them so. But I don't, now. Because what's more important, a cool band being cool again, or the people in it living their lives and being happy? Justine is an abstract artist, married and living in San Francisco; Donna is exploring improvisation and ecstatic feelings in film and sound, studying for a PhD in Glasgow; Justin plays with other bands, including Miki Berenyi's Piroshka, and, most recently, The Jesus and Mary Chain. He's married to Sharon Mew, who joined Elastica Part 2 as a keyboardist. Annie is somewhere being Annie. There has been some talk of Elastica reforming, but Justine won't do it without Annie, and Annie won't do it at all. A TV company is making a drama about a '90s indie band and is using Elastica as the template. Which sounds terrible, of course.

Do we need someone to act out what happened, to pretend to be a band we loved? Do we need the real band to play for us, to rattle out their album tracks in order, one to fifteen, for our delectation and delight? Is any of it necessary?

When really, if we want, if we think hard enough, we can remember Elastica clearly. See how frayed and brilliant they were, stepping forward in their jeans with their guitars, hammering out their short sharp songs, staring out as the sun set over Glastonbury, the perfect band. See? Cool.

Don't Look Back in Anger

OASIS

'Slide Away'

Oasis arrived ready. That's how I remember it. Some bands land, bang, fully formed, all there, with the songs and the look and the quotes and the playing live and the what-you-going-to-do-about-it attitude. With their own insider language that spans from conspiratorial to confrontational. Do you dare to approach? Will they let you in? Each member of the band is different from the others, but somehow, recognisably the same. A gang. A family – literally, in the case of Oasis. And just by existing, by walking into the spotlight, they shift our culture.

I first saw Oasis play the Marquee in 1994, alongside many other journalists and indie music types. We had been told already that they were good. I was working as a presenter on a cheap-and-cheerful late-night youth TV show with an audience corralled from the streets of Deptford (the production assistants would go out and persuade local teenagers to come into the studio), there to watch comedians and bands. The booker was good and we got great acts: the Manics. Senseless Things. Naughty by Nature. (I introduced Naughty by Nature while bouncing on a space hopper.

They looked confused.) Anyway, at a recording of the show, as I stood on a balcony trying to remember my script, a music promoter told me about Oasis. He told me about them in a confidential, insider manner, like, 'You'll want to know about this band, and you'll be glad I told you.'

He was right. A few months later, I went to the Marquee, along with everyone else, and Oasis were great. Impressive. Straight-forward. No messing about, no angst, no do-you-fancy-me hair-flopping, no throwing themselves from speaker stacks or writhing on the floor. Their music was familiar, The Beatles and glam rock swirled with a bit of psychedelia, and they played it confidently, without fuss, very loud. I thought: 'Are they playing too slow?' They looked out at the crowd, unsmiling, almost stock still. Noel watched his own hands when he was playing guitar, like he was checking he was getting the notes right. Liam sang up into the microphone, hands behind his back. They seemed so deliberate and unstoppable. The drums went onnne-twothree-four, onnne-twothreefour. They were completely intoxicating, especially Liam.

A big part of me thought, 'Oh, there they are'. I grew up in a nouveau-riche suburb of Manchester, a place where footballers and *Coronation Street* actors bought mock Tudor houses, once they'd started making money. Oasis were inner-city Manchester, and I knew lots of boys like that, because there was nothing to do in my suburb if you weren't interested in shagging a footballer, so I went into town, to the Haçienda and the Ritz, and to gigs. In town, there were lads like Oasis everywhere. They held their cigarettes like darts and only passed the spliff to you once all the other lads had had their toke. They said little unless they were drunk or on an E, and then they wouldn't shut up, hilarious but also quick to put you down. If you got too enthusiastic about something they would look at you, take a long drag and say, 'What's she so fucking excited about?' If you were like me at the time, which was like a puppy off a leash, this could be crushing, even as you laughed.

When I moved to London, I discovered that because of acid house and the reputation of 'Madchester', Manchester had a lot of kudos in the music scene. But, at the same time, quite a lot of people in London were scared of Manchester. They liked the Manc humour, the slagging and cockiness, but they worried that it might be directed at them. This was useful for me, because I wasn't scared of Manchester or Mancunians. So I was sent to interview many of the city's bands: New Order, Happy Mondays, The Stone Roses. The difference between those bands and Oasis was the desire for success, and the desire for fame.

Oasis seemed to distil years of Mancunian snotty romance – the walk, the style, the sneer – into something pure, boiling it down to its most basic, potent form, like potcheen. It was mesmerising, especially when it came with their astonishingly catchy, positive-yet-yearning songs. Those songs were ready to be sung on the terraces; out of the windows of late-night taxis; wobbling, drunk and teary, along the high street after closing time, with your arms thrown to the sky, bellowing the chorus into the faces of your friends. They were songs that had lived inside you for years but you hadn't quite been able to locate them. Until there was Liam on stage, chin up, hands hidden, beautiful and intimidating, singing those songs out into a crowd full of people that somehow knew them too.

Yet, the band wasn't accepted by everyone, not straight away. Some people thought the music was too meat and potatoes; the romance was too on-the-nose. Plenty of music journalists were underwhelmed. People like music for many different reasons. There was a way of writing about music back then, full of clever references, if-you-know-you-know jokes and right-on politics, that insisted you couldn't like certain bands because they didn't say acceptably thought-through things about class or they weren't cool. (Cool usually meant that the journalist didn't fancy his chances in a fight with the band.) All based on the idea that you can't separate the art from the artist, that only someone with impeccable politics can be allowed to dream up a tune and play it for an audience. This sentiment still exists today.

But still, even those who thought Oasis weren't all that could tell that a switch had been flipped. Oasis changed the atmosphere. They shook everything up, like the bad lads arriving at a party, the townies on the top deck of the bus. Scrappy, mouthy, up for a fight. Taking the piss. You wouldn't want to be on the wrong side of them, but if you were accepted into their orbit, well, you'd be untouchable.

In a time when there were many, many music publications, and they came out weekly, fortnightly, monthly, packed with information and gossip, reviews and interviews, Oasis were a gift. A gift of the gob.

Johnny Hopkins, a friend who I met in Manchester some years before I was a music journalist, started working as a press officer at Creation Records in 1993. He was six months into his job when his boss, Alan McGee, called him on his landline around midnight (this was pre-mobile phones). Johnny was asleep in bed.

'McGee was like, "Johnny, Johnny, I've got the perfect group for you."' McGee meant the perfect group for Johnny to do the press campaign. *Great*, Johnny thought. *But I'm in bed.* So, Johnny said to McGee, 'OK, let's talk about it tomorrow . . . And he's like, "No, Johnny, I've got to tell you now. I'm up in Glasgow, they look amazing, they've got these great songs, and they threatened to trash the place if they weren't allowed to play." I was like, "Great, Alan, that does sound up my street, and we'll talk tomorrow." He called me every half-hour about them until it was morning.'

Johnny already knew that McGee could be enthusiastic, especially when well-refreshed in the middle of the night. But at work the next day, he was given the Oasis demo tape. It had a homemade cover, which was unusual (most demos just had the band's name and a phone number scrawled on them). The cover had their name on it, in lower-case '90s style, over a Union flag swirling as though it was going down the plughole. The songs were great: ten bangers. Johnny thought they sounded like acid house, but played in a rock 'n' roll way. I'm not sure about this, but it's a nice way to think about them.

Soon after, Liam, Noel and Bonehead came down from Manchester to Creation's office, then in east London. 'They came through the office and there was this crackle,' says Johnny. 'They had this presence. We were on the floor above and before they even got up to our room, all the girls in reception were buzzing . . . You could just hear it through the building. All the lads were similarly energised. And they came up to the press room. There were three of us there, each sat by our own particular wall, and Liam, Noel and Bonehead walk in and stand in the middle in a triangle with their backs to each other, addressing the three of us. Like those speaker cabinets they have in some sound systems . . .

'And they boomed out this surreal dialogue, just sparking off each other. You could see shades of the early Beatles interviews on TV in America, but it was funnier and coarser and less mannered. It just flew out of them. They were unbelievably funny, individually and collectively. And there was a really good spirit between them, a strong bond.'

There are certain criteria that a PR (an A&R person, a manager, a record-label boss, a journalist) looks for in a new act. Usually, the artist will have a few boxes ticked, and will have the potential to tick the rest. Here's the list, according to Johnny.

- Great songs and the ability to play live.
- A strong image; look cool in photos (harder to achieve in an era without mobile phones: people weren't as sure of themselves in front of the camera, and the spectre of 'selling out', which included appearing even vaguely cheerful in photos, was always there).
- A clear sense of who they are, and a realistic sense of what they want to achieve. ('Very important', Johnny explains, 'because plenty of bands walk in saying, "We're going to be the biggest thing since whatever," and you know they haven't got the ability or the staying power, so you have to temper that for them. That's often the biggest part of the job.')

- Interesting in interviews.
- Strong work ethic.

You might think that most bands can tick these boxes easily, but they can't. Maybe the songs aren't there. Or the look is all wrong. Or the person leading the band isn't quite right. It's very rare that a band ticks all those boxes. But Oasis did. Plus they were fan-friendly.

'Fans could aspire to be Noel, because he was the leader, he wrote the songs, he was going to earn the most money,' says Johnny. 'And people could aspire, in their dreams, to be Liam, or to sleep with him. But they actually could be Bonehead, Guigsy or Tony McCarroll, because the three of them had that everyman appeal. That's really important.'

No band drops out of the sky. They just practise off-camera, to the side, in somewhere other than London. Oasis were The Rain for a little while, in early 1991: Liam, Bonehead, Guigsy, Tony. At that point, Noel was roadie-ing with the Inspiral Carpets; he was a guitar tech for five years and he was good at the job. A roadie's job is technical and physical: get the equipment in, make sure it's set up right, pass the right guitar to the right person at the right time, put it all away at the end of the gig. But there's another part to the job and that's to provide the relief: the jokes, the drinking, the couldn't-give-a-fuck-mate attitude. Noel was good at that, plus he enjoyed the travel, the hotels, the pay (£350 a week).

He once said to a journalist – who'd turned up to interview the Inspiral Carpets but found they couldn't be bothered – 'You know if I was in the band, I'd do an interview with any cunt.' So the journalist interviewed him, and Noel gave great quote. He said: 'Inspirals, Happy Mondays, Ride, Blur and all them lot, it's good that they're in the charts. Very very very healthy. Indeed.' And: 'I've seen gigs. I can judge how many people are in a fucking field. There's no point in putting on massive great big gigs outdoors on the fucking side of a hill and being shit. You can't get the sound right, the facilities are shit, you can't get the right support bands.' And: 'All I'm concerned with is what comes out of them speakers at the end of the fucking night and what goes onto records. What it's all about is the songs. And from the crew's point of view, it's all about taking loads of drugs and having a good time!'

By the time he joined Oasis, Noel had a lot of backroom knowledge. 'He was clocking everything when he was roadie-ing,' Johnny says. How the money worked, how the songs worked. How to set up gigs that make money and sound good. How the interviews worked. What he could and would do better when he was in a band. 'The momentum once we let Oasis out of the bag was insane. But it's all down to the work ethic. Once Noel got in that band, he just drilled them relentlessly, rehearsed them relentlessly. That is the person that he is.' And he was a natural when it came to the music press.

Before Oasis, there were plenty of Mancunian bands that had the songs, the looks, some of the this-is-our-show-now attitude. New Order, The Smiths, Happy Mondays, The Stone Roses . . . But they were less press-amenable. Morrissey was fantastic in interviews: he had opinions, he spoke in long, perfectly constructed sentences, he looked great in photographs. But he was difficult with anyone who wasn't completely on his side. Happy Mondays were caricatured by writers, and weren't that interested in doing interviews, though Shaun and Bez were brilliant talkers. New Order and The Stone Roses actively avoided most press. In real life, every one of those bands were friendly, but they often presented themselves as otherwise to journalists.

Oasis, on the other hand, enjoyed talking to the press, especially Noel. He loved talking, full stop. He phoned journalists up when he was bored, held court backstage, told hilarious stories, wound people up and enjoyed it all. The mayhem, the gossip, the challenge: no problem. He liked socialising, hanging out after the interview was done. When he moved down to London, he dated a couple of journalists. Liam was five years younger and more wary; easily bored, often upset. Still, they both informed anyone with a microphone or a tape recorder that Oasis were the best band around, that no other band came anywhere near, other than The Roses and The Beatles.

'As a PR, you've got few choices in what you do,' Johnny says, 'but the two main ones are either you lump your band in with the prevailing trends or you set up in opposition to everything else that's going on. With Oasis, that's the route we took. Because they weren't like anyone else. They weren't Britpop. They were Irish Mancunians for a start.'

1994 was Blur's year. *Parklife* had done so much better than anyone had expected, catching a feeling, creating a pop-culture moment. And at the start of 1995, everyone was quite friendly. At the *NME* Brat Awards in January, both Blur and Oasis won awards. Blur won four; Oasis, three. Noel and Damon had their photo taken together for *NME*'s cover. Liam was meant to have his photo taken with them, but he refused and, instead, Martin Rossiter from Gene stepped in. In the picture, he looks awkward, but Damon and Noel are smiling. The article about the evening reports that Liam shouted at the Manic Street Preachers when they were getting an award (James Dean Bradfield told him to 'shut the fuck up'), that he slagged off Shed Seven and Elastica when they were on stage, and that Graham from Blur tried to snog Liam, with tongues. There is a verbatim account of Liam refusing to have his photo taken with Damon, before challenging Damon to a fight and also arguing with Noel. Noel calls Liam 'fucking stupid'. Liam says, 'You can fuck off, as far as I'm concerned.'

On 20 February 1995, both Blur and Oasis went to the Brit Awards. Blur won four awards: Best British Single, Best British Album, Best British Video, Best British Group. Oasis won one: Best British Breakthrough Act.

The issue of *Melody Maker* of 22 July 1995 had a cover with the word 'BRITPOP' in big letters across it, and 'EVERYTHING YOU EVER WANTED TO KNOW BUT WERE TOO AFRAID TO ASK' underneath. The cover image is a photograph of gig tickets, CDs, promo photos, backstage laminates laid out on top of one another. The bands are Oasis, Blur, Pulp, Gene, Elastica, Sleeper, Suede, The Bluetones, Verve, Radiohead and Supergrass. There is no interview with Oasis inside, but the paper puts them second in a list called 'The Champions'. Blur are first.

On page five of the same *Melody Maker*, there are a couple of small news pieces. One is entitled 'OASIS ON A ROLL'. The other, 'BLUR GO TO THE COUNTRY'. The piece on Oasis reads: 'Oasis have a new single, "Roll With It", set for release by Creation on 14

August – the same day as Blur's "Country House", thus setting up an intriguing chart contest between the two biggest Britpop bands.'

Blur vs Oasis. It was not what it seemed. I liked both bands, and that was allowed. You didn't have to choose, though it was fun to do so. The controversial aspect for the indie music scene wasn't the simultaneous single release, but the fact that other people, people outside of music, were taking notice. Not the fans, but the proper journalists, the broadsheet writers in suits and ties, the tabloid gossip hounds, the paparazzi, the BBC news anchors and researchers. It's hard to grasp why it was considered such big news, but these might be some of the reasons. The commissioners and editors were in their forties, and remembered The Beatles vs The Stones, who were similarly set in opposition to each other; the bands lived close to the centre of London and went out a lot, so could be photographed easily; it was August, commonly known as 'silly season' for news coverage; there was an actual quantifiable result to the rivalry, like a football match. Who would win the match? The team that sold the most records in a week.

Still, the fuss was surprising. Indie music never went anywhere near the news. News ignored music, unless it was huge American acts, like Madonna or Michael Jackson. It was just a few weeks after the Glastonbury Festival, when Take That's Robbie Williams had played football backstage with Oasis, and got on stage with them too, high and manic with spiky bleached hair. I told my editors at the *Observer* about this, but they weren't interested. They didn't want me to write about it, didn't consider it news. Now, that potent mix of pop, indie and Glastonbury would be newspaper catnip. There would be a picture of Robbie Williams with Oasis on every paper's front page, from the *Daily Star* to *The Times*. But not then.

The *News at Ten* covered the simultaneous single release as Blur vs Oasis, but really, it was indie music vs the outside world. People were queuing round the block to buy the singles, sleeping outside HMV to grab records and CDs in different formats. They were doing this not for pop artists, or for American acts, but for British indie bands. It felt exciting and ridiculous, and hopeful. Because all those fans and all those musicians were on the same side, really. The fuss about Blur vs Oasis was about indie music moving in to take over the mainstream pop charts. This doesn't happen often, and once Blur and Oasis were at Number One and Two, that battle was won.

A few weeks before the Number One palavers, I did an interview with Oasis for the *Observer*, pegged to the release of (*What's The Story*) *Morning Glory?* It was June 1995, and as part of the piece I went to see the band play a secret gig in Bath Pavilion. At the gig, they played 'Morning Glory' and 'Don't Look Back in Anger' for the first time ever. Brand new songs played to an emotionally overwhelmed crowd of, mostly, well refreshed lads, who wrapped their arms around each other and shouted along, picking up the choruses in seconds. The ceiling was low. Everyone was dripping in sweat. And the songs felt like those lads' soul music, the tunes they would play when their babies were born, when their hearts were broken; to celebrate their lives' biggest moments or to soothe the agony of bad times. Songs that stretched forward into their future from somewhere in their past. Songs for the heart, not the mind. Songs that somehow, they already knew.

In July, I went up to Scotland to interview the band. They were playing two nights on Irvine Beach, a few miles outside of Glasgow. They played almost exactly the same set as they did in Bath, though they swapped around 'Live Forever' and 'I Am the Walrus'. They didn't play 'Wonderwall' – which seems ridiculous now – but they did play 'Don't Look Back in Anger' as an encore, and 'Slide Away'. Afterwards, I interviewed Noel in a portacabin near the stage. This was unusual: very few bands will do interviews after a gig. He had coke with him and we took a few lines. 'I'm on a line of coke every forty minutes,' he said.

Then everyone who had anything to do with the band went back to the hotel. If you're not in the band or working for the band, then hanging out in hotels after a gig can be odd. The environment is wildly charged. Highs and lows played out in over-lit lobbies with tapestry-backed chairs and patterned carpets, with stressed overnight staff who aren't paid enough to deal with all the mayhem. Sometimes they just give up, let the band serve themselves directly from the bar. If there's a piano in the lobby, it will be played. If there's a chandelier, it will be swung from.

I remember Liam coming into the hotel bar, swift, inscrutable, adrenalised. He shot Noel an unreadable look, and Noel ignored it, continuing to talk to the journalists around him: six of them, all from music papers. Soon afterwards, Liam lurched up from his seat, chucked a beer bottle at the ceiling and left the room. Liam brought his own energy, and his energy was: anything can happen. Not out of control, but uncontrollable, with no off button, no respect for social mores, all those unwritten rules that keep people from hitting each other or smashing up furniture or not kissing someone else's partner. He walked into a room and everything changed. The electrons shifted and fizzed. You couldn't take your eyes off him.

I was meant to be interviewing Liam as well as Noel, but it was impossible to organise. Oasis's manager, Marcus Russell, kept blanking me, and their tour manager, an ex-army type who nobody seemed to like, couldn't swing it. Liam was too intimidating to approach on my own. He padded around like an angry cat. Now I think: maybe he felt hurt. I was told, 'Liam will do the interview in the morning, don't worry,' and then, in the morning, Oasis were gone. Back down south to play Phoenix Festival.

Because Liam didn't talk, I needed more for the piece. So it was agreed that I would interview Noel again, over the phone this time when the band were in Japan. In between, the Blur vs Oasis single fight had taken place and 'Roll With It' had come in at Number Two.

Back at home, I sat on the floor of the lounge next to the answerphone machine, because that was the only way I could record the call. I asked Noel about Blur. 'The guitarist I've got a lot of time for,' he said. 'The drummer I've never met, I hear he's a nice guy. The bass player and the singer, I hope the pair of them catch AIDS and die because I fucking hate them two.' It was a joke – a joke with a punch in it, but a joke nonetheless. It didn't seem homophobic because I didn't think Noel was homophobic. He was just ranting, digging Blur out in public again, playing the now-what-are-you-going-to-do-about-it card. He could have said: 'I hope the pair of them get knocked down by a bus and die.'

Nobody at the *Observer* flagged the AIDS quote as being something to worry about. Not my editors, not the legal department.

(The lawyers were more concerned that something else Noel said, about Creation and drug-taking, was libellous. We took that bit out.) We gave the AIDS line so little thought that we didn't even use it as a pull quote. The pull quote we used was: 'He gets all these sex-starved young girls with big breasts. I get the psychopaths.' But when the interview was published, everything went mad. Lots of people were very upset. America lost its mind. Noel had to apologise.

'It just went a bit playground,' Johnny recalls. 'I had hundreds and hundreds of conversations with people on that Sunday, and the subsequent week. People saying, "You shouldn't say it – it's a homophobic remark," and I was like, "Is it a homophobic remark? Because if you're saying it's a homophobic remark, you're saying that AIDS is a gay disease. So, actually, you're the ones that are homophobic."'

I saw Noel at the *Q* Awards a few days later. I went over to him and said sorry, though now I wonder what for.

Sometimes grown-ups take notice of the noisy teenagers drinking in the park and decide to play a game of football with them, or teach them to play cricket, let them into the game, tell them how they should be behaving. But the teenagers never ask for the adults to do this. They're just having fun, in their own world, living their own lives according to their own secret rules that others don't understand.

Up until that interview, I felt like I was writing for people who were the same as me. People who understood the context. When you're writing for your friends, it's strange for your words to be pulled out and examined by others, who you never imagined would read anything you wrote. Even though I was a journalist and Noel was a star, neither of us understood what an offhand remark can do, how it can be snatched out of a conversation and turned into a quote so offensive that it immediately spreads across the world. Anyone tabloid-trained would have recognised what Noel said as dynamite, but I'd learnt to write on music magazines and nobody I'd interviewed had ever really been of interest to the 'real' press before. Nothing I'd written had gone viral before. We didn't even have the word for it.

Even though I don't believe his comment was intentionally homophobic, I wonder, a bit, if it served as a green light for people who actually were, whether it inadvertently welcomed in an audience who did think being gay was a bad thing. And then I wonder if we should have printed the comment at all.

In November 1995, Oasis played two sold-out gigs at Earl's Court. Johnny was there and at the end of the night he was walking towards the venue's massive staircase with one of the radio pluggers, enthusing about what a brilliant night it had been. They turned the corner and on the stairs was a group of blokes. 'They were just pissing down the stairs,' says Johnny. 'That was the moment we knew it had really changed.'

When I read my interview with Noel now, what stands out for me is a different quote. I asked him about what he had learnt from roadie-ing for the Inspiral Carpets and he said, 'I learnt that you'll get ripped off unless you're very careful. I learned you don't make money unless you're as big as U2.'

*

Oasis have always been a band that inspire passion, that get people singing, crying, yelling their emotions into the sky. But that straight-to-the-heart appeal – champagne supernova lyrics, enormous unapologetic tunes – also means that they wind people up. Or, if not them (Liam and Noel's humour usually wins through), then their fans. Pissing down the stairs, pushing to the bar, swaggering along the train carriage, shouting through the town. So it's interesting that 'Slide Away' has always been a fan favourite, because it's 'one for the ladies', according to Noel. He's said that Oasis should have played it live more often; that Liam's vocals on this track are some of the best he's done.

Noel wrote it after a row with his girlfriend Louise Jones, who he went out with whilst he was in Manchester. They split up in 1994, not long after Oasis got a record deal and he moved to London.

'Slide Away' is ambiguous as well as specific. There are no details to tie it to Noel's relationship: it's more general than that. The title implies both sex and drugs, and the love in the song isn't pinned down either. It could be about staying or leaving, sliding away but also giving all you've got, 'now that you're mine' but also 'I wonder where you are now?'

Liam's singing of 'Let me be the one who shines with you' is the key moment, the heartbreak, the shift. The song moves up the emotional scale until it hits 'Now that you're mine'; the opening of a window to a fresh cool dawn after staying up all night trying to sort things out. There's hope, and tenderness, and defiance, and an understanding that sometimes words don't work – sometimes love doesn't work – and the music has to say what you can't. Sweet and tender hooligan soul: what Oasis do best.

Hero for Our Time

PULP
'Common People'

At the end of 1994, in the calm-before-the-storm months between Pulp's *His 'n' Hers* album and the release of 'Common People', I interviewed Jarvis Cocker for the *Observer*. We were meant to be having tea at the Savoy – a hotel where he and Pulp had been feted just a few weeks before, for the Mercury Prize – but our attire was deemed inappropriate, so we had to leave and go to a wine-bar. I don't remember what I was wearing, but I wrote down the details of Jarvis's outfit. He wore: a knee-length fake fur coat, tartan scarf, tweed jacket, an inky-slinky purple shirt, burgundy needle cords, snazzy shoes with stack heels and his usual window frame specs. His hair was tufty. He towered over everyone, a well-dressed 6' 4" anglepoise lamp. The Savoy fashion police were wrong. He looked brilliant and he looked like himself.

Though Jarvis wasn't fond of interviews – 'I'm really bored thinking about myself, I'd rather think about anything else' – he was excellent fun. He spoke about almost winning the Mercury Prize; the judges had said *His 'n' Hers* had come a close second to M People's *Elegant Slumming*. 'We booed,' said Jarvis. 'We needed the money.' He pointed out how, if Pulp had won, the money would have gone to charity, because they'd have split it five ways, £5,000 each, and he'd have spent his winnings in Oxfam.

We discussed music. He wasn't a fan of bands who were 'like, we just want to talk about the music man, we just love to play, it's the spirit. I think it's an excuse for having crap lyrics. I'm talking about Primal Scream.' Who are Pulp for? I wondered. 'You buy a Pulp album,' said Jarvis, 'if you want a song about a wardrobe.'

The subject of couples came up, because of *His 'n' Hers*. Jarvis said he was quite bad at being a boyfriend – 'I don't do very well at all, it causes me a lot of trouble' – and terrible at confrontation. He sounded worried about the existential tedium that being coupled up could bring: the restaurant outings 'not talking to each other, just eating chicken kiev', the Sunday traipse around Ikea. He remembered the parties of his youth. 'We used to write a list of who you were inviting, and then try and think who might pair off with who,' he said. 'To me, all the milling around before was much more interesting and entertaining, people bounce off one another and then funny things happen.' He liked individuals, how they made a mockery of sweeping social generalisations, and told a tale about a Sheffield milkman who had a Rolls-Royce and went to posh nightclubs to pick up high-class women – but if they lived more than three miles away, he'd dump them, because he couldn't afford the petrol.

We talked for a long time, so there were some Jarvis-isms that I didn't put into the piece, such as, 'I've always thought content is more important than technical prowess. It's more important to have an idea and then work out a means of getting it across,' and,

'I can't imagine having a public persona and a private persona, that would be terrible.' Be original and be authentic, two completely admirable life tenets. He also said that he thought of life as being like a plastic bag, and you occasionally have to empty it out, because it's important to only carry around what you need.

And we talked about Pulp finally making it. As far as we knew, this moment was It, as good as Jarvis and his band were going to get. *His 'n' Hers* had reached Number Nine and was on its way to going gold, he'd got the cover of the *Observer* Life (before Blur and Oasis), he was being feted everywhere as the new king of indie, described by some magazines as 'Pop's Mr Sex'. There was a sense, perhaps, that Pulp's new songs were good and that the next LP might also be a success. But even so, it had taken sixteen years, over half Jarvis's life, to get to this high point. 'I wouldn't have done it if I'd known it was going to take so long,' he said. 'If someone had told me when we started, I'd say, "Oh, I can't be arsed waiting."'

We had no idea, really, what 'making it' was. What being paparazzi-stalked, followed-by-kids-round-the-supermarket, Oi-Jarv!, quick-pic-for-my-daughter, wear-a-disguise-at-Glastonbury-if-you-want-to-wander-about, *News at Ten*, national treasure famous actually meant, because we didn't know anyone who was like that. But Jarvis, being Jarvis, had a good idea.

'It's like running up a pyramid,' he said. 'You're running up, and then you're only at the top for a split second, and before you know it, you're actually going down. But you don't know you're going down until you start doing it. And so you never appreciate the fact that you were at the top.'

*

Jarvis formed Pulp in 1978, aged fifteen, in an economics lesson at school in Sheffield. He drew pictures of what they would wear, wrote out a short manifesto. Despite his specificities, it took several years for him to find the right combination of odd-bod musical talent that became Pulp. During that time, he tried and failed to go to Oxford University (at the interview, he pretended he'd read a book that he hadn't), lived in a drafty warehouse for a while (no chairs, so that nobody would hang around too long), signed on for ages. In 1985, he fell thirty feet from a window trying to impress a girl. He spent six weeks in hospital ('films on a Thursday night, wheeled beds in a row, they propped you up') and this time proved to be an artistic breakthrough. He suddenly understood that what he had to do was concentrate on small details in his songs; and that he needed to make something happen, rather than wait to be discovered.

Over the years, Pulp released several albums: *His 'n' Hers* was their fifth. It took until 1988 for the band to have a settled line-up (though this changed again, when Pulp fan/roadie Mark Webber joined as an extra guitarist in 1995; and at the beginning of 1997, when guitarist/violinist Russell Senior left). Jarvis had spent six years on the dole and got a full degree at St Martins before this. Still, they never gave up. Later, drummer Nick Banks said: 'We could see that we'd got something interesting to present to the world. And we'd got the undiscovered Pelé of music frontmen . . . He was an absolute nutcase, funny with it, and really interesting.'

Anyway, because they'd been around for so long, Pulp were often unfairly dismissed as also-rans. Most people interested in indie music knew about them – they'd got their first John Peel session in 1981 – but they weren't taken particularly seriously. They were seen as Crimplene, kitsch, small-time; charming enough, but almost a novelty act. But in 1991, they did a tour and anyone who saw them play realised that Pulp had changed. An essence had become distilled, they knew what they were about. They were fantastic and they'd been hiding in plain sight.

Wiser managers were hired; the band signed to Island Records. And from there, they just got better and better. Their songs became more acute and pointed: 'Razzmatazz', about one of Jarvis's exes; 'Babies', about hiding in a wardrobe of someone that you fancy. The atmosphere of the records – seedy and operatic, cheap and cheerful – and the subject-matter – deftly observed stories of relationships, watchful dissections of class – were all woven through with humour, and anger too. Jarvis presented them with panache: striking poses, pointing his long fingers, throwing sudden shapes, a dashing blade disguised as a corduroy-sporting geography teacher.

In March 1994, Pulp had a party to launch 'Do You Remember the First Time?' at the ICA, which featured a film they'd made of semi-famous people talking about losing their virginity, including Justine from Elastica, comedians Jo Brand and Bob Mortimer, Alison Steadman, John Peel, Vivian Stanshall. The band played, and they were completely brilliant. It felt like everyone was sort of . . . primed for the next stage. Especially Jarvis.

Club Smashing was a club night hosted by Matthew Glamorre, Martin Green, Adrian Webb and Michael Murphy. It started in 1991, moved around various venues (sixteen in total), and ended up at Eve's on Regents Street, opposite Hamley's, which is where it really took off.

Eve's was big in the 1960s, when it was frequented by spies, ambassadors and dancing girls; Christine Keeler and John Profumo went there. It shut in 1991, and when Smashing arrived a couple of years later, the club still had the same decor. Red velvet banquettes, fake palm trees. If you want to glimpse some of its style, you could check out the video for 'Disco 2000', where Pat and Jo Skinny, stylists, friends of Pulp and gorgeous people-around-town engage in a *Jackie*-magazine-type photo love story. Will they get it together? we wonder as Jo puts her handbag down on a fabulous dancefloor with lit-up coloured squares. It's Eve's dance-floor, and you can see the coat-check booth too.

Smashing became a default nightclub for the new Camden-come-Soho British bands, and because of the music it played. 'I just played whatever I wanted,' says Martin, a playlist approach which harked back to a pre-house-music era, where alternative club DJs would play any record, as long as they liked it. At Smashing, you'd hear Bowie, the Beasties, then a spot of Elaine Page, some hi-NRG, followed by TV theme tunes like *Pinky and Perky*. But also tracks that were being made right then, sometimes by Smashing clubbers. 'We played "Cigarettes and Alcohol" when it first came out,' says Martin. 'It was quite campy, you know: "Give me gin and tonic".'

Smashing's other USP was how its clubbers looked. Matthew, who'd run Taboo and was in the group Minty with Leigh Bowery, insisted that people make an effort to look cool. (He only let Oasis in under sufferance, telling them, 'Next time, boys, make an effort.') The Smashing clubbers' aesthetic was jumble-sale glitz. Suits that were slim and '60s mod-ish, or kick-flared and '70s, tracksuits like the ones you wore for PE as a kid, sleeveless mini dresses, nylon shirts, plastic macs, go-go boots. Haircuts that recalled *Alfie, À Bout de Souffle, Performance*-era Mick Jagger. Accessories included cigarette lighters in the shape of guns; biros with 2D people in their barrels whose clothes disappeared when you tipped the pen up.

It was a style that we continued, to various extents, at home. We lived in crappy flats packed with the unwanted tat of our childhoods: bubble lamps, swirly rugs, 1970s eiderdown covers, space hoppers, space guns, ashtrays made from toy truck tyres, records by Burt Bacharach, *Top of the Pops* cover versions, second-hand everything. Detritus that had been swept away by the aspirational, sharp-edged, matt-black 1980s.

Smashing understood this cheap, potent glamour. It welcomed it. 'It was a genuine scene,' says Martin. 'At the time we used to think, "Oh it's not like the '60s!" but, in a way, it was. It was the last period before the membership clubs came in and started separating people, because they were about whether you could afford it. Whereas we were like, if you had the right attitude and you liked the music and weren't there to cause trouble, then you were part of it all and you were welcome.' Jarvis got the title for *Different Class* from someone at Smashing who would say it to mean something extra special.

Gradually, remembers Martin, the bands that attended became big. First Suede, he recalls, then Blur. He describes one night when various members of Blur and Pulp turned up in cabs; Jarvis in the first one, with Alex and a couple of others; Damon in the second. 'Girls and Boys' had just come out, and a group of girls outside

Hamleys spotted Damon and started screaming. He had to be rushed downstairs and into the club. Jarvis, they didn't know. A few weeks later, when 'Common People' came out, the screaming was for Jarvis.

Pulp's 'Mis-Shapes' video makes me think of Smashing. In it, Pulp are playing on a nightclub stage in front of a mixed, suspicious nightclub crowd, who side-eye each other because of the way they're dressed. There are visible battle lines between the tribes: townies versus students, indie kids versus tough lads.

A few years later, when Britpop went mainstream, those tribal differences would become smudged. Damon liked Chelsea and walked like a geezer; *Loaded* celebrated alternative bands but also where's-the-fit-birds laddy-ness. But before then, the people who came to Smashing – and to nightclubs like it across the country – were the weirdos. The ones who were picked on at school for being different, who liked strange music, who knew they'd never win a fight but still went out in clothes that might provoke one: 'You could end up with a smack in the mouth, just for standing out.' Not posh, not hard; quirky and fun; cool in their own charity-shop manner.

It's interesting looking at the 'Mis-Shapes' video because the real git is played by Jarvis himself, and he isn't a football lad, because casuals knew how to dress. This Jarvis is worse. Hair slicked back, pencil 'tache, shirt and tie and the most terrible leather jacket in the world: grey, with epaulettes and a deep V shape. Sleeves pushed up, of course. A stringy Begbie, the sort of bloke who hated football, but liked the fighting. The twat Jarvis sticks a beer mat on to real Jarvis's shoulder, in the same faux bonhomie way that a bully would whack a piece of paper with KICK ME on it onto the back of a soft kid in primary school. It's the schoolboy version of a gauntlet being cast to the ground. But when the inevitable fight happens, caused by him spitting beer into Jarvis's face, it's not really violent, partly because if it were, the video wouldn't be shown on TV, but also because such scraps were scuffles really, as pathetic as the characters' inadequacies. (I remember a similar one at Dave Haslam's Temperance Club indie night at the Haçienda: two mullet-heads had wandered in, possibly lost on their way to Rotters. They started trying to beat up a friend on the dancefloor. We all jumped on their backs, there was a bit of rolling around and then everyone got up, they left and we carried on dancing.)

The video ends with a message, written on a toilet seat:

WE SHALL FIGHT THEM IN 'THE BEECHES' +
'THE KING'S HEAD' YOU KNOW THE SCORE
10 BLOKES WITH TACHES IN SHORT SLEEVED
WHITE SHIRTS TELLING YOU THAT YOUR THE WIERDO
FEAR NOT BROTHERS + SISTERS
WE SHALL PREVAIL
LIVE ON

Pulp's 'Mis-Shapes' and 'Common People' go together. They're both about being an outcast, because of your class and your taste, and they show who you're up against. The stupid thugs, the patronising posh. Both songs are bitter/beautiful anthems, a snarl with a smile, a funny story as well as a call to action. 'Common People' is stronger: it has a specific baddie, a silly well-to-do sculpture student who thinks that being poor might be fun and wants to try it out, visit its strange land like a tourist. It has that devastating bridge – 'If you called your dad, he could stop it all' – that huge last verse – 'You will never understand what it means to live your life with no meaning or control' – and the build to the howl of the 'you' at the end. It is vicious and sublime, and causes a near-riot every time Pulp play it.

Smashing was welcoming, but it wasn't designed for the normals. And it really was a surprise when Jarvis became famous. Not only had Pulp been going for so long, but Jarvis, as a personality, seemed destined to be loved only by outsiders. He was a demi-god among the art-school crew, those who were called 'alterno' at school, the not-good-at-sports contingent, the swots-turned-night-owls, and that seemed correct; but it was hard to imagine him becoming anything more. Who would accept such a lanky git as their superhero?

The answer, it turned out, was absolutely everyone.

There are two TV moments that helped define Jarvis. The first was his appearance on *Pop Quiz*. *Pop Quiz* was a telly show that had been on in the early 1980s and then was revived for a few months in 1994, hosted by besuited cheese-meister Chris Tarrant. Jarvis took part, on a team with Chesney Hawkes and Des'ree, and, after a slowish start ('I was completely pissed'), wiped the floor with everyone in the quick-fire round and swept his team to victory. We couldn't believe that anyone we knew would be allowed on a telly programme so seminal and yet so bland. And then for him to do so well . . .

'My finest hour,' he told me. 'I was really pleased it went alright, because I was sick of people letting you down and being boring and crap on things like that. It felt I'd struck a blow. Those kinds of things are important to me. *Pop Quiz* was important and that's why I did *Top of the Pops* as well.' On Pulp's first ever *Top of the Pops* appearance, playing 'Babies', he'd wiped his brow with a pair of spotty knickers and opened up his jacket to reveal a sign that said 'I HATE WET WET WET'.

Martin was at the recording of *Pop Quiz*, with Matthew. Afterwards, they and Jarvis got a producer to let them into the *Blue Peter* garden. (Another respected childhood relic. To anyone in their twenties at that time, the garden was the BBC's almost-Eden, a sacred space. When it was randomly vandalised in 1983, everyone was genuinely horrified.) In the hallowed haven, they all smoked cigarettes and bonded. Jarvis promised Martin that when Pulp landed a bigger tour with more money, they would pay him to be the DJ.

That was the Common People tour, in late 1995. The build-up happened over a year. When Pulp played Reading Festival in 1994, in an afternoon slot, they debuted 'Common People', and it was obvious it was going to be a hit: everyone went mad, even though they'd never heard it before. Martin got an early copy and played it at Smashing. And everyone went mad, even though they'd never heard it before. By the time 'Common People' was released in early 1995, Pulp fans were desperate to buy it.

It went to Number Two (Robson and Jerome kept it off Number One). Then, in June 1995, Pulp stepped in as super-sub late head-liners for Glastonbury's Pyramid Stage on Saturday night (they had two weeks' notice. The Stone Roses dropped out because John

Squire broke his collarbone). They were fantastic. The final song was 'Common People'; and everyone – everyone – sang along. A few days later, Jarvis said, 'I'm not usually a very demonstrative person, but I did find it quite touching when everybody was singing the words. I was thinking on a more cosmic level than I usually do. It had a significance beyond it just being us; it proved you can have 100,000 people crammed into one space without them killing each other.'

Suddenly, amazingly, Pulp were big – properly big, touring-all-the-time big, interviews-with-serious-journalists big. And so were other indie bands. The Blur vs Oasis palaver happened in August, a few weeks after Glastonbury. The mainstream press – tabloids included – were thrilled, and looking for more. When Pulp's 'Sorted for E's & Wizz' came out in September, with 'Mis-Shapes' as its double A-side, strange people (tabloid journalists) started trying to offer the band what looked like drugs, photographers ready to take pictures if they accepted. The song, which is definitely not pro-drugs, featured a photograph of a magazine page folded into a wrap on its cover, and a step-by-step diagram in the CD booklet on how to make said wrap. The *Daily Mirror*'s Kate Thornton wrote a front-page story, under the headline 'BAN THIS SICK STUNT'. There was a picture of Jarvis and the sub-header 'Chart Stars Sell CD With DIY Kids' Drugs Guide'. Inside, *Mirror* readers could vote on whether the track should be banned, by phoning a YES or a NO phone number ('Calls should cost less than 10p. Lines close at 6 p.m.').

Pulp were thrust into a new world, one which they'd had no truck with previously. They were bewildered by the extra attention, the open doors that had once been shut, the abrupt VIP welcome. The leather-jacketed 'tache boys suddenly giving you a wink and inviting you into the back room, but still slapping the 'kick me' notice on your back when you weren't looking.

Jarvis's second important TV appearance was more spontaneous. The Brits of February 1996 was a weird one; triumphant and sour, all at the same time. A shift towards the new, but not a complete one: though there were awards for Oasis, Supergrass, Massive Attack and Björk, there were also ones for Annie Lennox and Bon Jovi. Oasis won three – Best Album, Best British Group, Best Video (for 'Wonderwall', voted for by the public) – and were triumphant and yobbish throughout, with Liam accepting one by singing 'Shitelife' to the tune of 'Parklife' and pretending to shove the award up his bum.

There was also a special award for Michael Jackson – Artist of a Generation – presented to him by Bob Geldof; for what reason, nobody knew. Jackson took the opportunity to sing a hugely choreographed and OTT version of 'Earth Song', which involved several dozen children earnestly emoting and Michael busily kissing a rabbi before rising above the stage on some sort of holy crane, white shirt billowing, in what appeared to be a music-business-supported bid to become Jesus, or at least the Only Person who could save the earth, the seas, plus elephants and 'crying whales'.

Jarvis was drunk. Irritated by Jackson's pomposity and encouraged by keyboard player Candida, he and his friend Pete Mansell staged a very mild stage invasion. (Tricky and Massive Attack's Mushroom got up to join them, but were stopped by bouncers.) They hopped fairly easily up there, and, then, didn't quite know what to do. So Jarvis flashed his tummy at the camera and turned around, bent over and waved his hands near his bum, as though wafting a fart into the audience. Then they skipped to the back of the stage and ran back round to their table.

Thirty minutes later, Jackson's people called the police. Jarvis was arrested, taken to Kensington police station (Bob Mortimer went with him as his lawyer), questioned until around 4 a.m. and charged with actual bodily harm, as Jackson alleged that he'd hurt some of the performing children. He was released on bail.

Initially, the tabloids came out firmly on Jackson's side: 'The night our young dreams were Pulped' and 'Boy's true grit at the Brits' (about the child performers) said the *Daily Mail*; the *Daily Mirror* went with 'Jacko Rages at Yob Rocker' and 'We'll Sue Pulp Lout'. Even the *New York Post* had something to say, namely 'Rocker Beats Up Jacko's Kiddie Choir'. But very quickly, something changed. Not only did a video from David Bowie prove that no children had been hurt, but several pop stars came out in support of Jarvis, including Brian Eno, Bernard Butler, Everything but the Girl and, of all people, Jonathan King, who said, 'Jarvis was reflecting the feeling of 98 per cent of people in the hall.' Paul Weller's mum phoned the *Mirror* to say, 'Jarvis didn't touch those kids. He's a lovely bloke.' After a few days, the *Mirror* changed its tune – its readers were overwhelmingly in support of Jarvis – and decided that 'Jarv' was its new hero.

The charges were dropped. Now Jarvis wasn't just a hero to the mis-shapes, mistakes and misfits; he was the whole of the country's. It changed how everyone reacted to him; it changed how he reacted to the world. People were lovely to him – he didn't ever get the abuse that Liam or Damon did – but I once saw him in a Camden doorway, just standing, his back to a door, hiding from passers-by. He walked around as he usually did, but it wasn't the same.

'Perhaps a bit of a spell was broken,' said Nick later. 'Because [Jarvis] seemed to enjoy observing the oddities of life before that, and once everyone's looking at you, it's hard to look at the strange things going off around you without affecting those things.'

'The absolutely astonishing thing about that time', says Martin, 'is that the people who were in that moment became hugely famous without altering anything about themselves at all. Not their style or musical content or vision. They just refined their own taste and music and aesthetic and carried on with what they were doing.'

1996 was a turning point for Pulp. They became fashion darlings, invited to everything, performing for art shows and corporations, as well as their usual fans. Jarvis said, later, that by the end of the year, he had a form of nervous breakdown. Very early in 1997, Russell left; their next album, *This Is Hardcore*, released in 1998, was a deliberate rejection of all those new post-Brits jolly-up-Jarv fans, a dark and chilly dissection of drugs and sex, a series of filmic scenes that captured the panicked self-loathing, the disgust of middle age.

These days, of course, there is no way that the Savoy would refuse to serve Jarvis some Earl Grey and scones, and that's not (just) because he's famous. It's because in the mid-1990s, Jarvis, and Pulp, shifted the idea of what cool looked like, turned it right round to face the other way, away from beautifully cut designer wear, from a rock snarl and leather trousers, from cold money into something less cynical, more human and delightful.

Up until then, Jarvis had been an art-school clever-clogs tapping on the glass of the VIPs, not only because he wanted to be recognised (though he did), but because he thought it would be interesting. And the thing was, we all wanted him to get there. Because he might have seemed, to some, like an angular, strangely dressed weirdo. But to us, he was our representative, our secret agent. He was always an outsider. But somehow, in the mid-1990s, Jarvis became a winner. He hit the peak of the pyramid.

And then, like he said he would, he slid gracefully down the other side.

Lead-Singer Syndrome

THE VERVE
'Bitter Sweet Symphony'

We should start, of course, with the video. Let's watch it again. Here is Richard Ashcroft in 1997, a young man with the cheek-bones, the hair, the height, the intensity of the perfect rock 'n' roll star. Blue-white skin, shadowed eyes, broken nose. Build of a twig on a diet. Leather jacket over denim one (NB not a motorcycle jacket), black jeans, brown Clarks Wallabees. Ashcroft walks into shot, steadies himself, stands straight-backed in front of roadworks that stretch across the pavement (the bollards, the cones, the pallets, the sign saying Pedestrians with an arrow). He has something more than poise. Not arrogance, but something close. And why not? He is completely beautiful.

He looks up to the sky for a second, waits. A rollerblader skates towards him. He steps off the kerb and begins to walk straight ahead.

The video for 'Bitter Sweet Symphony' is what made Richard Ashcroft famous, took him and The Verve stratospheric, trans-formed him from the interesting, vibey frontman of a wig-out guitar band with a heavy-duty capacity for drugs and drink into an off-kilter national icon. It became a meme before memes existed: comedians made skits of it; there was an imitation video made for 'Vindaloo', the novelty football record by Fat Les; and over twenty-five years later, Richard recreated it for Sky TV.

And all that happens in the video is he walks straight ahead. Step by step, he pads through Hoxton, the grubby version that existed before it became a destination for balloon-huffing hen nights and ball-pit city boys. There are other people on the streets, moving in and out of shot, passing around him on the pavement. He just keeps walking. Moving forward no matter what: shoulder-charging one girl so hard that she falls to the floor; walking over the bonnet of a car that's in his way, ignoring the owner who shouts at him; disdaining the sexual interest in the eye-flick from another woman; banging through two tough blokes who turn, threaten him with violence, but let it go. On walks our hero, not oblivious, but purposeful, deliberately unaffected by others. Blinkered. The violins swell and repeat, swell and repeat. He sings of how he's a million different people and how he can't change, though he says he wants to. At the end of the song, he's joined by the other members of The Verve, who walk silently along beside him.

Like all the best pop videos, the one for 'Bitter Sweet Symphony', directed by Walter Stern, expresses an unspoken element of the song. Not a hidden message – the meaning of the song, that life is sublime but ruined by mundanity, is completely clear – but the soul of it. In a song drenched in filmic strings, Richard plays the narrow-eyed, impenetrable, lone gunslinger. (You know he'd look good in a poncho.) He arrives in town, changes it just by existing, then leaves, himself unchanged. No one can touch him, no one can hold him back, he's on a never-ending, forever solo, one-man mission. If he had a pistol, he'd blow on the barrel end like he was drying his nails.

The obvious echo of this video is the video for Massive Attack's 'Unfinished Sympathy'. That short, filmed in one steadicam shot by Dan Kneece, directed by Baillie Walsh who went on to direct the ABBA Voyage virtual concert, features singer Shara Nelson walking, solo but purposeful, along two LA streets south of Koreatown. 'Bitter Sweet Symphony' isn't a remix of it, not a cover either. Maybe a tribute.

There are other overlaps. The 'symphony' wordplay, the use of violins. The ache in the lyrics, caused by romantic love in 'Unfinished Sympathy', existential crisis in 'Bitter Sweet Symphony'. Shara likens herself to a soul without a mind, in a body without a heart: Richard sings, 'Well, I've never prayed but tonight I'm on my knees, yeah.' A sense of despair, but also a sense that life could be, should be, magnificent. With both, despite the lack of visual histrionics, we understand the singer is at their wit's end. What can they do? Put one foot in front of the other.

The difference, of course, is that where Shara Nelson moves steadily on, striding between people without touching them and without them touching her, a ghost in her own life, Richard Ashcroft barges through, makes contact, mows people down through his own unwillingness to stop. They turn to look at him a lot. He ignores them, doesn't deviate from his path. He hits and runs, at walking speed.

A few years ago, another ending was released to the video, one that was filmed at the time, but never used. In it, Ashcroft's continual bashing into other people ends with him being beaten up by the tough blokes (three of them), which, to be fair, would seem a likely consequence of his woeful pavement etiquette. We see the beating, and we see him on the ground close up, face bloodied. Then he stands up – of course he does! – and continues walking. In this version, the rest of The Verve don't join Richard. They stay in a side road and look at him with unreadable expressions as he moves on, away from them, into the night.

But in the video we all know, the band – Nick McCabe, Simon Jones, Simon Tong and Pete Salisbury – appear towards the end and start walking along too. Not quite with Richard – he walks slightly ahead – but either side of him, half a step behind. He doesn't acknowledge them. Are they supporting him as equals? Or following him, like they're disciples and he's their skinny Jesus?

Verve formed in 1989, in Wigan. Richard, Simon Jones and Pete all went to school together; they found guitarist Nick at their sixth-form college. Their shared interests were rooted in the tastes of the masculine north-west: football, music, drugs. Richard had been a football kid. He worshipped George Best, supported Manchester United and joined various small football clubs when he was young. But he didn't like sticking to a formation system, and gave up playing when he was thirteen. He broke one lad's ankle during training: Pete's, the future Verve's future drummer.

When Richard was eleven, his dad ('big feller, kind of strict'), who worked on and off in clerical jobs, died unexpectedly, of a blood clot on the brain. ('You work all your life, you're a slave to money then you die.') After a while, his mum got a new boyfriend, and Richard's stepfather, a clever and open-minded man, talked to his stepson about exciting ideas concerning the power of the mind, how thought could physically change things, move molecules, raise the temperature of the room. He bought Richard a motorbike when he was sixteen. Soon after, he and Richard's mum moved down to the Cotswolds and Richard moved in with Simon and his family.

Many pop stars and actors and other fame-hungry people in the public eye lost a parent when they were young. The pop psychology is pretty clear (you lose your source of love and you seek out more love, from an audience) but such a death can also act like a starting pistol. If you know for certain that life can be snatched away unexpectedly early, then you'd better get on with making your own time on earth mean something, make it memorable and epic and wild. No time to waste.

Verve's gigs were never small: Richard would picture himself playing at Madison Square Gardens and manifest that energy even for tiny venues. He'd climb the speakers, chuck himself off, crawl on the floor, howl at the mic from three feet back, even when there were only ten people there, and six of them had just popped in for a shandy. Not for him the traditional 'don't embarrass yourself' reticence of the northern man. He always had a sense of scale.

When he was living in Wigan, he would live for playing live. In 1992, he told *Melody Maker*: 'The 40 minutes I'm given to play live is such a fucking outlet. You've got a week of living in Wigan where you're a nobody . . . But for 40 minutes I can be someone, express all my fears, whatever. And that's what I live for, those 40 minutes. For three weeks, I'm nothing, I'm watching the television in a shitty flat above a chemist. But onstage, there I am. And there are 400 people, 200 people, 40 people, looking for something from you.'

Sometimes after gigs, the band would have excess energy to burn and they'd go to some woods outside Manchester, build fires, play music, drop acid. These happenings bled into their early studio work and they recorded their first album mostly on LSD. Though they're from Wigan, there was a psychedelic feel about Verve, a Liverpool 1980s 'head' sensibility, of taking hallucinogens and smoking heavy weed and listening to Pink Floyd. Nick's guitar sensibilities were always big – he made a wash of sound, layered, echoed, distorted – and the band backed him in that. The other factor at that time, according to John Best, who managed Verve from around 1992 to 1996, was Richard's domestic life. His girlfriend wasn't always keen on Richard skipping off to practise when he had things to do at home: while waiting for him, the band would jam for ages, creating enormous, proggy riffs and swirls and ambitious atmospheres. Then Richard would arrive, and scatsing over the top. Voilà! A Verve song.

When Richard and his girlfriend split up and he moved to London, with nothing more than a bag (he had all his belongings confiscated by his landlord, because Richard owed him £3,000), he stayed at John Best's flat for a while. John was living with his then-girlfriend, Miki Berenyi of Lush, and she had music equipment in their home. While Richard was staying, he started using Miki's gear and wrote a few shorter, more straightforwardly sentimental ballads – the ones which later became The Verve's hit singles. He also nicked quite a few of John's underpants.

It took a while for the idea of The Verve to take hold. They were mentioned in dispatches: a news story about them changing their name from Verve to The Verve, because of legal difficulties with jazz label Verve Records; an interview where Richard would declare, 'Our ambitions are great, but we don't know what they actually are.' For a few years, they were regarded by most as a talented lot, with an amazing front person, but not enough pop songs. And their off-stage habits were full-force. They all smoked spliff constantly, drank without stopping and hoovered whatever other chemicals were around. Their antics were notorious. On the 1994 Lollapalooza tour in the US, Richard forgot to eat and drink for several days, and ended up having seizures due to dehydration. Soon after, when recording their album *A Northern Soul*, with Owen Morris, the hard-partying producer of Oasis's albums, things got so out of hand that a studio engineer locked himself away. The band's work was wrapped around the partying. With one exception. Nick McCabe had just become a dad. He got up at a normal hour, added his guitar licks and otherwise stayed away.

In July 1995, three months after *A Northern Soul* was finished, just after 'History' was released and went to Number 24, Richard forced a Verve split, by leaving and getting the rest of the band to leave one by one, until only Nick was left. Then the others all joined up again, without Nick, and tried to recruit another guitarist. They had a go with Bernard Butler, who'd just left Suede, which proved unworkable (there was only room for one star, and that was Richard), and then put out feelers towards John Squire, but Squire said no. In the end, Simon Tong, a friend from Wigan, stepped in and the new version of the band spent most of 1996 recording *Urban Hymns*. At the end of the process, Richard decided that, actually, they needed Nick back. Nick turned up and added his guitar parts to 'Sonnet' and 'The Drugs Don't Work' in one take.

Photographer Chris Floyd was involved with The Verve around that time and when they toured the album. 'It was a bubble, a strange world of young men,' he remembers. 'Other than Kate [Radley, from Spiritualised, Richard's wife] who would just hang out with Richard, it was all blokes. It was like *Das Boot* crossed with *Lord of the Flies*.'

There was a sense that The Verve were about to break big, and Chris was employed by the record company to take pictures of this important time. So he was part of The Verve's crew. But he was also often asked by papers and magazines to take pictures to accompany their interviews, which made him press. He was an insider and an outsider, someone who moved between roles. This could make things difficult.

'There was a lot of suspicion and paranoia in the band towards the press,' he recalls. 'People just didn't trust you. There was a constant feeling that people were trying to stitch them up. That probably came from the *NME, Melody Maker, Sounds* weekly papers culture, which was quite combative . . . Now, things are completely different, aren't they? It's all mutually beneficial, so bands put up their press on social media and say, Thank you so much! and @ the writer. Hashtag "love you". But then, the paranoia was rife.'

The paranoia was partly because it was important to The Verve, especially Richard, to seem credible, authentic, the real deal. Not plastic, not shit. Invulnerable musically, but also in how they looked and acted. It can be hard for young straight men – especially young straight men who grew up in 1970s and '80s northern England – to be anything other than bulletproof. The Verve, northern men all, had been socialised never to expose their feelings, never to get excited or enthusiastic or curious or silly. Don't show yourself up. Game face on at all times, no emotional expression, in case someone starts taking the piss. That's what the bowl walk is about (which Richard has, just not quite as obviously as, say, Liam Gallagher). It's an open-armed step into a potential fight, like, 'What are you gonna do about it then?' You need an armour that means that nobody can find your weak spots, because other people can be violent and cruel. They can't be trusted.

'If you combine that paranoia with a lot of weed,' says Chris, 'it creates quite a heavy atmosphere. As a bloke, you didn't feel like you could speak much, because if you said anything that stepped out of line, someone would pounce on you and you'd be separated from the herd and ostracised.'

Twenty years later, Chris spoke to Nick about that time. Nick had been very difficult to work with, intensely suspicious of Chris. But, years on, he was apologetic, saying that back then, he genuinely couldn't believe that anyone might be on his side.

That same mistrust and desire to be cool was at play when Richard performed. Off camera and tape, Richard was very funny, says Chris: a brilliant mimic, great at voices, quick-witted, charming. But he changed when a camera came out, or when a journalist turned up. 'It was like he had a shell around him, a coating. He was implacable, and sort of humourless. He just wouldn't show that lighter, funny side.'

There was a schism in the band. Richard kept himself separate, with Kate, which stoked the rest of the band's paranoia, whether knowingly or not. After all, Nick had already been kicked out once, only to be invited back in when Richard needed him. Sometimes the others wondered if they were The Verve, or Richard Ashcroft, plus backing band.

'Richard had a ruthless streak,' says Chris (others say this too). 'He kept himself apart from everyone, in his own space, holed up with Kate. He's a classic performer, and has the narcissism and ruthlessness to go with it. You'll never know who he is.'

Richard sounds like an extreme sufferer of LSD: lead-singer disease. But there was also a brilliantly out-there side to him, which, pre-'Bitter Sweet Symphony', earned him the nickname Mad Richard in the music press (he hated this). He might have suppressed his funny side in interviews, which made many journalists dislike him, but he showcased other aspects. In rambling sentences that sort of made sense and sort of didn't, he tried to express the vastness of the thoughts in his head, about life and the universe and what music meant and could mean. Not for him the dinky tales of imagined suburbanites, neat snapshots of contemporary British life. Richard was about the big stuff, about rising above the mundanity of existence whilst knowing the depths, the unexpressed extremes. For him music was life or death, and life was hard to understand, which might go some way to explain lyrics like 'There ain't no space and time to keep our love alive, we have existence and it's all we share', from 'Space and

Time' on *Urban Hymns*. He was always searching for the epic: 'The attraction of our band is the abandon,' he said. 'People feed off a band when they know you have no boundaries.' And that's why playing live was so important to him (he once called himself 'the ringmaster, the conduit'. He also said he felt no pain, 'like an electric eel').

The profound musings of a misunderstood prophet, or the pompous half-thoughts of a loon? 'I'm unreadable, you can't pin me down,' he said. 'Because I haven't yet pinned myself down. I don't believe I ever will.' He told journalists he believed he would be able to fly 'in a few years time . . . through meditation', that 'the mind can change molecules in water', that his stepdad raised the temperature in a room or made sticks in water turn round just through the force of his mind. But he also said: 'Any time I've said something that has ever meant anything, it doesn't look good in print. Real people and real things seem to lose their power when you see them in a pile of magazines.'

Two quotes seem to sum him up. The first is from a 1995 interview in *Select*: 'Everyone else is mad, not me. People have been blackmailed into believing certain bands are the real thing. And I am the real thing. I walk onstage and I perform in the way Ian Curtis performed, in the way Iggy Pop performed. It's real, you don't know what you're feeling. It's not madness, it's something that should be embraced.'

And, from a 1998 *Rolling Stone* interview: 'I'm a firm believer in songs coming from an unlimited pool, and you have to be in a certain state of mind to get them. You don't know why you're in that state of mind. Sometimes it's a dangerous state of mind. But

I know where my influence comes from. It comes from the universal mind, mate.'

The universal. When a song arrives, like any artistic creation, it can feel like it's been beamed down from above, like you've connected to something bigger than yourself. It's the same when a gig takes off, when the fans and the band and the music and the moment create something more enormous and meaningful that anyone there could express on their own. We can all believe in the universal, if we allow ourselves to do so, mate.

Though it would have been nice if he'd squirrelled in a few jokes, Richard was talking a kind of truth. And in the 1990s, when many music fans had been involved in the acid-house explosion, where house music and ecstasy flung open the minds of uptight young men and freed them to dance, what Richard and The Verve represented was a bridge between the full mind expansion of drugs and dance music, and the feet-on-the-floor musicality, authenticity and look-at-me frontman of a rock 'n' roll group.

One more factor: The Stone Roses, and how long they took to make their second album. It's hard to explain how much The Roses chimed with the men of the north. They absolutely worshipped them: their heart-catching tunes, their snotty attitude, their dress sense, their wit, everything. The Roses were unbelievably missed when they were gone. The northern soul was desperate to be filled again, and in the hiatus between The Stones Roses' eponymous first album in 1989 and 1994's *The Second Coming*, bands like Oasis and The Verve formed almost specifically to step into a Roses-shaped gap. When The Stone Roses finally properly split, in 1996, those bands were ready to step up. And the audience was there, waiting, in their Reni hats, Adidas and parkas. Ready for another northern group to understand that even the most insignificant life has grandeur and sweep to the person who's actually living it.

The Verve sold millions of records across the world, won Brit Awards (they didn't turn up, but played a housing charity gig instead) and broke up in 1999, when Nick could no longer handle the pressure and excess. He left in the middle of a tour in 1998, and the band continued for a little longer, then split. They reformed again in 2007, made an album, but called it a day in 2009.

Other than Richard, the members of The Verve have played in different bands and for different artists: The Shining, Cathy Davey, Gorillaz, boletes, Black Submarine, John Martyn, Black Rebel Motorcycle Club, The Charlatans.

Richard has continued to perform under his own name. He still headlines enormous gigs. In 2018, he made an appearance on BBC breakfast TV with Naga Munchetty and Charlie Stayt. They struggled to contain him. Richard spoke directly to the camera, said hi to his family, told other kids on half-term holiday not to eat Kraves, the sugary breakfast cereal. Later, he lay down on the sofa in his shimmery suit. When Munchetty asked him why he was wearing shades, Richard said that, although he respected what she and Stayt did for a living, 'I'm the only one who can wear sunglasses right now.'

'Music becomes like a religion,' he said, about wearing his sunglasses. 'Rock 'n' roll is like a religion, so don't ever question one of the key attributes.' Meaning: it was part of his faith to look like a rock star, at all times. Then he jumped over the back of the sofa, and walked up to one of the set's fake windows. 'Life feels like *The Truman Show*,' he said. 'I just want to say hello to Manchester.' He pretended to bang his head on the window. 'Oh, it is *The Truman Show*!' he said, then walked back to the sofa and launched straight into promoting *Natural Rebel*, his latest album. It was a fantastic performance. Everything he said was accurate and funny, but the way he said it, without adhering to established TV interview rules, proved impossible for the presenters to handle.

'Bitter Sweet Symphony' has a life without its video. It appears in *One Day*, in *The Simpsons*, at the end of *Cruel Intentions*. Famously, there was a huge legal fuss about the four-bar sample of a David Sinclair Whitaker arranged instrumental version of The Rolling Stones' 'The Last Time', attributed to the Andrew Loog Oldham Orchestra. It led to The Stones getting all the royalties as writers of the track, until 2019, when Mick Jagger and Keith Richards ceded the copyright to The Verve.

But the video is very different without the music. If you take away the music, it's just an unsmiling loner barrelling through dirty streets, contributing nothing, hurting people, making things worse, embarrassing himself. Without the music, you think: That guy's life seems terrible. He's a madman. With the music, though, he really does seem like he could be a '90s be-Wallabee'd Messiah.

The It Girl Diaries

SLEEPER
'Inbetweener'

Sleeper might be the quintessential Britpop band. Not only did they make perky, wry, memorable guitar-based pop tunes while wearing neat polo shirts and jumping up and down, not only did they boast a photogenic frontwoman with a great haircut and a knack for quotes, their time in the spotlight maps Britpop's time perfectly. They bubbled up in 1994, went big in 1995 with their album *Smart* and even bigger in 1996 with Stephen Street-produced *The It Girl*, then bowed out – their own decision – while they were still big, in 1997. They were the support act for Blur during *Parklife*, and the Manics on some *Holy Bible* gigs, played to 65,000 people as REM's support at Milton Keynes Bowl, and were headliners themselves for the tour of their platinum-selling album *The It Girl*. They clocked up a succession of hit singles and albums, including five in the Top Ten, and would have had more if their record company had done what it was supposed to, such as press enough copies of their 'Inbetweener' single for the amount of people who wanted to buy it.

Sleeper covered Blondie's 'Atomic' for Danny Boyle's *Trainspotting*, (it's playing when Renton first sees Diane in the Volcano nightclub); they blasted through *Top of the Pops*, breezed in and out of Radio 1, *The Word*, *The Chart Show*; survived beery, leery *TFI Friday* more than once, playing live, Louise performing in small skits (here she is playing a supply teacher, here cracking jokes with George Best), gamely smiling and wry-browing her way through Chris Evans's deliberately unnerving questions.

Sleeper songs were made for the radio: chock-full of hooks, with snappy titles ('Sale of the Century', 'Delicious', 'Vegas', 'What Do I Do Now?') and lyrics that didn't sneer or condescend. They made appealing music videos: larking about in a supermarket with Dale Winton, doing a grocery dash; on a plane full of Elvis lookalikes (Louise as the white-booted air hostess); in a red room with a waterlogged floor (Louise fully clothed, submerged, hair slicked back); glimpsed through tall windows in atmospheric rooms like noir film stars. They worked hard, turned up, the men in the band almost ignored, dismissed as three interchangeable 'Sleeperblokes'.

Above all – and this was their winning card, as well as their Achilles heel – Sleeper had the unbelievable made-for-pop asset of Louise Wener. Singer, songwriter, stylist, band leader; quick-witted and controversial in conversation, cute and gamine on camera; prickly and clever, but soft-voiced, with a gentler vibe in person than her opinions sounded when written down. She was interviewed over and over, about her sex life or her relationships or what it's like being a sex symbol or what it's like being a woman in a band, her answers never boring or bored. She was snapped in minidresses and boots, skinny jeans and sandals, with her round eyes and much-imitated short haircut. Plastered across the music press, again and again, especially the weekly inkies.

Sleeper existed because Louise willed them into being. She and Jon Stewart were in a band, and a relationship, for several years before they had a hit. They'd met at university in Manchester in the late 1980s where, Louise has said, 'it seemed that every second person was a budding rockstar'. When they moved to London, in the early '90s, they spent a couple of years not knowing quite what they were doing, how they might fit in, what exactly they were up to. Then Louise's dad died of cancer, and her grief kicked her into action. 'I am fearless in this period,' she wrote later, 'a living breathing streak of brunette ambition . . . done with second best.' She knew the competition, understood the pop moves. She and Jon had worked on their songs. They recruited Andy Maclure and Diid Osman from a *Melody Maker* advert.

There was something about that moment – the irrelevance of grunge to UK life, mixed with the call-to-arms of riot grrrl; the dull passivity of shoegazing and the end of 'baggy' indie-dance music – that indicated that music might be about to shift, that it might be time to revisit the sharp and spiky three-minute pop song. Louise felt it. She thought they could do it. But their band didn't have the music business connections, no journalist champions, no friends on the scene. So Louise set about creating them. She faked a positive *NME* review and sent it to A&R scouts, she put out a call for actors to be in a pop video so an important gig was filled with enthusiastic fans. And, soon after, they were signed.

Their record deal, with Indolent, was atrocious. She knows that now, of course. The band signed away their rights to six albums for the un-grand total of £12,000. (As compensation, perhaps, the record company man offered Louise her first line of coke straight afterwards.) They would end up selling a million records, their album *The It Girl* going platinum, and the others silver (*Pleased to Meet You*) and gold (*Smart*). They would make a bit of money from publishing. But from that record deal they made: nothing at all.

Still, back in 1994, deal signed and witnessed, a thrilled Louise, Jon, Diid and Andy set about their new job as a professional band, writing and rehearsing, casting old songs aside, working, working, working until they had a brace of new ones.

In January 1995, they brought out 'Inbetweener'. A song about life in the suburbs – Louise grew up in Ilford and Gants Hill, a London suburb – it's a deft sketch of a young couple who aren't that sure about each other but are dating anyway. There are neat details that place it in era and area. She goes to see naff-tastic striptease hunks The Dream Boys, 'got tickets from Keith Prowse'; he reads racy (but old, even then) Harold Robbins novels; they're so far out of London that their suburb isn't on the A to Z maps which everyone used to get around. It's about limited options. And, for the female character, it's about making the best of it whilst knowing you're going to leave. The guitar siren-chops in the background; Louise speaks-sings until the chorus, which is surprisingly sweet and hooky. In the video, Sleeper chuck stuff around a supermarket with Dale Winton. Louise looks cute and blinks a lot.

Once 'Inbetweener' fired the starting gun, bang: it all went off. Three years of proper pop madness, of TV and touring, promoting and playing, of chasing fame and being chased for being famous.

In 2010, Louise wrote an excellent book about it, *Just for One Day: Adventures in Britpop*, that skims over certain details and highlights others. It was all she'd ever wanted, being in a band, and she was sharp enough to know she should savour the experience, even at the time.

'It's funny,' she says now, 'I don't remember being tired, ever. It's like you're running on adrenaline and energy. But you realise suddenly you've got a Sleeper bus and you've got trucks. At one point you're supporting Blur and jealous of them having a cheese board, and then suddenly you've got your own caterers providing the cheese, and they're making you Christmas dinner in July because you fancy it when you get off stage. It's like this absolute circus mentality.'

The best parts were the small moments. Thinking up tunes on the top of a night bus, writing the riff to 'What Do I Do Now?' on a bus in Texas. Working on 'Sale of the Century' all night with Andy in their tiny attic flat and then going to Hampstead Heath to watch the sun rise. When she thought up tunes, she didn't write them down. She believed that if they were good, she'd recall them.

Fun bits. She remembers being up a New York skyscraper to do an interview about the space race, because *Smart* had astronauts on its album sleeve, 'and they thought, "OK, these guys must know everything about space."' They went on a Japanese telly show to be poked by a padded stick in some sort of competition that they had to win in order to be able to play their single. They were chased by Bangkok school kids, because there were so many at the signing, running along corridors and out into Tower Records. 'Ludicrous. But brilliant.'

She remembers the video for 'Statuesque'. All of them stoned, her sitting on top of the trunk of a Cadillac convertible, cruising around Los Angeles in the milky West Coast light, thinking, 'This is it, we're going to break America!

'And we got arrested! We thought the police were coming for our bag of weed, because we were all stoned. And they just said, "Ma'am, will you please get back in the car? Please don't do that, ma'am . . ."'

And she loved the playing, the being onstage, the audience. The 'sweaty clubs, the fag ends and lager'. The colours and shapes and feelings of playing live are still part of her now.

There were other aspects that were more difficult. The so-called scene was . . . odd.

Because Britpop might have been an idea dreamed up by journalists, but it was an idea that was coming true. It started as a way to cover exciting new groups not yet big enough to justify a two-page feature, a label invented to create a buzz around something that didn't fully exist as yet. As the old newspaper adage has it, three's a trend.

But there *were* a lot of bands coming up that were reacting similarly to what music could be. Those bands had been playing the same venues, knocking about the same clubs, sleeping with each other, making friends with press officers, with journalists, with other people the same age with not much money but a lot of ambition and opinions. There was a scene.

'That part of it was real, in the sense that Camden, that part of north London, felt like it was owned by certain bands,' remembers Louise. 'And there was this strange idea that we were all part of this whole.'

Yet there was no supportive camaraderie. Quite the opposite.

'Everyone was *savage*,' she says. 'Everyone was super competitive. Partly because they knew that it could crack at any moment, it could go. So the pressure was ferocious. There was this huge competition, like, who's got the most column inches? Who's got the front cover? Checking midweeks and comparing. Just this constant analysis and worry. And so this idea that we were hanging out, buying each other pints – well, that didn't happen for us.'

Still, Louise wasn't naive. She understood the assignment. If there was a competition, she was in. She was up for it. And, she felt, she was prepared for some of the less pleasant parts of the job. She'd grown up on the outskirts of London, so she understood the uncool part of pop, the Radio 1 roadshow naffery, the *Top of the Pops* DJs surrounded by girls. All that ''ello, darlin'' slap-you-on-the-backside, golf-club heartiness, that winking, sexist cheese. She could see it for what it was.

'I was expecting all that bullshit from the Radio 1 DJs,' she says. 'But I wasn't expecting it from the guys in their Dr. Martens. Those guys who thought they were the most right-on, cool people in the UK. They were the worst.'

She'd never really read *NME* or *Melody Maker* when she was growing up. She hadn't cared about them. She liked Bananarama as well as David Bowie, she'd been obsessed with taping the Top 40, rather than listening to John Peel. She'd been a *Jackie* photo-story model (respect). 'I hadn't ever read those papers,' she says. 'It wasn't until we were in a band and we were going to be in them that I was like, "All right, I'm going to have to suss out what this is".'

In the way that optimistic young women do, she assumed that

the men of the music press would be fine with her. She was wrong. She sat down with one inkie journalist, and before he switched on his tape recorder and asked his questions (requiring Louise to provide detailed analysis on feminism, the class system, oh, and what she felt about teenagers masturbating over her), he said, 'I'm going to *get* you.'

'You'd be called a tart, you'd be called a madam, and that would be fine,' says Louise. 'You'd have letters in these papers saying I should be burnt as a witch, things like that. This was standard. It was just completely acceptable.'

Her very existence seemed to rile these men. Maybe because she was attractive and funny, but not making music that they could like (too lightweight). Maybe it was because, having split up with Jon, from 1995, she was going out with Andy. So she wasn't going to shag them, and she wasn't shagging someone they respected (fancied), like Damon, or Liam, or Brett. What was she doing, being so fit and yet so unavailable? Why was she in a relationship with someone they thought wasn't up to scratch? Someone that, if they were honest, they felt superior to. I mean, Andy was the fucking drummer.

Maybe it wasn't just Louise's un-single status, though. Or her music. There are plenty of men who feel anger towards women they find attractive merely for existing. We could analyse why, but why bother, when they clearly aren't going to do it themselves? Who wants to know the reasons behind calling a young woman names? There are no real reasons.

Louise took some of these encounters and worked them into her songs.

'Took a man from Stepford with a tape recorder/Got his ego broken, so crestfallen', from "Lie Detector", that's one of those guys', she says. 'One of those interviewers. You'd go in and give them nothing that they wanted, and they would write shit about you.'

She quickly learnt that the weekly music press was ideological, obsessed with being PC, ethically correct, with their chosen musicians listening to the 'right' records, coming from the 'right' background, saying the 'right' things.

'It was like you had to prove yourself', she says. 'How deeply did you worship at the altar of indie? And if you've grown up with pop music, and you hadn't sort of differentiated, it was like you were already wrong. It felt like being in quite a contrived space, like I was working out the whole time how I had to play it. I worked out a way, but I felt constantly like it was a little mini war of attrition.'

No wonder indie women started dressing like men, in trousers and big boots.

'We had steel toecap boots, we had little leather jackets', she laughs. 'We wore cardigans, for fuck's sake! It was a defensive move. But even with all of that, it was still, "Who's the most sexy?"'

Which was difficult – conflicting – because part of Louise wanted to enjoy being desirable. It's an enjoyable part of being in a band. 'Guys enjoy that at the front of bands – it's accepted that if you become a rock star, you immediately get the keys to being a sex symbol. That's part of the deal.'

'I was a really unattractive teenager, as most teenagers are', she says. 'I had acne, I wore glasses, I'm asthmatic, I have birthmarks – I was super self-conscious. And then I suddenly went into this transition. What you want to do is to be able to enjoy that and not have it be the thing that defines you, or not be denigrated by it. Like, this is just a little extra superpower that I have. But what I actually am is a lyricist, and I write melodies, and actually, I do that really fucking well. So just once, maybe say so. It wasn't a huge ask, I don't think.'

Outside of the inkies, in TV and radio, it was pretty awful too. Louise remembers going on a TV show.

'*The It Girl* had just come out, gone platinum, a Top Ten album that I'd written, and they go, "We're just going to get the cameraman round because he really fancies you, so you can look at the cameraman and tell us what you think and whether you fancy our cameraman." And that was a standard interview, that was just normal. And you're like, "OK, so that's what I'm here for."'

Then there was the time that a powerful industry man, who Louise spent a fun evening out with after a work event, saw her in the street. He looked her straight in the eyes and said 'Cunt', then walked past. She hadn't slept with him.

Now, she thinks that women were 'trying to find their way, trying to expand what it was to be a woman in a band' in an industry that had never belonged to them, 'working out how to be in that space'. Which was the right thing to do, but nobody wanted to help. 'It felt like no one had our back,' she says. 'I just thought it'd be different. You felt like you were engaged in some strange sort of war, and it was really unpleasant. It was grim.'

Because, of course, the music business, making records, the media, the whole shebang was set up around power. 'It's the whole point of it. Like, what's your power position, where do you sit? What leverage do you have? And that's true with every part of the process. You're always looking at where you sit in the structure.'

So if your record deal is bad, and you're undermined by the media, you're always going to be in a precarious position.

'Because of the way that the media was, because of the way that I felt represented, it took me a long time to think of myself as a musician, or as a songwriter. Or that those are my skills. I was just a mouthy bird who didn't wear a bra.'

When Chris Evans interviewed Louise on *TFI Friday*, he asked her about her relationships, with Jon and Andy – she brushed it off, with a, 'Yeah, I'm working my way through the band. We're getting a string section, so I'll have more'. He also asked her about male groupies.

'Well, the boys in the band, they get loads of girls,' said Louise. 'They're in gangs and they come straight up and say, "Do you wanna fuck?" The guys give me poems or flowers and they're really shy and they're a bit scared.'

That encounter – preserved on YouTube – reminded me that in 1996, I wrote a piece about indie-music groupies. It seems a strange commission now, but back then, not only did I write about it for *Select*, but Steven Wells wrote almost exactly the same article for the *NME*. There was a testosterone-fuelled recklessness in the air, fuelled by the new lad mags like *Loaded* and its sleazier, duller copycat *FHM*. A do-whatcha-like straight-as-a-die sexuality that presented itself as adventurous adult-baiting, where the new rebels knocked over the tables at the party, drank all the booze and grabbed at the girls because it was funny. Groupies seemed to be part of this atmosphere, and the music papers wanted to be sexy, too. Hence the feature.

When I read the piece now, I think, Hmmm. The sex is consensual and pretty tame – mostly blow jobs – though there are a couple of tales of more than one man having sex with the same woman. Many of the stories came from the women, rather than the musicians. A couple of the women worked in the music industry and enjoyed casual sex with their colleagues: so, not really groupies, more friends with benefits. I didn't anonymise anyone in the bands. I did change some of the so-called groupies' names.

In a few stories there is, without doubt, an unequal power relationship. And there's judgement from a few of the men, that the girls are asking for it, so they got it, and then they're kicked out. That age-old conscience transfer of wanting to do something you're unsure about, and then, as soon as you do, hating the person who helped you to do it. Misplaced self-hatred. Shame-shifting.

In the piece, I asked women in bands if they got groupies like the men in bands did. Singers such as Lesley from Silverfish, Tracy and Melissa from Voice of the Beehive, a couple of other women (not Louise) who didn't want to go on the record. They all said no, other than the wafty sad-eyed poem-writers.

But off the record, more than one told me that, though they didn't get male groupies, they did get the occasional creepy music journalist, pushy, sexual, who wouldn't leave them alone. Separately, they told me the same names, over and over. I did nothing about this, other than tell other women those names.

One of the so-called groupies in the piece, a teenager, said to me that she didn't really know why she wanted to sleep with bands.

But she did know, really. She explained it perfectly. She said: 'It's an immature thing, wanting to be famous myself. Cos I can't sing, I can't play any instruments, I'm never going to be in a band myself. But perhaps, you know, I can touch that stardom.'

You can touch that stardom. But you can't catch it. You don't catch stardom by standing next to a star, or by giving a star a blow job. And you don't catch it by interviewing it either, by asking irrelevant questions about politics or masturbation, trying to trip someone into saying the wrong thing. You're not going to be a star if you undermine, or flatter, or otherwise subtly bully a real star into sleeping with you.

To be a true star, as opposed to star-adjacent, you need to be an artist. You need to make your art. And that art – the elusive piece of work that might give you that fame, that spotlight, that attention you crave – comes from having an idea, catching it when it's alive, making it blossom into something real, and then doing it again. Keeping on going until you get there.

Pick up the guitar, write the lyrics, and have a go. You are allowed to do that. I wish I had said that to the girls that spoke to me.

It was Louise who pulled the plug on it all. Sleeper's third album, *Pleased to Meet You*, was due out and their first single was 'She's a Good Girl'. But BMG, Indolent's parent company, decided that the week that 'Good Girl' came out would be the week that they stopped discounting their singles. Which meant that 'She's a Good Girl' was double the price of every other single out there. It went in at Number 28. Two months later, Louise called a band meeting and said they should split up.

'I couldn't face what was coming,' she says. 'I had absolute clarity about what it meant. You get a lower chart position, and suddenly your tour support goes, your marketing budget goes, everything just steps back. So you have this very slow, graceless withdrawal, like a slow death. And I just couldn't fucking bear that. It was the right thing to do. But it wasn't easy. It was really hard.'

They went out with a bang, at a sell-out gig at Brixton Academy.

Louise lives in Brighton now. She moved there with Andy when she was pregnant with their second child. We never met during the 1990s, but thirty or so years later, I went to Brighton to talk to Louise for a live podcast she hosts. She was the interviewer, I was the interviewee. 'I much prefer it,' she told me.

Before we did the podcast, we chatted a bit about Sleeper's return to making music and touring. She hadn't been able to be in the band for a long time, partly because she hadn't wanted to, and partly because she and Andy had kids, so it was difficult. When they returned, their youngest was only ten, and their attempt to mesh domestic life with being in Sleeper was almost impossible.

'I lost count of the number of times that we'd get the phone call that one of the kids had puked, or got a fever,' she remembers. 'We were just about to go on stage in Newcastle and we got the call from their grandparents, like, "Yeah we're in A&E, we think she got appendicitis . . ."'

It's not easy to sustain a band when you have young children, clearly. But a lot of women left before then.

'A lot of the women walked away from it all,' says Louise. 'They left. Guys stayed in it, and got more successful, and they took away that [female] heritage, even if most of us were still doing stuff, whether it was at the margins or other side projects. I think a lot of women just felt like, "That's not for me. I can't do that, I can't be that, and it doesn't give me what I had expected."

'The strangest thing about all of that time', says Louise, 'is that the bit you don't consider is the absolute best part. Making songs is what it's about.

'I wanted to be in a band because I wanted to be on stage,' she says. 'I thought, "We're going to be famous, we're going to be rich, and it's going to be great," and all that stuff seemed like it was the *thing*. And it's not. None of that stuff that surrounds making music is the thing.

'But it never gets better than the moment that you come up with a melody, or a bit of song and you play it to someone, and realise, "Oh, that's good. We can do something with that." And you all get together in the rehearsal room, and it turns into something great. And then you play it in front of people, and then you record it. That process of it, of creating something from nothing. *That's* the joy of it.'

Back to Black

GARBAGE

'Only Happy When It Rains'

All bands are an accident, happy or otherwise. The hardest part of being in a band is creating it. Somehow the right musicians need to be drawn to each other, to locate themselves among all the other artists, weirdos and chancers out there who think that music is the answer. How do you find the four or five people that can somehow spark into the exact, yet indefinable, mixture of talent and sound, personality and drive, laughs and cussedness that makes a band? The hardest part is creating the band. (The second hardest part is being in the band.)

And there is a parallel universe where Garbage doesn't exist. Where Steve Marker doesn't switch on MTV's *120 Minutes* on 12 September 1993 and idly watch a video for Angelfish's 'Suffocate Me', the one and only time that the video is played on the network. He turns off the TV and gets a beer and doesn't see the smudgily provocative lead singer or hear her intimate, scary vocals. Or he does see the video and forgets the name of the band. As it was, he only half-remembers that name (Angel-something? Scottish?)

when he mentions it to his fellow music-experimenters, Butch Vig and Doug Erikson.

In that parallel universe, maybe Butch and Doug don't agree with Steve that this obscure female vocalist could front their new studio project, their sort-of band sort-of idea. At that time, they were thinking, well, it might be fun to have a lot of different front people, so that each track had a different vocalist. And high-profile people would want to sing on those tracks because, within the alternative music scene in early '90s America, Butch Vig had become a huge name. He'd produced albums by the Smashing Pumpkins, Sonic Youth and L7. But the game-changer had been Nirvana's *Nevermind*, the 1991 breakthrough LP that changed everything for everybody in the grunge scene. Butch was a big deal, as a producer.

Perhaps, in this parallel universe, after *Nevermind*'s success Butch decides to simply carry on producing. There were a lot of offers for him to do so and it would have made sense, given that he and Steve had set up a small studios, 'Smart', in Madison, Wisconsin, where they lived. They'd met at university and had set up the studio partly so that Doug's band could play and record there. Why not continue doing the thing they're known for, that makes money and will continue to make money, due to points (the royalty percentages paid to producers for their work on an album)?

But Steve was getting involved with hip-hop and Butch was excited by music other than grunge, by the sampling and heavy sounds of rap, especially Public Enemy, and they all wondered if it would be possible to make alternative rock in a similar way, to make music created by machines, taped and twisted in the studio into songs that sounded heavy but alive and, if not happy, then vibrant.

They'd all been making music – either in bands or producing – for quite some time. And now they were in this small, sleepy town in Wisconsin, up past Chicago and a little to the left, making music and wondering what to do with it. So when Steve suggests the woman from the Angelfish video as a singer, they think, well why not?

At twenty-seven, Shirley Manson had already had ten years of being in a bad. That band was Goodbye Mr. Mackenzie, a fairly successful Scottish pop-indie group, where Shirley was the backing singer. But it had split up and splintered into Angelfish, with her on lead vocals. Angelfish wasn't really working. Outside of that, Manson had worked at Miss Selfridge for five years on a make-up desk until she was taken off for being bolshy with customers. She'd gone clubbing a lot. She'd lived in a house with other creatives, with friends of friends, sleeping on the floor. At one point she'd sunk very low – 'crushing depression, struggling to get out my bed before four in the afternoon' – only continuing because one pal kept getting her up to go for a walk.

More complicated than she first appeared, Shirley was a mix of rebellion and self-loathing. A happy childhood had changed into a terrible time at secondary school, where she was relentlessly bullied by one girl for around a year, often just for having red hair. Her bully robbed Shirley of any kind of joy. Her unhappiness turned into rebellion. She started smoking and drinking, bunking off school and cutting herself.

Though she doesn't cut herself now, she understands what it's about. 'It's to do with your inability to deal with how you feel about yourself as an adolescent, your sexuality, your breasts, your pubic hair or whatever,' she's said. 'And for me it all turned into a feeling of self-hatred. The sensation of never feeling good enough or pretty enough will always be there. It's a constant dialogue, and you just learn to be more powerful than that other voice.'

But back then, she was less in control. She joined a drama group, which helped – but a predatory adult man there groomed her into sex, which didn't. After that, she had several sexual partners, one of which was Martin Metcalfe, the singer in Goodbye Mr. Mackenzie. She joined the band. Later, she recalled her position there as 'a completely disempowered creature'. But she worshipped Siouxsie Sioux and Patti Smith. She loved playing live. She knew what she wanted. She just hadn't yet had the opportunity to achieve it.

Shirley arrived in Madison in summer 1994. The first hotel she stayed in smelled of old men and had a mirror on the ceiling. She moved to another, which is where she lived, on and off, for the next five years. For a while, her situation wasn't much better than when she was in Angelfish: she was skint and she wasn't quite in the band yet.

'I was a nobody, a nothing, given this incredible opportunity,' she tells me from LA, where she now lives. 'And I was totally aware of that, I wasn't stupid. I'd been in a band that had struggled for ten years, so to be invited into this endeavour was a big deal. But my friends have postcards to this day from me, writing in complete distress from Madison saying, "Jesus fucking Christ, I don't know what I've done," and, "This is going to end very badly."'

Every day she walked through the heat or the cold in her big boots to the studio. Madison was small and collegiate, with no city culture, and extreme weather. 'Hot and muggy in the summer, freezing cold in the winter. I had no money and no credit card. No friends, no family, no nothing. And I couldn't drive.' She could see that the band had something, a patchwork of ideas that might work. But they weren't a band. They were an idea of a band. 'I was trying to join an idea of a band with one producer and two musicians, but they all got automatically ascribed this fine mantle of producer too. So, three producers and then I could be the singer. But that's not a band. I was *glaringly* aware of how difficult a sell this was going to be. I thought it was doomed to fail.'

Shirley had never written songs before and had no production experience. What she was about was performance. She could sing, and show out, and get an audience going. She knew how to create an atmosphere with her voice, how to play it down to draw a listener in; when to whisper, when to scream. She knew the importance of a look and an attitude. She'd spent years playing live, selling songs to a handful of people or to indifferent half-crowds.

The UK music scene, even if you were living in Edinburgh rather than London, was close-up and scrappy and DIY, on top of itself. Sub-cultures and trends changed fast, ate themselves from within, spat people out. In Madison, everything was more laid back. Flannel shirts, a big drinking culture. Not just the band, but the whole town. Shirley set about feeling her way into her new job. The boys were encouraging but it was still a strange situation. She was paid per diems (a daily wage) for three months – a trial period – and only ate one meal a day.

She remembers them playing her 'Stupid Girl'. She thought, hmmm. She wasn't mad about singing something that could be seen as putting women down. 'It was not a title I would have ever come up with,' she says today. But she was very far from being an equal within the band as yet. 'I was this invited guest, which was really uncomfortable and weird,' and because of this, she had to approach altering some of the words 'in a very gentle fashion'. Not her natural technique. Still, she felt upbeat because the song sounded so good, with its Clash drum sample, its energy: 'an extraordinary sonic tapestry, very carefully and beautifully put together'. She hoped her personality could make the title work.

It took a few months for Garbage to work out what being in this sort-of-band, this studio project, might entail, how it might play out. It was still so early. Yet, almost immediately, there was music industry interest. The band released 'Vow' on a CD compilation for a UK magazine, and suddenly there were record-label reps making the long trek to Smart. One arrived with an ice sculpture. Somebody else turned up in a garbage truck (geddit?). Shirley thought: 'Holy shit. Well, if these idiots are going to fucking fund this, then so be it. Let's go for it.'

The speed of everything meant that she, too, started working fast. Elbowing her way in. She found herself excluded from a lot of the label meetings because she still wasn't yet part of the band. One time, she was upstairs while a meeting was going on and decided to write a song – 'the first song that I'd really written, chords and melody, that I brought to the band'. She finished it in the time it took for the meeting, played it to the band afterwards, and they recorded it in about an hour, which was unbelievably quick for them. The song was 'Milk'.

Gradually, all four of them were starting to understand what being in this strange project might mean. And then there was another meeting, with their record label's head of PR. Even now, Shirley remembers the sting of it. 'He said to me, "Nobody's going to want to talk to you, it's all going to be about Butch. We'll try and get you a couple of interviews, but be aware that it's all going to be Butch-driven." To be told that by one of the heads of your label is hard. Because they're basically saying, "Well, you're not special enough to do your job. You're not a frontperson. Sorry, but you're going to have to take a back seat." It's like a fucking punch in the face, you know? And I was like, "Yes, well, we'll see about that."'

In the UK, Garbage's first single was 'Only Happy When It Rains'. Another song that Manson had to make her own; another one where she hated the title. For her, it was too close to 'Happy When It Rains', by The Jesus and Mary Chain, influential Scottish indie doomsters signed to Creation. The JAMC were one of the coolest bands out there, and they were her fellow countrymen. So Shirley was inwardly cringing. But when she heard the rough demo, 'I was like, "Oh, thank fuck. It doesn't sound anything like it, I can relax."' There was a snippet of a lyric idea; she took it, wrote her own words and made it her own.

Plus, she loved the concept. 'It's so Scottish.' Humour and pess-imism – a potent mix that she identified with. 'I understood what the boys were trying to say. They didn't pick me because I was Scottish. They picked me for other reasons. But here I am.'

Her Scottishness worked well with Garbage; 'grit with humour' is how Shirley describes her national character. Tough and funny, a bit more red-blooded and hardened than their softy English counterparts. And that delight in the dark side of things, mixed with a come-on-then wit – 'pour your misery down on me' – turned out to be what Garbage was best at. A band that knows that life isn't always joyful or easy, but takes the hard times, the insecurities, the mess, the heartbreak, and turns them into something ferocious that also makes you smile.

'Only Happy When It Rains' was Garbage's first single in the UK. It went in at Number 29, and stayed in the charts for three weeks. Not so long, but it's still hugely popular; their most licensed track, used all the time on TikTok and Instagram Reels. Unusually, the chorus comes banging straight in: no verse, no music before the vocals start, just crackle, children laughing, the sound of rain, a clicking drum. And each line is like a tongue-in-cheek slogan, almost a mickey-take of grunge's gloom.

Shirley wasn't completely involved in creating the music as yet. But she took over when it came to the visuals. 'The video for "Only Happy When It Rains" is like the launch of Garbage as an idea,' she says. 'Video in the '90s played such a big role in breaking a band, or any artist. Having videos played nonstop on MTV. And MTV *loved* us. We made really good videos. That's something that I will take a lot of credit for. I knew what I was doing. I understood what a video is supposed to do. I made sure it was strong.'

The first UK video had to be a statement. She styled the boys, put them in eyeliner, black nail varnish, big collars and suits. No way were they going to 'fall into the abyss of anonymity', she says. And no way was she. In America, the look for alternative women at that time was still quite grunge-affected and androgynous. 'Everybody was in flannel shirts and boots, and deliberately messy fucked up hair,' she says. 'Most of the girls were not wearing much make-up because they wanted to be taken seriously, as an alternative female perspective.'

This was not Shirley's style. In Scotland, she'd been a clubber, in little lycra dresses. She thought, well that would work on MTV: 'Neon colours.' Plus, she says, she was thinking of Kylie Minogue. How Kylie had been sexless and cute, a girl-next-door, and then had changed when she'd started going out with INXS shag-meister Michael Hutchence. 'All of a sudden, she transformed herself into a super-amazing-looking pop star,' Shirley recalls. 'Having been Charlene from *Neighbours*, with her permed hair and '80s garb, she became Sex Kylie.' So she brought that sex-pop element and her own British clubbing gear to her video-style, and, as an ex-Miss Selfridge make-up queen, she added heavy slap. 'Here are the false eyelashes and the eyebrows and the lined lips. Everybody can fucking kiss my arse . . . there was that, plus my boots. I had to wear boots. It was that weird mixture that I think made me stand out.'

The deadpan look into camera, the stomping and kicking, the insolent delight in the grubbiness of the warehouse they're in (at one point, she's singing in a toilet). There is no pretty or twee or clichéd sexy in Shirley. Around her, Butch drums and Doug and Steve play until they start wrecking their guitars (a rock platitude, but also a signal of a move away from grunge and into the more modern world of sampling). The band's performance is intercut with scenes of strange characters in animal onesies and masks looking spooky in a landscape. The colours are distorted, the neon pink and blue of Shirley's minidresses bleeding out from the monochrome background. It's all there. The fun, the confrontation, the grime-glamour, the defiance. 'My only comfort is the night gone black.' The wit and the darkness. Garbage as an idea.

Garbage appeared on *Top of the Pops* for the first time in 1995, to play 'Only Happy When It Rains'. Shirley wore clompy boots, black nails, black trousers, a black spaghetti-strap top. The only colour was a long bright pink boa hanging on the microphone stand. She looked cool. What she didn't look was Britpop. Because how could Garbage be that? They were three-quarters American and one-quarter Scottish, and you'd be hard-pressed to find many Scots who call themselves Brits. Plus, the idea of Britpop, the fundamental concept, the starting gun, was a reaction against American grunge.

'We were the odd fish in the cool gang, for sure,' she says. 'We didn't belong, and we weren't embraced by any scene. Nobody claimed us. We were the odd one out.'

Garbage were outside the hot drama and frantic gossip and weekly reporting of the UK music press. They weren't hanging around Camden with inkie journalists or drinking with other bands. But that doesn't mean they didn't slot into some of the other ideas swirling around at that time. 'I was bold and a show-off, and I knew that I wasn't going to get completely annihilated by press or promotion because I knew my own self,' says Shirley.

Shirley was a perfect fit with the unspoken Britpop belief that front people were important. The idea that indie music was better when it was delivered by look-at-me show-offs, that alternative sounds should be given personality by an actual personality, someone who looked brilliant and attracted attention and who had something to say.

Punk and post-punk had given many alternative pop stars to the UK; Adam Ant and Robert Smith and Siouxsie Sioux bursting out of *Top of the Pops* and music magazines to grab the attention of both pop-lovers and doomy teens. But by the early '90s, for quite some time, within indie music, it had been credible to be anonymous. To disdain press coverage, to refuse to be on the cover of your records, to treat fame like an embarrassing coat to be shrugged off and left on the floor in the corner. Only sell-outs wanted their photo taken. If a cool band agreed to a picture, they would be looking away, or to the ground. My Bloody Valentine and The Jesus and Mary Chain and New Order all made amazing music, but they flinched from fame. Added to this, rave had contributed to the idea that hit tracks could be made by anonymous people, that you didn't have to cavort in *Smash Hits* with a pineapple on your head to qualify as a popstar.

But now there was Jarvis Cocker, Brett Anderson, Damon Albarn, Liam Gallagher. Indie singers with strong opinions and excellent faces, made for photos and interviews. An understanding of the fun of fame, the joy of fans being allowed to fancy the lead singer, and the lead singer enjoying that.

And there was something in Shirley Manson, something tumultuous and unsatisfied, that could only be sated by being in a band, and being seen in a band. 'When I was onstage I didn't feel scared,' she said once. 'The perverse converse of how other people experience being onstage.' By being an alternative pop star, stepping up to the mic, going to stage-front and showing the world the version of herself she wanted to show, she eased something inside herself. Plus, she was really good at it. She looked cool, but her stage persona was fiery. She gave young girls confidence, just by being in front of them, looking stroppy and different and holding her own. She had nerve (she had a nerve). With some bands, you might get more than one person to have a crush on. With Garbage, really, there was just the one. Shirley Manson.

What was interesting was who crushed on her. From the start, it was girls. Teenage girls, the beating heart and driving force of all popular music, can sense something in a pop icon that they might not quite know themselves. Manson was funny and front footed, quick to call out stupidity, ready with a joke and a put-down. But distress was always close. She had self-harmed as a teenager and had suicidal urges. She struggled with depressive thoughts. She was creative and confrontational, but also fragile and vulnerable to criticism.

Actually, Shirley thinks now, part of what you feel in 'Only Happy When It Rains' is the fuck-you energy of teenage girls. She had a direct link back into that; her own teenage difficulties had formed her. 'When I was growing up, to be a girl was to be told to minimize the space you took up: "Close your legs. Don't be loud. Smile. Be cute. Be attractive. Be pleasing." But I was a rebellious kid, and I wasn't going to sit in the corner and be quiet,' she told *Rolling Stone*.

'I was very dark, unable really to control my thinking – until I joined a band, funnily enough,' she says. 'And then things got a lot easier. Like, I had other things to think about. I had a way of coping with my spirit, for better or for worse, for good and bad. I had this energy and I didn't know what to do with it, but once I joined the band, I funnelled it into that.'

Girls can sense that darkness. They know it, they live it, they love it. Some men, not so much. A complicated woman is not one they want to deal with. Though Shirley enjoyed almost all of her press encounters – 'I was really good at press. I was able to hold people's attention for a decade, you know? And I enjoyed it' – there were male music writers, especially in the UK, that sneered at her; dismissed her as too mouthy and not good-looking enough.

'It would just be the odd piece that fucking stung,' she says, 'but it made me insane. I didn't care if we got a bad review elsewhere because it didn't feel personal. But when we came to the UK and we got a bad review, it crushed me. And some of the press was very misogynistic and sexist, glaringly so. Comments about my body, my face, my shag-ability. How crazy I was. Because I was outspoken. That's very personal and hard to throw off. I think many female musicians would complain about the same things.

'I arrived at a time when it was just men that were adulated. Our culture is very comfortable adulating men. Not so comfortable praising women then, and still not very comfortable with praising women. In the '90s, a man could write one song, and then disappear forever, and he'd be lauded as one of Britain's greatest songwriters and talents to ever have lived, and garner a bunch of awards, and always be given a second chance, and put at the top of a festival fifteen, twenty years later. It's wild. And it still remains that way.'

Shirley assumed – like every young woman living, working and enjoying their life at the time – that she would be treated as an equal. She thought that being a great frontwoman was the same as being a great frontman. But when she cut her hair off, her record company got upset. When she said what she thought about certain issues, there were comments. (An A&R man told her that he masturbated over her pictures; she was meant to be pleased.) Within the label there was a belief that she wasn't always an asset. Too mouthy, too difficult. Not pliant, not pleasing.

'I was blind to the system I was actually up against,' she says. 'And as you get older, and you learn more, and you educate yourself, and you have more experience, you start to see things a little clearer. I am shocked at how little I saw. I never really understood what was going on a lot of the time. It's just as well, because I probably wouldn't have been able to get out my bed in the morning.'

And there was the other side to it all. The camaraderie of women who were also going through the same. Because the other thing about being in an American/Scottish band, one that knew how to tour and to play live, to put on a show, night after night, was that Garbage fitted into a US alternative scene that was changing and expanding, coming to the fore, shifting the focus from pop.

'It was an amazing time for alternative women,' says Shirley. 'Arguably, the only time the female alternative perspective has enjoyed a place in mainstream culture. I don't think it's really happened since. There we were, hanging out with Hole and No Doubt, with Gwen Stefani and L7 and just all these incredible bands. It was wonderful. I felt like, "Oh my God, finally I'm with my people. This is my world. I understand this language." I was so excited to be there, and privileged, and inspired by it.'

It gave her the energy and determination to keep going. When the boys got over their aversion to playing live, Garbage went on the road, all around America to sell their album, and then, a couple of years later, for *Version 2.0*, and on and on, trailing along under big grey skies on a tour bus for months and months. Three years after selling four million copies of their first album, Garbage were playing an actual county fair, with pigs and chickens, and a local hall in South Hadley, Massachusetts, as well as big venues on the coasts. But it didn't break them. At no point did they chuck it all in and go home, like so many British bands did. Because they weren't British. Their home – other than Shirley's – was America. Big, scary America, where if you make it, you last. And they made it, and they lasted.

'I cringe sometimes when I think back,' she says. 'But I also think I did my best. I was so young and naive. And I put up with a lot of shit that I wouldn't put up with now, you know? Women aren't allowed to progress. We keep having to prove ourselves over and over, restarting. You're not allowed to hold on to your agency, to build a full career, like a man is. But, you know, I'm still here.'

She laughs.

'And that's because, like many women from back then, I am,' says Shirley, 'an unrelenting cunt.'

Dark Star

PJ HARVEY
'Down by the Water'

'I am constantly fascinated by the difference between someone opening their mouth and speaking, and someone opening their mouth and singing.' Polly Harvey once said this to me and I think about it quite a lot. Especially when considering Polly when she talks (composed, careful, warm, physically still) and Polly when she sings (depends what she's trying to convey, how long do you have?). Polly playing live has long been something to behold.

The first time I saw PJ Harvey perform was in 1992, at Legends in Preston. PJ Harvey were a three-piece band at the time – bassist Steve Vaughn, drummer Rob Ellis and Polly herself – arranged democratically on stage: Polly on the left, Steve on the right, with Rob on drums, at the back, in the middle. All very equal; though, really, it was hard to tear your eyes away from Polly. Small frame encased in an all-in-one, vest-topped, black body suit; stompy fuck-off boots; one big hoop earring; dark hair in a bun. She stood still and straight, no jumping about, no guitar hero poses. I don't remember her talking to the audience. Her expression was, mostly, calm, sometimes amused, which showed itself in a flicker around her eyebrows, a twist in her mouth.

Without her guitar, you'd have thought Polly was a dancer. But it was there, slung quite high across her body. And God, she made an enormous noise, both with that guitar, which she made thrash and squall, and with her voice, which moved from a whisper to a howl to a growl to a lament, like living, out-loud turmoil. I remember the audience wasn't huge but it was rapt, almost stunned. A bit of jumping about to 'Sheela-Na-Gig'. No phones in those days, of course, so no look-away distractions. I was reviewing the gig and I wrote: 'With a wide-open wail, she draws you in and then roars and soars and seethes until your insides are turned outside and your heart is left twisted round your breathing apparatus.' By you, I meant me – and all the other people in the room. Especially the women.

Polly was compelling. She was beautiful. But – and this was unusual for the time – her magnetism wasn't to do with her sex or sexuality. Though she made what Courtney Love called 'angry vagina music', onstage, at that time, she rarely ignited her femaleness, her femininity. Despite her lyrics, her live persona wasn't directly concerned with being a woman, or even with the women in the audience. No 'girls to the front', no virgin/whore discussion, no L7 drop-your-trousers rock-shock, no 'shut up men let the women speak'.

She spoke to a different part of womanhood. Something perhaps more extreme, to do with how your body separates from or meshes with your mind, how your female physicality might stop you from accepting yourself. There was a twig-snap fragility to Polly. But, along with that, and opposite to it, an absolute belief in what she was doing. It was mesmerising. There was an 'of course' to it. Why would gender come into this? it said. What's the problem? When you're this good, what is there to discuss?

A couple of hours before the gig, I did an interview with Polly and the band. It wasn't an easy one. ('There's so many things that I don't think it necessary to talk about, like our backgrounds,' she said to me. 'It makes it very difficult for people like yourself.') Still, it was interesting. Polly, who wrote all the songs, described how she did so in her head, without touching an instrument, mulling them over, sometimes for months: 'Sometimes I don't hear the music or the words, I'll just have a feeling I want to get across . . .' she said. 'I think about music all the time, there's nothing else I think about, whatever conversation I'm having, whatever film I'm watching, whatever book I'm reading.'

She was polite, with a lovely Dorset burr and contained body language. No extraneous movement. She included Rob (chatty) and Steve (less so). 'Sometimes I sing the songs to Rob and Steve,' said Polly.

She said that she thought people missed the humour in the songs, such as when she went into a falsetto (the band were working on 'Me-Jane' at the time, which *is* funny). I thought of 'Sheela-Na-Gig' and said I thought she was right. 'I would like it if we sounded like a fairground ride,' said Polly, who was living next door to a fairground at the time. 'One thrill after the other, whether it was making you unhappy or really scared . . . There's such a fine line between something that's really funny and something that's really horrific.'

Funny/horrific. Right from the start, she walked that line. The very first time PJ Harvey performed was in 1991, at a skittle alley in Dorset. There were about fifty people there and, Polly remembered later, 'with the first song, we cleared the hall, so there were only about two people left'. A woman went up to Rob, in the middle of a song, and shouted at him: 'Don't you realise nobody likes you? We'll pay you, you can stop playing, we'll still pay you.'

Stop playing, nobody likes you. You're not funny, you're horrific. Or the situation's a bit horrific, but you find it funny. An uneasy combination, and there was always something about Polly that made people uncomfortable. The *New York Times* called her a 'guitar-toting succubus'; many pieces, even rave reviews, used words like 'screeching harridan', though there was usually a question mark after those words. She scared the horses, scared the men. When Courtney Love called Polly's songs 'angry vagina music', she also said, 'The one rock star who makes me know I'm shit is Polly Harvey.'

It was that, really, that created the unease. Polly was, from the start, obviously, clearly, very good. She made the sort of music that male music journalists loved – noisy, syncopated, dynamic, blues-based, quiet–loud guitar rock songs – but made it without fuss, or pose. She gave it dignity, not status.

And, perhaps even scarier, she used it to sing lyrics that picked at the relationships between men and women, or at the very nature of being one or the other. 'Sheela-Na-Gig' is about a woman being rejected for being too forward – *you exhibitionist* – her childbearing hips being too much for a prospective lover.

'Rid of Me' is disdained, obsessional, scary, erotic, driven love: 'I'll make you lick my injuries/I'm gonna twist your head off'. 'Dry' is sexually specific and '50 Ft Queenie' is the triumphal stomp of monster (drag?) womanhood: 'I'll tell you my name F-U-C-K . . . force ten hurricane . . . bend over Casanova'. 'Man-Size' is similar to '50 Ft Queenie', but different, about the exhilarating joy of banishing femaleness – *get girl out of my head* – and behaving like a manly man, using measurements and maths to assert 'Good Lord I'm big'. It could be from the viewpoint of a man or a woman, though I always thought of it as a woman using macho tropes to get herself through life. In the video, Polly sings it with masculine gestures whilst sporting a top with a Marilyn Monroe graphic and a pair of white lacy pants. Recently, I saw her play it in a long white shift dress and white ankle boots.

Where were the jokes, the winks, the seaside sauce? Against the grain of the bubbling English indie music scene, Polly ignored The Kinks, The Beatles, David Bowie, The Smiths. Her songs contained the beauty of Björk, the darkness of Tricky, the off-kilter awkwardness of Radiohead. They were intense. And the people who liked them understood that intensity – not a trite passion but something built of loss and experience, an existential human pain as well as a delight. The grinding gears, the screeching brakes, the smash of it all. She wrote several of her songs in her late teens, though she wasn't in a full relationship until she was twenty. It was just her imagination, her occupying of a mood. Later, Polly became an artist that could bring music up from place and time. But in her early '90s songs, the place she drew on was the body;

she transported herself into particular moods and physical sensations. Visceral.

'I just wanted to say something that hadn't been said in that way before,' she said later. 'I was trying to cause a riot in one way or another.'

Dry came out in 1992, and then *Rid of Me* in 1993. *Dry* was produced by the band and Howard 'Head' Bullivant in Dorset. It was the first chance that Polly had to make a record and she thought it would be her last, 'so, I put everything I had into it, it felt very extreme for that reason'. *Rid of Me* was made in two weeks in Minnesota with Steve Albini. Polly and Albini connected in interesting ways. 'We were both equally offended by the way women are treated in the music industry,' said Albini later, 'coddled and treated as if they're incapable of making their own decisions.' But, in the studio, Albini sometimes found himself treating Polly in that very way. 'He got really angry with himself,' said Polly. 'I think that made him feel a bit uncomfortable.' That discomfort around masculinity is what makes the album so great: Polly both desires its swaggering charms and rejects them entirely. (As an aside: *Rid of Me* inspired Kurt Cobain and Nirvana to make *In Utero* with Albini in the same bang-it-out-in-a-fortnight way, in an effort to reclaim their raw punk roots after the huge success of *Nevermind*.) Anyway, *Rid of Me* came after the end of Polly's first serious relationship. It was a difficult time: she'd moved from Dorset to London to study sculpture at St Martins, a degree which she never finished; the band started touring a lot, including across America; they swapped record labels from indie to major; after one tour, the band split up. She moved back to Dorset, near to her parents.

Polly grew up in Corscombe, a small village of a few hundred people near Yeovil, on a small-holding with her older brother and her mum and dad, who ran a quarrying business. Her family was loving, but not huge talkers. Her parents adored music (they'd wake the kids up by playing Jimi Hendrix or Captain Beefheart records at 3 a.m.) and her mum got London bands to come and play in local halls. They'd stay in the Harvey family house and give the young Polly music lessons.

(The mere fact that Polly came from the countryside slightly spooked the music press, especially when she told them tales of twisting off the testicles of baby lambs, or pulling dead lambs from birthing ewes. Resolutely city-centred, journalists wondered if it meant that she was sort of posh, or maybe weirdly innocent. She wasn't a working-class hero, anyway, nor definitively art school. She was disqualified from some sort of important club.)

When she was growing up, Polly spent all her time with boys, because it so happened that the kids that lived nearby were all boys. 'I wanted to be a boy so much,' she said. 'I used to wear male swimming trunks until I started developing breasts at twelve or thirteen.' She liked Action Men. She'd wee sitting on the bowl of the toilet, facing the lid. She only grew her hair as a teenager because she kept getting told off when she went into women's toilets. Until her teens, she made her family call her Paul. Perhaps because of this, her teenage years were hard: 'I was a classic tortured teenager.' She suffered from self-loathing and depression.

'I don't even think of myself as being female half the time,' she said later. 'I never write with gender in mind. I write about people's relationships to each other.'

But she was a woman. So, once she started making music, she was constantly compared to, or set against, other female singers. Especially, she noticed pointedly, if they had brown hair. There were connections drawn with Kate Bush, Patti Smith, Tori Amos, even with pop-folk-one-hit-wonder Tanita Tikaram. Polly was asked a lot if she was a feminist. She said – and this was deemed quite outrageous at the time – not really. She might be, but she wasn't sure. She hadn't done the research. 'I don't know what feminism is,' she said once. 'People attack me for that, saying, "You must find out what it is and see," but I don't have the time. I don't have the energy. I'd rather read a book.' Another time: 'I hate the word feminist. It can do so much more damage than good. All I want to do is write honestly, and I'm a woman.'

Those terms, that conversation, simply weren't anywhere near what she was thinking. Not what she was dealing with. She was often surrounded by men – we're talking the music industry, after all – but she didn't find that a problem, as long as they were on the same wavelength.

Clearly, it was strange for Polly – as it is for many women artists – to be treated as a woman before being treated as a musician. She kept wrong-footing journalists, not saying what they would expect. Her jokes landed oddly. She told a French TV presenter that playing guitar in front of a bass amp was 'a sexual experience'; she said that sex was a very natural thing to write about. 'For me, music is a turn-on,' she told Q magazine. 'It's not something to do with your head, it's to do with your body, which is a very sexual instrument. To bring sexual elements into the lyrics to go with the music just makes perfect sense to me. It just happens.'

Polly once said that reading the press about her in the 1990s contributed to her having a nervous breakdown. There were so many words spewed out, by all of us music writers. So many magazines and papers competing with each other, unpicking music to its constituent parts, talking to and across each other about tiny incidents that happened at gigs or something funny someone did at an awards ceremony. The '90s music press was like social media before it existed. The hot takes, the side swipes, the purse-lipped judgement, the readiness to cancel people for the tiniest of seemingly unacceptable actions, especially around sexism. The outraged responses to something someone else wrote or said, the oppressive little club of it all. Who's the funniest? The most outrageous? The monthly papers joined in, but it was the music weeklies that drove it. The writers tried to out-cool and out-write and out-right-on each other.

And the writing about Polly could be vicious. One writer, in a singles review (a singles review!) called her a 'pretentious bitch', and wrote, in capitals, 'GOD I HATE THE WAY SHE PREENS HERSELF IN THE VIDEO'. The video was for 'C'mon Billy' and featured Polly playing the part of a garish Moulin Rouge-style prostitute, a theatrically disturbing exaggeration of a stereotype. In the same review the writer wrote: 'Not that I have anything against people who bare their breasts and then pretend they're making a statement.' (Love the use of 'people' in that sentence.)

'Bare their breasts' refers to a photograph on the back of *Dry*, which showed Polly floating in the bath. The picture was cropped just underneath her breasts. The photograph, along with the cover shot of *Rid of Me*, of her flicking her sopping wet hair, was taken by Maria Mochnacz. They were beautiful images. They caused no end of a furore, which became even more intense a week or so later, when she had her photo taken, topless but from the back, for the front cover of the *NME*.

Polly was interested in art. She chose the image because it worked with what she was saying on the albums. At no point had she considered the potential moral quandary of the photographs, and how this would be discussed in the music press. (She didn't take advice anyway: she just presented the album, with the photographs she wanted to be used, to the record company, and that was that.) All those different emotions, the guitar, the sound, the use of words and imagery in her records, the intimate, funny, frightening songs about what a female body could be, how it could behave, and the media discussion was, essentially: tits out – good or bad? When she played, sometimes men shouted that. Show us your tits.

'Down by the Water' is the first single from Polly's third album, *To Bring You My Love*, and it's known as the PJ Harvey song for people who don't like PJ Harvey. It has recognisable Peej elements: it's creepy, menacing, oblique. But *To Bring You My Love* is the first time she works with co-producer Flood (later, she describes their musical relationship as 'two bells ringing with the same note') and there's a noticeable emotional change. 'Down By the Water' has strings, electronica and a lush arrangement, and although it's about murder and loss, or at the very least bad interfamilial dynamics, after *Dry* and *Rid of Me*'s indie blues noise, it's practically a pop symphony. The verse and chorus are clear and catchy, the story is told so that we understand, the plucked strings add punctuation. It's a gothic country song, based on a traditional US folk song, 'Salty Dogs Blues' – 'I heard her holler/I heard her moan' – with murder on its mind: 'Little fish, big fish swimming in the water/Come back here and give me my daughter.' Brrrr. It's a pretty tune, but the atmosphere is chilly and ominous, the whispered fish refrain like a curse. Though she seems to blame the river, we know the singer murdered her daughter.

It marked a shift from what we might call grunge Polly – clear-faced, plain-outfitted, taking on the men at their own guitar job – to theatrical Polly. Exaggerated glamour, OTT femininity, a near-drag version of womanhood. Long dark hair cascading down her back. Scarlet satin, blood-red mouth, glittering eyes, thick clumped eyelashes. A warped glamour puss, a heroine, a belle dame sliding into a flood, floating down a river, hair a swirling cloud. The video that came with it – PJ in her long dress dancing, and then in the water, going down down, her silver shoes a-glitter – was played a lot on MTV, and 'Down by the Water' got to Number Two on the US's Modern Rock Tracks chart.

There's an element in PJ Harvey that went unacknowledged for a while, even by Polly herself. The desire to be a star, a front person that everyone looked at. She had been so shy as a child, and she was still uneasy with journalists. Despite her natural desire for privacy, she engaged with the press gamely enough, because she understood that in order to get her work known, to get people to listen and know about it, she had to talk to journalists. 'I want to be seen by as many people as possible and sell as many albums as possible and I know I have to do interviews to promote these things,' she said. 'I am ambitious in what I do. I want to be the best.'

And being the best also meant being centre stage. Which

fitted with the time: indie music had become crowded with show-offs, bustling with lead singers who searched out the camera, who were there to perform. Though she was quiet about it, Polly wanted to be seen, to perform to people who were dying to see her. I asked her about it recently, if she remembered that feeling of wanting to shine fitting in with other mid-'90s extroverts. 'Yeah, it was shoegazers before that time, wasn't it?' she said. 'People looking down at the floor.' She stepped into the spotlight.

We first saw Polly as a star in her 1995 Glastonbury appearance. There we were, gathered in front of the Pyramid Stage on a sunny late afternoon, expecting our regular low-key, black-clad, noisy guitar queen. But on Polly stalked, to give us something else. In a hot pink catsuit, with lurid, smeared make-up – black eyebrows, blue eye-shadow, fake lashes, slash red mouth – she was a warped and deadly version of female sexuality. 'Joan Crawford on acid,' she called the look later. Her body formed strange angles. When she played 'Down by the Water', she stood still to hit two wooden claves together, utterly serious in her unserious leotard. Funny and horrific, right there. She was mesmerising.

But she also seemed vulnerable, very thin, sort of stretched and tight. Particularly because she wasn't playing guitar. Guitars hang in front of you like a shield, but also like a big fuck-off gun. She had neither at Glastonbury. No protection, no weapon. With that performance, with her painted face and her tiny body, striding on heels, twisting and writhing, she gave us an unsettling grotesquery of femininity, its fragility and eroticism and look-at-me power. It blazed out of her, manic and violent.

Everyone who watched knew there was something wild and unusual about her performance: not a traditional rock showing out, but an acutely strange, extreme theatrical presentation that seemed to be seeping into the person who offered it to us. Was there a danger that the smeared mask of make-up might become her actual face?

It was as though she had taken all her anger and desperation around femaleness – the 'Rid of Me', the 'Man-Size', the '50 Ft Queenie', the 'Dry' – and turned it into something else, something physical and unpretty. If she was going to be judged as a woman, then here was the most extreme version.

'I'm not a removed person, no matter what I'm doing,' she said once. 'I've always been very visceral, in that I feel things very deeply.'

I saw PJ Harvey play 'Down by the Water' very recently, at a festival, in the pouring rain. It remains the song of hers that everyone knows and it was the one that got the biggest cheer, from sodden tank-topped young people and from middle-aged indie fans in their sensible kagoules. Polly owned the stage, but far less manically than in 1995. She struck angular poses: one outstretched leg, her arm pointing up, a living arrow. She turned and waggled her bum, deliberately, slowly. It got a cheer. She talked to the audience, in a warm and conversational manner, thanking us for staying to watch her even though the rain was lashing. And then, she used that same instrument – the voice that talks, the voice that sings – to give us 'Dress', '50 Ft Queenie', 'Man-Size'.

When she played 'Down by the Water', she hit the two wooden

claves together, still fascinating, still ominous, glowing in her ghostly white shift. The rain hammered down. The whispered curse shimmered out into the night, over our dripping heads. You couldn't take your eyes off her.

What You Get When You Mess With Us

RADIOHEAD

'No Surprises'

There are some funny little memes and videos about Radiohead out there these days and they mostly joke that the band make white guys' music, that they tap into something profound but hidden in emotionally stunted men. They highlight Jonny's guitar, the judder and scrape of it, as a key. There is a bit of truth in this, which is why the memes are funny. Radiohead are a stadium-filling band that make music that expresses the deeply felt, rarely acknowledged, oddly complicated emotions of the decent and frustrated. And when those feelings come, they can burst out jagged and wild.

It seems unbelievable now, but in the early 1990s, these international art-rock sensations/extreme musical experimenters/ chart-chewing tune-delighters were just another English indie band trying to make their way. Trying to get their music out to an audience, to work out what they were doing and who they were for. Then, Radiohead wore Adidas T-shirts, leather coats, silly sunglasses. They got some bad reviews: 'pitiful, lily-livered excuse for a rock 'n' roll group', 'make-weight cock-rockers', 'they fail to provide the vaguest suggestion of dark intrigue'. They were teased for being serious. Some writers were rude about singer Thom Yorke's looks and the intensity of his delivery.

Based in Oxford, Radiohead didn't hang out in London and as they were signed to a major label (Parlophone/EMI), their indie credentials were deemed dubious. Their music wasn't part of a scene, their influences (REM, Talking Heads, Pixies) weren't of the moment. There was always a distance between them and the frenzied chatter of whatever London was celebrating from week to week. But they still played at the same festivals, were reviewed by the same journalists, turned up at the same awards ceremonies, chugged around the small college venues playing short sets alongside Kingmaker, The Frank and Walters or The Sultans of Ping.

They did interviews. As people, they were a delight: simultaneously extremely nice, warm and funny – bassist Colin Greenwood especially, has a way with a joke – and ever so slightly removed, in the manner of distracted professors, as though half their mind was off thinking about complex number patterns but the other half was enjoying your company as a distraction, while those thoughts were spinning. And Thom was especially different; separate because he was the frontman, but also because there was something about him that couldn't settle. He seemed to stalk through life like a wary cat. He clearly found aspects of his job a real challenge; including, often, interviews. Imbued with a high-wattage star quality and a mesmerising stage presence, there was also an exacting emotional intelligence in Thom that could make interviewers feel like they were missing the point – the Radiohead reason – by several miles. (He once interviewed himself, for *Dazed and Confused* magazine, and, said, to himself: 'I think this discussion is so fucking lame. There's no point in continuing it, really.') And, underneath it all, something seething. A palpable anger. You'd consider whether to take Thom on in a fight. At 5' 5", he wasn't tall, but there was a feeling that if he started punching, he'd never stop.

So not clubbable, not out with all the inkie journos getting convivially drunk. But still: lovely. And by anyone's standards, but especially those of the music business, Radiohead were clever. Artistic, immensely gifted and future-thinking (later, Colin would make a gag that *OK Computer* was called that because they were all OK at computers), plus thoughtful around politics and climate change. What's not to like? Hmmm. There were several people I knew, including some journalists, who just couldn't stand them. Too earnest, too gloomy, too swotty, too right on. Not enough funk and swing in their rhythm section, nothing to dance to. Not rave enough. Not punk enough. Not pop enough.

Anyway, as would become clear, none of this mattered. Because within a few years, Radiohead would move up and away from every other band in the UK. In 1994, a tuftily bleach-blond Thom was on the cover of the *NME* with Justine Frischmann and Brett Anderson ('a haystack between two Hitlers', said one wag). The coverline was 'TAKE BRAT AND PARTY!' because the *NME* awards had temporarily been called the Brat awards. Three Brit-poppish icons, each clutching an award in the shape of a hand with the middle finger raised ('Creep' won best single). Radiohead next won an *NME* award four years later, in 1998, for *OK Computer*. An LP so un-Britpop it might as well have been made by Snoop Dogg.

What determined Radiohead in the 1990s were two things. First: they knew what it was like to have a big hit. 'Creep', their first proper single, came out in 1992 (it got to Number 78), but was then re-released in '93, and became a humongous anthem, a calling card of a track. Even now, it's the song they're most known for (like, in a different way, the Beastie Boys' biggest track is still '(You Gotta) Fight for Your Right (To Party)'). 'Creep' was a teenager's outsider lament that was somehow both creepily desirous of, and sadly yearning for, a woman's beauty; given edge and grandeur by Jonny Greenwood's guitar slash and the full majesty of the grunge chorus. The 1993 release went to Number Seven in the UK, and – perhaps more importantly – was celebrated on the student radio stations of West Coast America. It was huge on the alternative scene and broke them in the US, easily, in a way that British bands could only dream of. Well: perhaps not easily. Off the back of its success, they had to play it every night on a seemingly never-ending two-year tour.

From then on, Radiohead had no need to chase a huge smash single, because they'd done that and they knew first-hand what it meant. It meant everyone at a gig waiting for them to play that one song, people coming backstage looking for 'the "Creep" guy', or taking a very literal view of how Thom viewed himself. 'Creep', which the band called 'Crap' after a while, stymied them, fixed them, pinned them to a board like insect specimens. 'It was a lesson,' said Thom later. 'The way that modern music culture works is that bands get set in a period of time and then they repeat that small moment of their lives for evermore . . . And that's just what we weren't going to do.' It took a lot of determination, self-belief and a faith that they could write better songs, play more interestingly, say something stranger, to break out. After 'Creep', they wriggled away from being precisely defined, over and over again.

And the other thing about them at that time was that none of their albums after their first, *Pablo Honey*, were immediate hits. Many people initially dismissed *The Bends* as not up to much – an album that boasted 'Fake Plastic Trees', 'High and Dry', 'Just' and 'Street Spirit (Fade Out)' – and then, with repeated listens, changed their mind. (Still: no *NME* award, not a peep.) With *OK Computer*, I have a very specific memory of driving back from 1997 Glastonbury on a precipitous weekend comedown. At the time I had a soft-top car, and we put the roof down and listened to *OK Computer* and, after a while, I looked in the mirror at a friend in the back seat, who'd had no time for Radiohead because he thought they weren't sexy. He was crying, and he wasn't sad. 'How do they do that?' he said. Radiohead made albums that were growers, that took their time weaving themselves into your world, but once they were wrapped in and around and through, they never left. How do they do that?

Radiohead, because of 'Creep', and because of who they are, kept consciously avoiding making their big pop record. There are two obvious times they were meant to do it. Once, straight after *Pablo Honey*; and again, after *OK Computer*. Both times they took a sideways leap. They kept swerving off the accepted path. No

Parklife, no *The Joshua Tree*, no *What's the Story?* They didn't want
the lifestyle and they didn't want the trajectory. So they kept steering
away from the next obvious move. Which is admirable, but, you
would think, a commercially unsound move. But the really odd
thing is, it didn't make much difference. Everyone still loved them.
Somehow, throughout their career but especially in the '90s,
Radiohead managed to make offbeat art-rock appeal to the masses.
How do they do that?

'I don't think that any of us in the band quite understand what
exactly is happening musically when things click,' Thom once said.
'It's like there's a collective consciousness within the five of us when
we're working that does it.'

There have always been five. Ed O'Brien thought at one point
that Thom didn't appreciate their fiveness, because it's Thom who
drives the thing that is Radiohead, and he can be obtuse and tricky,
go off on his own tangents. Every band needs someone with the
bit between their teeth, who can't rest until they achieve what
they've imagined. In Radiohead, that's Thom. So, yes, five, but 'we
operate like the United Nations', Thom says. 'And I'm America.'

Radiohead met at secondary school, the fee-paying Abingdon
School in Oxford. When Thom went to Abingdon, he lost all his
old primary-school friends. 'They blanked me,' he told me when
I interviewed him. 'One of them once got his older brother to kick
the shit out of me and throw me in the river, just because I'd gone
to that school.' Thom hated Abingdon, the boys that went there,
the competitiveness, the lack of girls. He got into several fights.
His saviour was the music room.

Colin was in Thom's year but had different friends. They met when they were fifteen, through crashing the same parties. Colin wore unitards and listened to Alien Sex Fiend; Yorke wore thrift-store suits that his mother altered to fit him. 'He'd be in a cat suit and I'd be in a sharp suit,' Thom said. Ed was recruited because he looked like Morrissey. Jonny, Colin's younger brother, was in Thom's brother's band, but was poached. Once drummer Phil Selway came along for the ride, On A Friday was born. The name Radiohead, from a Talking Heads' song, came after they were signed.

Actually, they could have been signed when they were around eighteen, but Thom really wanted to go to university and study art (he did English Literature and Fine Art at Bristol), so the others did too, apart from Jonny, who was still at school. Off they went – Colin to Cambridge, Ed to Manchester, Phil to Liverpool – meeting up in Oxford at weekends and in holidays to see if they still liked making music together. They did, and after university, Radiohead got a record deal pretty quickly.

Thom believed his time at art school gave him many things. He met his first wife Rachel there and it taught him, he said later, that the only way through a problem is to keep working. That approach – thinking in an art way and continuing to work even when everything, creatively, seems to be going awry – helped Radiohead get through the '90s.

'No Surprises' was made in that way. Though it was the fourth single from *OK Computer*, it was the first one they completed for the album, and it was a hard song to make. So hard that they've used it, over the years, to remind themselves of how difficult the process can be, 'just in terms of when we're in the midst of a song and we don't know whether we're completely wasting our time', says Thom.

There are some odd things going on in 'No Surprises', to do with speed and, in the lyrics, to do with interior and exterior forces. Thom has called it a fucked-up nursery rhyme, which is pretty accurate, especially given the pretty glockenspiel motif. (In *The Royle Family*, it's used as a lullaby, Caroline Aherne's Denise and Craig Cash's Dave playing it to Baby David in his cot.)

The words are about keeping things together by keeping stuff down. A heart that's full up like a landfill doesn't only reference Thom's obsession with how we dispose of the detritus of modern life; it's about what we do with our emotions. If we bury them and get on with life, they don't decompose. They stay as they are; there, but submerged. Ignored, so we can continue without drama. Such a pretty house and such a pretty garden, no alarms and no surprises; a quiet life's appeal. But a quiet life can also deaden. A job that slowly kills you, and you know it. You're being buried alive along with your emotions. Who would dare give such thoughts air, let the dark things come to the surface? Not you, but they leak anyway; they seep and ooze and spread and gradually they overwhelm.

In the studio, the only way the band could make the song work was to slow it down completely – 'It had to sound like we'd all taken Mogadon,' said Thom – make it almost too decelerated to play. This proved so difficult that Nigel Godrich, the producer, let the band play it at the speed they wanted and then slowed the pace of the recording. (An old Beatles technique.) It makes the music sound strung out, hazy and fragile, a bit off, so that Thom's vocals, the scary lyrics, can sit properly.

And a changed speed was also important in the making of the video for 'No Surprises'. Radiohead had already commissioned a selection of excellent videos, for 'Fake Plastic Trees', 'Just', 'Street Spirit (Fade Out)', 'Paranoid Android', 'Karma Police'. But Grant Gee's clip for 'No Surprises' is up there, one of the greats. Inspired by two things – 'a job that slowly kills you' and a moment from *2001: A Space Odyssey*, a shot of David Bowman's face in his helmet, just at the point when he realises Hal the supercomputer has lost it – Grant decided to film Thom's face in close-up, singing inside a specially made helmet that fills up with water.

Like the song, the video was really hard to make. Adrenalised, under pressure, with a helmet on his head, Thom couldn't hold his breath for the minute and twenty seconds required. He had to build up to get there, going underwater over and over for a little longer every time – and Grant sped up the song a tiny bit too, matching it to the camera shutter speed, so Thom had to hold on for a minute. It's still a very long time.

He takes a deep breath on 'silent' and drops his head into the water for the instrumental middle eight, looking straight out at us, eyes open. He doesn't move, but we can see his increasing struggle with the lack of air, the seeping panic. His face changes colour. The music seems to go on forever, and he's fading, until his voice comes back in and he raises his chin up and out. And when he bursts up through the water, shudders back into breath and starts singing again, it makes me cry. Who knows why? The determination, the length of time under there, the tension – you can't believe how long he's under for – and then the triumph. Combined with the lyric, the pretty motif, the image and idea of someone gradually, gently, going under until they suddenly fight to the surface and start breathing . . . It gets me every single time.

Once, I was on some sort of larky '90s telly thing, with Thom and Hooligan, the lead singer of These Animal Men. Hooligan and I were messing about, making stupid jokes. Thom, as I remember, was more dignified and polite. We were there to review various new pop videos and he took them seriously. One featured lots of anonymous kicking legs, dancing a little like *Moulin Rouge*, but more ambiguous, not so sexy, a bit threatening in their repetition. I dismissed the video with a flippant joke. Thom pointed out the director's ambition, how the idea was great, but just needed development. He made me feel a bit ashamed of myself.

All of Radiohead were great at acknowledging other people's art, and incorporating it into their world. Stanley Donwood creates their intricate, thoughtful album covers. And they commissioned brilliant pop videos, for which we should all be grateful. At that time, MTV was still an important music platform, and pop videos were thought of as vital promotional tools. And Radiohead's were shown loads on MTV, because they were always interesting. (So were others: Michel Gondry's shroomy fairy-tale animation for Björk's 'Human Behaviour'; Chris Cunningham's sensual white robots for her 'All Is Full of Love'; the Beasties' Spike Jonze-directed 'Sabotage'; Aphex Twin's terrifyingly crackers Chris Cunningham horror-shows 'Windowlicker' and 'Come To Daddy'. Cunningham also made the eerie floating underwater 'Only You' for Portishead.

Jonathan Glazer made Jamiroquai's immortal slip-slidey 'Virtual Insanity'.)

Radiohead videos kept them in music fans' minds in the times between albums, and guided them, really, as Radiohead grew into the band they needed to be. Their songs, which gradually expanded from Pixie-esque noise and furore into sublime, scratchy explorations of existential dread and internal panic (but with tunes!) were made for the medium, especially as the band themselves were up for exploration.

Their best of that era are 'Just', 'Street Spirit', 'Karma Police' and 'No Surprises'. 'Fake Plastic Trees' is pretty good too: the band in a stylised supermarket being pushed around in individual shopping trolleys. 'Just' is a short mystery film: Radiohead are playing, wildly, properly in a small hotel room, while, on the street below, a man in a suit falls to the pavement and won't get up. 'Street Spirit' – a beautiful, eerie, stop-start night scene with the band and others dancing and moving in an Airstream park, directed by Jonathan Glazer – ushers in a new Radiohead. It's unsettling but gorgeous. 'Karma Police', also by Glazer, is a sort of horrible joke: an un-drivered 1970s Chrysler car, with Thom in it, slowly chases a man along a long road. It's often cited as one of the best pop videos ever. Though, for me, the claustrophobic almost-drowning and triumphant defiance of 'No Surprises' will always beat it.

A lot of their videos were works of art, but uneasy ones. Unnerving. Radiohead were not having quiet lives, then. The touring that they did across the '90s was insane. Well over a hundred gigs a year across 1992, 1993, 1995; close to that in 1994,

1996, 1997; and still more in 1998 and 1999. Plus all the associated interviews, the photos, the shaking hands. They didn't really stop for a decade. It killed them and it made them stronger; fed into their ability to play, but made their recording sessions fraught and argumentative. Each one of their albums, right up to 2000's *Kid A*, was a kind of band torture. *Pablo Honey* wasn't too bad, because they didn't know what they were doing; but all the others were a reaction to touring, or to what was expected of them. Each album, they felt they had to push away from everything they'd done before, because they'd been doing the same thing over and over.

In various studios, they argued and created, created and argued. Made their art and worked through the difficult times. *OK Computer*, their strange magnificent epic, was recorded in a lonely country mansion owned by Jane Seymour. The band were convinced the house was haunted; tapes kept being messed with when no one was around. That paranoia bled into their music. It took them ages to finish the LP, and actually, when they brought it out, they thought everyone would laugh at it, it was so sprawling and silly and overwrought. But no: in the end, everyone loved *OK Computer*, though the jokes seemed to pass them by. (The lyrics to 'Karma Police' are really funny: 'Karma police, arrest this girl, her Hitler hairdo is making me feel ill' – which seems very definitely about Britpop – plus 'this is what you get when you mess with us', which is . . . sort of a threat and sort of a 'well, you know what we're like!' shrug.)

With the touring, the press, the pressure – from themselves – to keep changing and getting better, Thom said that, in the second half of the '90s, he felt like music, which had been his way of dealing with life, had become his oppressor: 'Sold to the highest bidder and I was simply doing its bidding. And I couldn't handle that'. He was close to quitting, over and over. Even when playing Glastonbury, in an astonishing performance on the Pyramid Stage in 1997, widely acknowledged as one of the festival's best ever, Thom nearly walked. Everything was going wrong, the equipment kept blowing, they couldn't hear. At one point during the performance he went over to Ed, tapped him on the shoulder and said, 'I'm off mate, see you later.' Ed said, 'If you do, you'll probably live the rest of your life regretting it.' And Thom thought, 'Good point'. He didn't leave. He worked through the bad bits.

Still, he came off stage at the end of their performance and said, 'I can't do this any more'. And then Radiohead carried on touring for another year and a half.

'When the *OK Computer* thing stopped,' said Thom later, 'I had no connection with that sort of emotional range any more. I didn't have any emotions at all for a long time.' It broke all of them. After the '90s, their albums were made in different ways, delivered differently too. No interviews to explain the process behind them, a pay-what-you-want idea of value. And a gradual realisation, especially for Thom, that what seemed to be internal – I have these feelings, and they are buried deep and I find them hard to articulate – was partly caused by external factors. Not just the weird existence – the slog – of being in a band, but being in the world when the world is what it is. How you're conditioned to be in that world, what you're expected to do, how you connect (or don't) to it. 'A lot of the problems I had were external,' he said, 'to do with my immediate environment, my upbringing, the way I saw the external world. And I had internalised them because that was the only thing I knew how to do.'

'The environment' means a lot of things, as does 'caring for the environment'. 'I'm quite an absorbent person,' said Thom. 'I have quite a low shield, or force field or whatever, so I can get very affected by things around me.' What had seemed like inner demons came partly from the outside, caused by a job – albeit a glamorous job – that slowly kills.

Radiohead's '90s music was driven by emotion that comes out sideways. Wild frustrations with yourself, or other people. With a political system or a music business that requires you to behave in certain ways, to pay back all that money and good faith, to pay your dues, for longer than you could ever imagine. 'No Surprises' understands that; it shifts between interior lacerations and exterior resentments. When Radiohead play it live, the audience always joins in with 'Bring down the government, they don't speak for us', a unified defiance against the system that lifts the whole song. Not-quite-grown-ups trying to work out how they really feel and how they've been made to feel, and the difference between those two things, and all of that confusion and emotion bursting to the surface. And the audience sings it back.

Radiohead have never won the Mercury Prize. They've never won a Brit Award. They've never changed their line-up. They didn't get stuck into hard drugs, though they got very friendly with booze and weed. They stuck with touring, even when it nearly killed them, they changed how they made music so they could cope. They created songs that they believed in but didn't necessarily know that anyone else would understand. Somehow, they manage to be both over- and underground.

Not so long ago, Colin talked about success. He said being successful is like 'slow-drying glue that sets around you, that slows you down and gums you up'. Because success means you have to do the same trick over and over: perform it in Italy, in Australia, in Japan; talk about it in the UK, in Mexico, in Spain. Explain it, and have yourself explained, repeat, repeat.

'And while all that's happening, your own life's going on at the side of it,' he said. 'With your own relationships and your own experiences, and that becomes sort of calcified as well. And the whole thing just grinds to a halt, really. And then you suddenly find yourself in the paper or on the cover of a magazine and your life and experiences have become summarised.' Pinned and labelled, an insect on a board.

'The trick is', said Colin, 'to try to be in the corner of people's vision.' To wriggle away. To be in the full glare of the spotlight, and deliberately take one step sideways, so you're not too brightly lit and you can still see.

The Misfit

TRICKY
'Aftermath'

Tricky was the wrong sort of working class for Britpop. Not lairy, not London; not bullish, not northern. Not chippy, but not chirpy either. He was like Britpop's shadow. He unnerved people.

I interviewed him a couple of times in the mid-'90s. One interview took place in New York, and I remember being struck by his way of speaking. He spoke in an accent which, to my northern ears, was a soft one, a rolling, rounded, country-ish sound. But his voice was wrecked: a crunchy low growl, a Dalek rasp. More than that, how Tricky talked was remarkable. I'd ask him a question, and he'd go off, delivering long sentences that swooped between feelings, sentiments that seemed to emerge, charge up and then dissipate as he spoke. He'd move from sweetness to threat to despair to humour, all in thirty seconds.

His music was similar: beautiful intimate sounds mixed with menace and anguish, a pure feminine singing voice next to an unsettling mumbled rap, heart-shattering bass alongside whispery hiss, rock riffs and half-heard found sounds. Emotions banging up against each other. A dream and a nightmare melded.

In New York, when we finished the interview, the American photographer came in to take his picture. Unlike British people, who use humour to connect, Americans often use work to establish a reciprocal status level, asking you what you've been doing recently, telling you what they've been up to. Like: my work makes me worthy, how about you?

The photographer said that she'd recently photographed Madonna, and, unexpectedly, Tricky exploded: 'Fuckin' Madonna! Fuckin' Madonna! Who gives a shit about fuckin' Madonna?' I wanted to laugh, but the photographer was scared and upset. She left. He didn't have his photo taken that day.

Still, that wasn't the time with Tricky that really stuck with me. That was when we were in Bristol, and we ended up talking about Tricky's uncle, a man who'd got into trouble throughout his life. His uncle had been in prison for murder and Tricky said he thought about that a lot. Not the prison bit (he knew what that was like), but the murder.

'How can you live with that in your head?' he said. 'How could you sleep? You'd see it every time you shut your eyes. Someone dying in front of you, because of what you did. I don't see how you could live with it inside.'

Tricky came from Bristol. Bristol, to non-Bristolians, seems like a rich place, pretty, un-industrialised, built from cream stone on hills around a river and boats. A collection of cute villages rather than a city. I had friends there who I'd visit during the '90s, and I was always struck by how laid-back everything seemed, how little got done, how packed full it was of attractive hippy-tinged stoners knitting their own yoghurt, ho ho.

Knowle West, where Tricky is from, is not like that. It's the most economically deprived area in Bristol, an insular place with its own rules, where everyone knows everyone and certainly knows when an outsider turns up. Its rough reputation meant that most non-Knowle West people stayed away. Tricky loved it. He was proud to be a Knowle Wester. Generations of families stayed in the community, and his family was no exception. His mum's side had been in Knowle West for years: his great-grandparents, his grandparents, his mum, uncles, aunts, cousins, siblings, all there.

His real name is Adrian Thaws, and he grew up with his grand-mother, Violet, after his mum, Maxine Quaye, died when he was four years old. Maxine died by suicide, possibly due to her not being able to cope with her epilepsy. (Tricky would give different answers when journalists asked.) He was raised by tough women. Violet taught him to steal; his aunt taught him to fight, sending him to boxing classes when he was fifteen. 'I've seen my grand-mother fight in the street,' he remembered. 'I've seen my auntie and my grandmother have fistfights, I've seen my grandmother grab my auntie's arm and close it in the door and break her arm, fighting over meat.'

He didn't see much of his dad, Roy, who was part of the Studio 17 sound system, mostly because the other half of Tricky's family blamed him for Maxine's death. (One uncle threatened to kill him, as soon as he got out of prison.) Tricky's family stretched across different households, but a lot of the men in his family were missing, not around. 'I've seen my uncle go to jail for seven years, then ten years my other uncle, my dad never rang,' he said later.

'Women keep it together, keep the food on the table, defend the children, if anyone fucked with us they would be down the school. I've never seen men do that for me, I've never seen men there for me like that. All I know is women.'

He was close to a couple of his cousins. But his sister grew up in another house and, when she came up to Tricky at an awards ceremony in the 2000s to say hi, he didn't recognise her. ('I was like, "Babe how are you, you look very familiar." And she was like, "Yes, I'm your fucking sister."') Families are complicated, even when they seem simple. Tricky's family was more complicated than most.

Knowle West was a white community – a 'white ghetto', Tricky called it – and he was raised 'as a white kid, but with Jamaican roots'. For Tricky, race wasn't the main factor in his younger years – 'we weren't seen as black, we were seen as Knowle Westers' – it was poverty. 'We were all poor together,' he said. 'Where I grew up, my white friends would get arrested as many times as me. I've seen policemen beat up my white friends while I've never been touched. Poverty's the link.'

Where he grew up was very different to most people in the mid-'90s music industry; but it was also *how* Tricky grew up that differentiated him. 'I was always in a dream-like state,' he said later; not quite present, living in another world.

When Tricky was very young, Violet would stare at him, smoking, catching the ash in her hand. She believed that his mum Maxine's spirit was inside him. She let him skip school and watch horror films with her. 'It was like growing up in a movie,' said Tricky. 'She used to sit me in the middle of the floor. She'd be playing Billie Holiday, and would say things like, "You look like your mum," watching me. I was always my mum's ghost.'

Later, he connected the horror films with his mum in a different way. 'I always thought, "Where does my name come from?" Adrian. There's no one in my family named like I'm named, so where the fuck does my mother get that name from? I saw *Rosemary's Baby* when I was a kid and it was like, "and he shall be called Adrian". I was like fuck – I'm the devil.'

Ghosts and violence, love and the devil, seeping into a young soul. No wonder Tricky was different. He'd go out in his teens wearing a dress. He was trying to look like the girls in Malcolm McLaren's 'Buffalo Gals' video, plus, he said, 'going out in a frock was just a recipe for a good night out', meaning a bit of chaos – though pop psychology would also point to his family role models, his lost mum. He faded in and out of bad-boy scenes. He managed to fit in with everyone, but he absolutely didn't at the same time. At home with spirits, accepting of a darker side, a person who picked up on atmospheres – or a person who created them.

'Aftermath', which he made in his early twenties, is something like the sound of those spirits: eerie, stoned, off-centre, other-worldly. There's a hiss that sounds like a fire crackle. The bass shudders. Tricky's spoken voice isn't synched with Martina Topley-Bird's singing one; instead, they repeat what each other is saying, just off-time, moving in and out. She sings his voice, his feminine side. 'Aftermath' is heavy; fragile and sensual as well as scary. And, in 1994, when it was released, it wasn't really like any other record out there.

*

After a few years, Tricky and Violet moved to Totterdown, slightly closer to the city. Tricky had a step-grandfather who he disliked, so he didn't come home much, got into a bit of trouble, dealing weed, breaking and entering (he was small, so he'd go through the bathroom window and let his friends into the house). At seventeen, he was sent to the youth-custody wing at HMP Horfield for passing fake £50 notes. 'Prison is just mind-numbing,' he said later, in *Hell Is Round the Corner*, his autobiography. 'Twenty-three hours a day, watching the walls. That, in a way, was my journey. Shit food, bored out of my mind . . . I made a life choice right there. I knew that life wasn't for me.' He was there for two months. Nobody visited.

That life wasn't for him. But what was? Though he was obsessed with music from a young age (especially 2-Tone and The Specials' first LP), Tricky didn't really have the drive to make it, or even an idea that he could. As a teenager, he did some rapping with the Wild Bunch, the loose DJ/rap group that turned into Massive Attack when Nellee Hooper moved to London to produce Soul II Soul, and DJ Milo left too. Massive Attack were a collective with a sound-system approach, as opposed to a band one: roles weren't entirely fixed, there wasn't really a front person. The beats were based in dub and hip-hop; lyrics and sounds were sampled, slowed down, bent around, re-upped. The main protagonists were 3D (Robert Del Naja), Daddy G (Grant Marshall) and Mushroom (Andrew Vowles). Shara Nelson and Horace Andy were the singers. Tricky rapped, had ideas for beats, produced, came and went. Massive Attack were older than him. Grant had almost ten years on Tricky; 3D was focused. Tricky wasn't in the same headspace: 'I was living a different life. I was still knocking about the streets getting into little bits of trouble here and there.'

There's a film that was made about Massive Attack around then, *Just a Matter of Time*: an ambient examination of being a Bristol band that involves a lot of mooching, and a fancy dinner at the end. Most people call the film 'Where's Tricky?' because Daddy G and the others are always looking for him, but nobody knows where he is. (He turns up at the end, banging on the door like a scary bailiff.) It was based on real life: Tricky, easily bored, would disappear quite suddenly on what would seem like a whim to others, but not to him. He wouldn't turn up for videos, or interviews. Instead, he'd follow music – gigs, sound systems – to other cities. He'd chase the fun. He once moved to Birmingham for nine months because someone told him there was a good squat there.

Still, he co-wrote three songs for Massive Attack's first album, *Blue Lines*: 'Blue Lines', 'Five Man Army' and first single, 'Daydreaming'. *Blue Lines* changed the landscape of British hip-hop, using American hip-hop production methods rather than its mic techniques: sampling, layering, atmospheres. The rapping on the album wasn't braggadocious, but muted, downbeat, quiet. Plus, perhaps more importantly for Tricky, everyone who worked on *Blue Lines* was an artist who learnt how to make music by being obsessed with music, by knowing the sounds they wanted, going into a studio and either making them themselves, or getting someone else to. 'You can listen to music until you become music,' Tricky once said.

Blue Lines gave Tricky a wage for a couple of years; but that messed him up. With a wage, he didn't need to work, so he had a lot of time to do what he liked: smoking weed, drinking, going to bars and clubs. After a while, he wanted to make harder, darker, more confrontational, personal music. He did a couple of bits on Massive Attack's second album, *Protection*, then left. No plan.

Tricky's solo career happened by accident. A series of accidents. In the early '90s, he met Martina Topley-Bird, a rebellious fifteen-year-old into American alt-punk bands, who was at boarding school in Clifton. She was sitting on a wall outside his cousin Michelle's house, humming, and Tricky asked her if she could sing. Then, Mark Stewart from the Pop Group had a day's studio time booked (not a professional studio, a room in a squat); but he couldn't use it. He happened to bump into Tricky, and donated the studio time to him. Martina finished her GSCEs and turned up drunk on cider with her mates. Tricky made 'Aftermath' with her.

'Aftermath' is built around two slowed-down samples: Marvin Gaye's 'That's the Way Love Is' and LL Cool J's 'Eat Em Up L Chill'. The deceleration makes everything askew, slightly trippy. Tricky wrote the lyrics for him and Martina on the spot, and they held the mic together, so he could go over the melody and words with her. It sounded good, so Tricky kept it like that.

His lyrics come to him off the top of his head, triggered by a single phrase. For 'Aftermath', it was 'Your eyes resemble mine/ You'll see as no others can'. His first ever lyric. Later, he said, 'I didn't have any kids then, so who am I talking about? My mother.' He found out that his mum used to write poetry but had no way of doing anything with it. 'It's almost like she killed herself to give me the opportunity, my lyrics,' he said. 'I think I've got my mum's talent, I'm her vehicle. So I need a woman to sing that.' After 'Aftermath', he often wrote as a woman, or mixed up the traditional gender expectations: 'I like putting women in a male role, have the woman play the strength and the man be the weak.'

When 'Aftermath' was done, Tricky took it to 3D, for Massive Attack, but D didn't want it. So he just kept the cassette, carried on partying.

His cousin Michelle was the one who pushed him into doing something with it. Tricky remembered meeting a weed-dealer who'd said, 'If you ever want to do anything, I'll give you some money,' so he went to him and got £500, pressed some white labels and took them round Bristol and London record shops. That was the start. Someone at Island Records heard it, offered him studio time (he made 'Ponderosa' with Howie B), and then, a deal.

Tricky made his debut album *Maxinquaye*, named after his mum, in a small home studio in a rented room in London, with producer/engineer Mark Saunders. *Maxinquaye* was itchy, glitchy, interior, paranoid, intensely experimental; a scary voodoo melange of mumbles, threats, drug flashbacks, the sound of water drops, creaking chairs, a gun being cocked, the needle reaching the end of a record. 'They label me insane. I think I'm more normal than most.' Tricky's voice was low in the mix; Martine's (and other singers like Alison Goldfrapp) turned up higher. Masculine words in a beautiful broken light-blues voice. It was inevitably the first vocal take that was used; Tricky's concentration would only last so long.

Though 'Aftermath' sets the tone for the rest of the album, it's a mishmash of styles, from the Michael Jackson 'Bad' sample on 'Brand New You're Retro', to the thrash of Public Enemy-cover 'Black Steel'. Tricky used some of the lyrics he gave to Massive Attack for *Protection*; he nicks a sample that Portishead also used on *Dummy*. There's punk in there, indie, dub. Everything has an atmosphere and that's partly because he didn't understand the rules. His flat was full of vinyl – Mark Saunders remembers that you had to be careful not to break the records as you moved around – and Tricky would pick out two tracks and put samples together, even though they didn't fit. Mark would have to make sense of it all.

Tricky's approach was instinctive and punk. 'I'm not part of anything, I'm me, I like hip-hop, I like indie music, I grew up through all of that. All I can do is represent myself. *Maxinquaye* was my fuck you to the world, there's nothing like this in the world . . . I wanted to make something that no one's ever heard before, I wasn't interested in anything else.'

Like Tricky, *Maxinquaye* didn't fit in with what was going on. No sharp sounds, no bright colours, no '60s references, no ironic wink, no stepping into the spotlight. Instead: doubt, paranoia, fuck-you interior sounds. It was completely alien to everything else. But it was successful – in at Number Three, selling 100,000 copies in just a few months – and that changed everything. Tricky was an artist designed for the underground, someone who could only work and live fully if he was operating outside normal life. But he became known almost overnight, instantly recognisable and celebrated by music-lovers and the creative cognoscenti. Shoved suddenly into a world of artistic acclaim, promotional duties, also bizarrely cheesy awards parties and strange celebrity situations. How would that work?

The answer is: it wouldn't, really. 'When the album went in at Number Three I just thought, "That's it, it's over,"' he said. 'I've done it now.'

But the music industry wouldn't accept that. There were obligations to be met, press to be done, gigs to be played, a whole master plan of touring and recording. Tricky found it hard. 'I'm not dealing with it very well,' he said in 1997. 'Things haven't changed for me since I was fifteen. I'm still the same person. My career has run off so fast that I need to catch up with it. I need to stop smoking spliff, I need to stop drinking alcohol because I'm scared.'

He didn't feel like he should be there, on magazine covers, invited to fashion dos, nominated for three Brit Awards in 1996: Best British Male, Best Dance Act and Best Newcomer. His rivals: Paul Weller, Edwyn Collins, Van Morrison, Jimmy Nail, Massive Attack, Eternal, Leftfield, M People, Cast, Elastica, Black Grape and Supergrass (Weller, Massive Attack and Supergrass won). He felt 'lucky, then I felt very misunderstood, then I felt suffocated'.

Tricky was such an anomaly within the music industry. For ages he wouldn't even sign a formal contract with Island. He started playing gigs before he knew how to, really: with Massive Attack, and as support for PJ Harvey. He smashed in with his talent, hopped right onto centre stage, and then refused to do what was required.

Despite everything, he could be great to be around, madly charismatic, funny, with an infectious laugh. But also, clearly, a loner. I thought of him as a witch. Not a wizard: too hokey and bearded, too conventional. A witch. Muttered incantations, forced to live outside the norm, consulted by the heartbroken and those wanting revenge. Understanding pain. Spitting curses. Casting spells.

Tricky's extreme sensitivity, his almost psychic ability to sense moods and take on vibe-shifts and internalise consequences meant he was like a lightning rod for the darker moods of humans, both his and others. His emotions came straight out; other people's emotions leaked in. Liam Gallagher tried to goad him at the 1996 Brit Awards; Julian Palmer, A&R for Island, had to keep them apart. 'I told Liam he didn't want to try any of that working-class macho stuff around someone like Tricky.'

There was no posturing. Tricky felt everything deeply, especially the nasty side. He said in one interview that if he saw someone looking sad, he couldn't stop thinking about it. 'I was in Paris doing a photo session and there was this old lady, and she looked very old and very sad. Now, that catches my eye, and it really, really hurts me. I don't like feeling like that. But it's something I can't control. It hurts me to such an extent that it confuses me.'

Press was difficult. Tricky was an instant press darling – not only great with quotes but with an ability to make any clothes look good. Music papers, style mags and broadsheets queued up to feature him. But those interviews often went haywire. Tricky had his own standards and it was easy to fall foul of them.

An interviewer could say the wrong thing, and Tricky would immediately chew them out. He was touchy, because of the weed, and because, he discovered later, he had candidiasis, a fungal infection brought about by excessive use of asthma medication, that threw his moods into wild frenzies. Cally Callomon, who worked at Island, called him an 'adventurous spirit' but 'suspicious because of his background'. 'You didn't know which Tricky you were meeting on any given day,' he said. 'He can be an affable, bouncing energy ball of ideas. He can also see people as rivals or competition.'

Also, the very nature of an interview was a strange battle for him. Journalists, whether style ones or news ones, want quotes, facts, explanations. They want to *understand*: who are you, and how did you get here? But that's not what Tricky wanted to tell them. Giving intimate details was not part of his world. His grandmother taught him to never give his real name to the police. Telling a stranger who you are is not part of many people's culture.

I remember moving to London and going to my first after-work parties. Free drink, what's not to like? But the people could be strange. Some would stick out their hand and say their name and their surname, and then where they worked. Like this: 'Stewart Stewartson, the *Independent*.' And then they would say, 'And what do you do?' This would always make me and my friends laugh. What do you mean, what do you do? (Loads of stuff, thanks!) It just wasn't how anyone normal would operate. In clubs and pubs, in life generally, you can strike up a friendship with someone, go on a full adventure for a few hours, a few days, and never know what they do for money. You're lucky if you can remember their name, and you certainly won't know their surname.

Anyway, who knows who they are at twenty-one? Or even at fifty-one? One interviewer asked him if he was trying to discover his inner self in the music. 'God no,' said Tricky. 'I wouldn't know where to start looking.'

Sometimes a piece about Tricky would be published and he would hate it. He threatened to break a *Face* journalist's legs for writing about Martina and their baby, Mazy. He confronted another journalist, again from *The Face*, backstage at Glastonbury 1996, and there was a scuffle; the journalist got a dig in the head. (The journalist was phlegmatic about it: 'People get hit in pubs all the time,' he reasoned.)

'I had a lot of problems – depression, mood swings, temper tantrums,' he said later. 'Someone would get my room service order wrong and I'd smash up the room. People around me found it very difficult. It's astonishing how dark your life can get without you even noticing. It slips and slips further away.'

The thing is: no one cared. Tricky was hugely charming and attractive, his music was enigmatic and enticing, a work of art. He was loved by people that might have rejected him if they'd met him in everyday life. It made him edgy. But how he felt was unimportant. It was who he was that mattered. Famous people queued up to meet him. He often blew them off. His hangover was too bad for him to meet Madonna. He had the flu the day he was meant to meet Prince. He did meet Kylie Minogue, Nicole Kidman, Naomi Campbell, Damon Albarn. Because they were just there, in the dressing room after he'd played a gig, hanging out, wanting to meet him. He made a track with Damon but it didn't work out. He went out with Björk for a while.

David Bowie wrote an almost unreadable essay about Tricky

for Q, in which he imagined talking to him. In the essay, Bowie has Tricky saying things like this: 'Let me tell you stories. I'm like Jesus . . . Did you know that cars can fuck you up through your body. It's the energy, any 15-year-old kid can tell you this. I get rude, knocking crockery, but I'm not the kid any more. I graduated. I'm no more the hard affair.' Who knows what that meant? But the very fact that Bowie wanted to write it showed the effect Tricky had.

People would look at him, because they recognised him; he thought they were asking for a fight. He shouted at a woman who was staring when he was with Ben Affleck – it turned out to be Ben Affleck's sister.

Famous people, non-famous people. Tricky just continued doing what he did. He became friends with Terry Hall and Shaun Ryder. At the 1996 Brit Awards, he sat drinking with Shaun, watching the Brits go to everyone else. Tricky said, 'How come me and you don't win stuff like this?' And Shaun said: 'Because we're ugly. We're ugly inside.' Their demons showed.

So, a born frontman who hated the spotlight; model-beautiful but bored in front of the camera; good at parties but a complete loner; gave fantastic quotes but hated interviews; liked people but would turn nasty in a second; a constantly inventive artist with an underside that the industry couldn't really cope with.

You could have guessed it all from listening to *Maxinquaye*, Tricky's whole young self put into his first work of art. His mum speaking through him, his childhood and background. His struggles came from where he was from: inertia, suspicion, late nights, darkness. It's not often that you hear from people that the press like to call the underclass. It's only because Tricky is so talented that it got through.

The aftermath of 'Aftermath'. Even for the hugely well-adjusted, even for the people who always wanted to be famous, fame will wreck you. 'Fame does cause mental illness,' Tricky said once. 'It has to. If you can feel people looking at you, that affects the way you walk, the way you talk. You can't be your natural self and that's what causes sickness. It wasn't healthy.'

Since *Maxinquaye*, Tricky has released fifteen other albums, created a record label, acted in one film and co-directed another. He's kept moving, from city to city: New York, LA, Paris, Berlin, Bristol, Toulouse, often relocating to places where he isn't recognised. His music has changed too. 'All my other albums since *Maxinquaye* were saying "fuck you", he said. 'I was making records deliberately so they wouldn't get on the radio. It was "fuck everything, whatever you like I'm going to make the opposite kind of album". He's spent millions on not very much and had to pay back hundreds of thousands in tax, which he earned by touring.

I went to see Tricky play recently. As ever, he stood in darkness, deflecting attention onto others on stage through the lack of spotlight on him, the way the sound was mixed. The crowd wanted more of him; he couldn't, or wouldn't give it. If you come from a place that has always been rejected, then the attention of others can feel completely wrong. Even if they relate to you because they've felt rejected too.

The Possibilities Are Endless

EDWYN COLLINS
'A Girl Like You'

We could easily make an argument that Edwyn Collins created Britpop; we could also argue that he was a Britpop one-hit wonder, with 'A Girl Like You'. Both these arguments are sort of true, both are sort of not. So let's try them out.

Edwyn created Britpop because, in 1979, he created Orange Juice, the tuneful, quirky Scottish post-punk band that made music usually called 'jangly'. Orange Juice were odder than that description sounds, though: somehow Edwyn, and a varying selection of bandmates, squished disco together with spindly chiming guitars, put Edwyn's smooth crooner voice to work on wry, conversational lyrics, and added an unmacho-yet-fuck-you punk sensibility, to create an entirely new, instantly classic post-Buzzcocks-pre-Smiths sound. You know that sound: it's the sound of indie music. And Orange Juice, along with others, gave us variations on the classic indie look: short back and sides with floppy fringe; turn-up jeans, short-sleeved shirt, Oxfords, hooded jacket; bootlace tie, country styling, quiff; shorts, kids' sandals, shirts fastened all the way to the top. Crucially: they wanted to be stars, but not sell-outs. They argued in the *NME* about such stuff.

Orange Juice's first singles were released on Postcard Records, an independent Glasgow-based record label set up by Alan Horne that lasted barely two years, and in that short time put out records by Orange Juice, Aztec Camera and The Go-Betweens. Then off Orange Juice went to Polydor and, in 1983, brought out 'Rip It Up', a hiccupy, unique pop song that not only nicked Chic's guitar approach and made a sound-and-lyric tribute to the Buzzcocks' 'Boredom' in the middle eight, but hinted at an acid-house future too, as the first Top 40 record to feature the squelch of a Roland TB-303. It went to Number Eight and was marked by an under-statedly rebellious *Top of the Pops* performance, where bass player David McClymont, mortified by the *TOTP* dancers in their work-out shorts and ankle boots ripping up some paper to illustrate the song, and – perhaps more relevantly – heroically twatted, stopped pretending to play the bass and instead lurched off the stage to gently head-charge Orange Juice's saxophonist, Jim Thirlwell, like a mild-mannered buffalo. Then he stumbled back onstage to do the same to drummer Zeke Manyika. The camera pulls away but you can see Edwyn laughing. Orange Juice were barred after their performance.

It didn't really matter, as after 'Rip It Up', none of their singles got anywhere near the Top Ten. Orange Juice split in 1985. Soon after, Edwyn brought out a couple of solo singles on Alan McGee's Elevation, a joint Creation/Warners record label. (How much more indie-into-Britpop do you need?) Orange Juice were hugely influ-ential, not just with musicians (The Smiths to Franz Ferdinand) but with 1980s pop kids, too. As teenagers, me and my friends all loved Orange Juice, from 1980's 'Falling and Laughing' to 1984's brilliant 'What Presence?!' The young Keir Starmer was a fan. Funny, clever, tuneful, cute, inventive, rebellious, artistic, they were a massive band among indie fans, but made little impact on the charts.

So, there's our first argument. Edwyn and Orange Juice invented indie music. He once got stopped on a London street by some Mancunians, who told him this exact thing: 'You're Edwyn Collins, you invented indie!' And then, a few years later, indie morphed into Britpop, which took it from outsider status into the centre of pop culture.

Here's the second argument. Edwyn's surprise 1995 hit single, 'A Girl Like You', gave Britpop a huge singalong hit, while also being nothing really to do with Britpop at all. Its guitar sounded like fuzzy Isley Brothers, its drum loop was from the 1965 Len Barry soul song '1-2-3', there was a vibraphone in there (played by the Sex Pistols' Paul Cook), and some 'yeah, it's alright's from the Subway Sect's Vic Godard. All completely undercut by the weird response noise that comes after Edwyn sings 'I've never known a girl like you before': that oh-poor-ickle-you piss-take scuzz of 'wah-wah-wut-wah-wut-wi-waaah'. Like telling a sad story and your best friend imitating you crying.

'A Girl Like You' wasn't Britpop, but the two overlapped: in the middle of the '90s, a Britpop subset sprung up, a small groovy '60s-style scene, where easy-listening nights were held in glitzy, velvet-banquetted cabaret clubs, and Mike Flowers Pops bounced into the Top Ten with cheese-tastic reworkings of Oasis songs. Edwyn's 'A Girl Like You' was a credible, Northern Soul version of this, a song that recalled a John Barry lounge-pop past while also being spikily original. You could imagine it in a Tarantino film. It was a catchy, indie-pop hit, made with guitars and an off-kilter, no-compromise attitude by a man with his own outsider style. So: Britpop-esque, at least.

Not that the UK took much notice of any of this at the start. 'A Girl Like You' came from Edwyn's 1994 album *Gorgeous George*, his third solo effort. With no record contract or publishing contract at the time, he'd made the album on his own, in his self-built studio, with friends such as Paul Cook and ex-Orange Juice bassist Claire Kenny. The late 1980s had been tough for Edwyn. He and his wife Grace Maxwell lived in a one-bedroom flat in Kensal Rise, north-west London, and they had very little money: at one point, in 1989, Grace went to Cornwall for a bit, taking their bank card, and, says Edwyn, he was left living on 'rice and salt'. Another time, he asked Grace when they were going to run out of money. She said: 'Three weeks ago, don't worry about that.' In 1990, their son William was born. Edwyn believes that he was their good luck charm.

Still, 'there was a period in the early '90s, when Edwyn couldnae get arrested', remembers Grace. She was, and is, his manager, and she arranged a lot of meetings with record companies, from majors to indies. No one was interested. Edwyn was, she says, 'a cheeky bastard, smart Alek-y' and had alienated a lot of people. 'I'm not like that any more,' says Edwyn.

It wasn't just him though: the early '90s were a tough time for many 1980s indie musicians. When acid house came in, its alien modernity seemed to wipe everything clean; plus, indie fans and writers were brought up with the mod-punk idea of anyone over thirty being disqualified from making music due to their age. (Paul Weller, too, after The Jam and The Style Council, was ignored for a while, but made a '90s comeback.) But Edwyn is a determined person. He decided to build his own studio. Then, if he couldn't make a success of his own music, he could produce other people's.

So, he made his studio and he made his album *Gorgeous George*. It was licensed to the small indie label Setanta and released in autumn 1994, with 'A Girl Like You' as the single. 'A Girl Like You' wasn't playlisted on Radio 1; it wasn't stacked in the right chart-counting record shops. It got to Number 41. And that was it. Except, in Belgium and Australia, 'A Girl Like You' went down very well. It inched its way to Number One in both countries. And gradually, gradually, things began to change.

'Something weird started happening,' remembers Grace. 'We had one of those old all-in-one phone-fax machines in the flat, and every time I picked up the phone, or put it down, it would be something good. A good fax would come out, I'd get a good call . . . And it just didn't stop. I'd pick up William from school, come home, give him some pizza, and the phone would be going into the night with calls and faxes from America. By the time we were into the beginning of '95, "A Girl Like You" was a runaway hit.'

Which was great, but they didn't have any infrastructure to back it up. The calls were saying, 'A Girl Like You' is being played a lot on radio here, so where are the singles for people to buy? Grace employed her sister, and they scrambled to get licences with different record labels all over the world, at speed. Nine different labels in the end, Grace says. There were calls for Edwyn to do promo, too; press interviews, TV appearances, live shows.

He was booked to appear all around the world to promote the single, and did so for the next year and a half. Some memories. He was told to make a new video for the American market, and he and Grace flew over there on Virgin Upper Class, a first for both of them, to make it. 'There was a cast of thousands,' says Grace. 'And it cost thousands, too.' The video was never shown on MTV, which preferred Edwyn's original video, which cost 'about 2p'. 'A Girl Like You' was a hit across South-East Asia, and Edwyn went to nine different countries there, with a promoter ('a gangster') who was an old friend of Imelda Marcos. She insisted that he go on a Philippines TV show where a children's five-piece dance troupe called The Universal Dancers were deemed essential to his appearance. 'Your record is only big because of these dancers.' No kid dancers, no Edwyn. He complied.

It was going so well around the world, that Grace and Edwyn remember being on a plane on tour in Germany, a bit bored, and Grace decided to make a 'fuck you all' list of all the people who would be pissed off about Edwyn's moment in the sun. 'It was a long list,' she recalls. 'It went on and on. I kept adding to it. Great fun.'

That list included people who hadn't supported the song when it first came out. And in early summer 1995, Edwyn and Grace decided it was OK to re-release 'A Girl Like You' in the UK. They'd resisted for a while – 'I didn't want the same thing to happen again,' said Grace. 'No playlist, not in shops, I couldn't put him through that again' – but, with the right infrastructure, they re-released 'A

Girl Like You' in June 1995. It went in at Number 13, then, over six weeks, climbed to Number Four, and took another six weeks to fall out of the Top 40. A genuine hit.

At home, though, there was some confusion as to how to treat Edwyn. The music press loved his past, and had respect for it, so couldn't sell him as a new, fresh pop star, which is how he was being sold across the world, 'literally everywhere except the UK', remembers Grace. Here, she felt, everyone was like 'we know him, we know what he does'. 'I was a has-been,' said Edwyn. 'So the *NME* and *Melody Maker* tried to categorise me with Blur and Pulp and everyone. With Britpop. And I thought, "I have nothing to do with Britpop."'

And he didn't, because he wasn't hanging out in Camden, and he wasn't part of that scene. And he did, because of his history, his taste, and the people he influenced. He appeared at several festivals, and got on well with Jarvis. He wound Oasis up, because he kept getting Noel and Liam confused; he enjoyed the daftness of Supergrass and loved 'Alright' as a song.

After a while, though, he hated it. Not the song; it being a hit. 'It wasn't fun,' he says. 'It was exhausting.' It gave them respect for people like The Spice Girls, said Grace. All that promo, 'and it doesn't really mean anything'.

'A Girl Like You' was Edwyn's brief, hectic moment in the sunshine, slightly extended by the track's refusal to ever really die. You can hear it in 1995's indie movie *Empire Records*; in 2003's big-gloss film *Charlie's Angels: Full Throttle*; in 2022's horror flick *Goodnight Mommy*. It plays over the end credits of an episode of *The Crown*. It's in *Sabrina the Teenage Witch*; it's in *Ted Lasso*.

'That record had the most unbelievable built-in impetus of its own,' says Grace. 'A resilience of its own. Even when we were scrambling around, trying to catch up with it, there was nothing I could do to fuck it up. It's as if it was saying to me, "OK, you, you lot are useless . . . catch me up. I'm off." It had a life of its own.'

Edwyn continued making music, and producing other people's music. He had two strokes in 2005, with severe effects. He lost the ability to use most of the right side of his body, and, initially, couldn't read, write or speak. At first, he could only say four things: 'yes', 'no', 'Grace Maxwell' and 'the possibilities are endless'. But he continued: learning to draw with his left hand, gradually getting better, working in his studio (which is now in Helmsdale, in Scotland), producing, performing. When I speak to him and Grace, Edwyn is funny and articulate.

And none of this, both he and Grace say, would have happened if they hadn't stuck to being independent. Not selling out. The actual indie-ness of indie music: which some Britpop people understood, and some didn't.

'Here's the thing,' says Grace. 'It was Edwyn being independent that saved him. You should always hang on to your music rights. Do not sell them. Don't do any deals with record companies unless you're doing them from a position of extreme strength. All that we have now, the life we have now, a lovely old age . . .'

'Young at heart, Grace!' says Edwyn. 'Young at heart.'

'Yes! Every bit of it has been made possible by "A Girl Like You". It's been thirty years. And it still sustains us.'

Party Politics

STEREOLAB
'Ping Pong'

Stereolab make music that sounds like a groovy party; one set in 1960s Paris or early '70s New York, or anywhere where the party-goers are in slim trousers in the vicinity of a bubble chair. Stylish, clever, classy, hip. A Stereolab single is the one a young woman with a sharp haircut and minidress puts on the record player before lighting a cigarette and dancing by wafting her hands in front of her face. That music could be based in Krautrock or Velvet Underground drone; it could be a take on elevator music; it might be dreamy pop made on analogue instruments or by hitting a tea tray with a mascara wand. It doesn't matter. The vocals are airy and light. That woman is dancing and that party is seriously cool.

The party is in a warehouse with gloopy projections on the ceiling, or it's in an apartment with a silver floor. In the corner, lounging on a modular sofa, leaning against a bare brick wall, or maybe looking out over the city from a balcony while smoking, there are other young people and they are discussing politics in an intellectual manner. Or art, or – most likely – other people's music.

Stereolab, as an entity – a Stereolab *thing* – isn't only about the music, though the music is seductive. It's about an idea of music: the idea that music itself can be an idea. You can set yourself boundaries or creative rules, you can build songs by taking specific elements of pop and pushing them very hard in one direction. Why not take the minimal amount of guitar chords and set them to rev around themselves over and over, layering themselves on top of themselves? Why not add the futuristic optimism of a Moog synthesiser and some pretty, aloof vocals that move between la-la-la and deconstructing capitalism without changing emotional tone? And then, why not keep doing that until you don't want to any more?

Two things that Tim Gane, Stereolab's songwriter, once said explain some of what the group is about (they don't like the word band, and they usually spell 'group' as 'groop'). 'Pop isn't technique, it's about ideas, and that's what makes it the ultimate music.' And, 'I don't want to be eclectic, it's about getting the fullest and deepest out of one area. Because that restriction actually gives you more freedom.' The area? Velvet Underground, Neu! Suicide, 'space age bachelor pad music', 1960s French pop. Trance pop that sounds like it's going somewhere, somewhere more idealistic, revolutionary and avant-garde.

Stereolab were always resolutely indie: they set up their own independent record label, Duophonic, before they released a record. Also, determinedly stylish: their sleeves had their own aesthetic, even their own Stereolab character, taken from a 1969 Swiss political comic ('A figure of the establishment who is eventually shot by the forces of the revolution'). They have a longevity stemming from them owning their own work, and being hugely prolific during the '90s, but also from their cussedness. When they signed to a major label, Elektra, for their US deal, they put a clause in their contract that said if Elektra didn't like any Stereolab album, they had ninety days to release it or the band could take it away and put it out on another label.

And, though they never had huge pop hits, Stereolab were Britpop influencers, infiltrators, spies in the midst. They went out a lot in Camden; they were friends with bands that weren't seen as Britpop but played on the same bills: Gallon Drunk, Huggy Bear. Laetitia Sadier is the French voice on Blur's 'To the End'. They palled about with Bikini Kill, played Lollapalooza with the Beastie Boys. They were part of an art-pop underground that didn't smash into the mainstream but stayed on the outside, ploughing individual furrows and influencing others.

Stereolab are centred around two people: Tim and Laetitia. Tim came from Ilford in Essex; Laetitia from Vincennes, a Parisian suburb. They met when Tim's band, McCarthy, played in Paris, in the late 1980s; soon after, Laetitia moved to the UK.

By the early '90s, they were living in Brixton, close to the Academy, in a grotty rented house along with Susannah, a French friend of Laetitia, and Gina Morris, a budding music journalist. It was far from salubrious.

'The house was freezing cold, and there was this locked room on the ground floor that we couldn't get in, with the landlord's stuff in,' Gina remembers. Tim and Laetitia had the biggest bedroom, as they were a couple; they were also the default heads of the household – 'the mum and dad' – for no reason other than their coupledom, and that, compared to Gina and Susannah, they were relatively straight (no drugs).

Tim was very quiet at the time – 'Laetitia would speak for him,' says Gina – but Laetitia wasn't. 'She was really funny,' remembers Gina. 'Much more than ever came across in interviews.' They'd already set up their own record label to release their music, with Martin Pike (it ended up with two branches: Duophonic Ultra High Frequency Disks, for Stereolab's UK releases, and Duophonic Super 45s, for other bands. A little later, it would release music by Yo La Tengo, Huggy Bear, Broadcast and an early version of Daft Punk).

Gina wasn't into the same music as they were – she liked grunge, whereas 'they wanted to be avant-garde agit-pop' – but when Tim and Laetitia needed other people to make Tim's songs into a Stereolab reality, she said, 'Well, I can help.' So on and off for six months, they'd all sit in Tim and Laetitia's bedroom, on the bed or on the floor, and work on the songs. Tim had a Moog, a guitar and a four track; Laetitia had books of notes for lyrics; Gina 'made some noises', meaning she sang countermelodies. 'All the songs were fully formed in Tim's head,' says Gina. 'He was a real Brian Wilson type.' He would give Laetitia the melody and she would come up with the words.

They played a few live gigs, which were chaotic. They enlisted other friends to play, so that the stage was crowded; six people working away with little audience engagement. Gina remembers being booked to support The Wedding Present, in front of 1,500 people, for their second ever gig. 'When we came off, David Gedge was standing there and gave us a look,' she said. 'We were pretty shambolic.'

Gina was friends with several *NME* writers (she went on to become a music journalist) and got Stereolab into the 'On' pages and their singles reviewed. The early reviews were savage, and often focused on the fact that there were two female singers, Laetitia and Gina, comparing the band to Lush. One even assumed that Gina was the lead. It couldn't last. One day, she and Laetitia bumped into each other on the landing at home and mutually decided that Gina should leave.

'And they got Mary [Hansen] within about six months and she was so brilliant,' said Gina later. 'Just perfect for them, her voice was so complementary, she was so fantastic visually, she could play guitar.' A little later, keyboardist Katharine Gifford also started working with them, along with Sean O'Hagan, from the High Llamas.

Stereolab eschewed the traditional 'we all met at school or through a *Melody Maker* ad' band line-up. A little like The Fall with Mark E. Smith, if Tim and Laetitia are both in the group, then that group is Stereolab. From the start, they had different musicians come in and out of the band, though Mary and Andy Ramsay, who is still Stereolab's drummer, were there for the longest. 'It was desperation really,' said Tim in 1993. 'We needed people to play on our records, or to play live. But they had different bands, and they had to go back to those.' But it was also how he liked Stereolab to work: not only because he was the songwriter, but because he enjoyed hearing other musicians playing a song that they hadn't worked on for ages. It gave the sound a freshness and, he said once, it was nice to listen to his own songs as though they were someone else's, like they were new.

After a little while, Stereolab moved from making their music in their bedroom into a studio. For their third LP, *Mars Audiac Quintet*, they were at Blackwing Studios, inside an old church in south London. Tim had an idea for the album – he wanted every track to have the same three chords going through it ('actually a single chord with two movements on top') – though that only worked for five tracks. He had the songs all worked out on a four track and recorded onto cassette, but before they entered the studio, none of the other Stereolab musicians had heard them before. No working it out at home, or in rehearsal. Stereolab weren't about jamming to find the tune. Rocking out was anathema to them. The ideas were there already – the tune, the concept, the demo – the studio was about bringing them to life.

'It could be quite hard,' says Paul Tipler, the engineer for *Mars Audiac Quintet*. 'Tim would write a bass line on his guitar and then expect Duncan [Brown] to play it straight away, even though the frets are much further apart on a bass so it was much trickier, and Duncan hadn't heard it before.'

But everyone was game and it was fun in the studio. Sean O'Hagan added strings and harmonies. To achieve the chiming repetitive underscore in an analogue pre-cut-and-paste computer era, drummer Andy had to play a deadpan beat and then go into sudden 'Hawaii Five-0 mode' whenever Paul clapped his hands. Andy also remembers the video for 'Ping Pong', the album's single, being filmed in the summer of 1994, during the World Cup. The video has a dreamy, sunny vibe; a feel of the day after one of those groovy parties. In a sun-drenched tower-block flat, up in the sky above the city, the group hang out. They play games on the coffee table – chess, blow football – and gaze at architectural models with intensity and a just-on-the-verge humour.

Intermittently, the scene is intercut with other images. Sometimes fun ones: a UFO hovers outside; the window is used as a screen for old-school computer game *Pong*. There are architectural drawings. These hint at what the song's actually about. Because despite Mary's ba-ba-ba's and Laetitia's detached delivery of the pretty tune, 'Ping Pong' is a political song. Laetitia's lyrics are about how capitalism ends up turning back on itself, and wrecking people's lives in the process.

The lyrics are serious stuff, asking the listener to consider the historical pattern of the economic cycle: 'Three stages stand out in a loop/A slump and war then peel back to square one and back for more'. It's not exactly girls who want boys who like boys to be girls. Capitalism's never-ending death spiral over the guitars' never-ending chord churn.

Laetitia could sing about what she wanted, as long as she stuck to the tune, so she did. And her tranquil delivery – she could have been musing on love and ice cream – belied her subject matter, which was revolution. It was this mad tension in Stereolab that made what they did so unique. The way the words worked against the sound of her voice (once described as 'strawberry milk'); how the groovy '60s party Moog sat over the '70s drone sound of minimally changing chords; how Laetitia, an emotional, energetic and political person, submerged her personality into an effortless vocal. You don't have to shout to be radical. All these elements, that appear weird when written down, sound warm and engaging and light in a Stereolab record.

You could see *Mars Audiac Quintet* as the peak – perhaps the end point – of a certain form of Stereolab, the one which drew on Velvet Underground, Suicide and Neu! to make a looping, barely changing, dense guitar background and top it with Laetitia's light, cool vocals, with Mary's ba-ba-ba-ing chiming in and out. Over the next few years, they started investigating a jazzier, more easy-listening sound, then a sprawling, spacier feel. But in December 2002, Mary was killed in a traffic accident in London, when she was riding her bike. She was just thirty-six. 'Mary was a great spirit in the band,' said Tim. 'She was like a sister,' said Laetitia. Her death broke the band for a while: they stopped recording for a year; soon after, Tim and Laetitia split up. They returned to make *Margerine Eclipse*, which contains 'Feel and Triple', their tribute to Mary.

Throughout, and now, they still sound like Stereolab: all their records sound like Stereolab. And whenever you play a Stereolab record – or even when you hear them sampled, on a Busta Rhymes track, or by J Dilla and Madlib – there's a portal back to the sort of party where Dadaism is discussed alongside politics, where art and ideas and music are there to try and make life not just cooler, but better. A loop. An endless experimentation in the same groove. Peel back to square one and back for more.

Teenage Kicks

ASH

'Girl From Mars'

Two facts about Ash in 1995. Ash fact number 1: they were young. Teenagers, still in sixth form. So young that their manager had to visit Tim Wheeler and Mark Hamilton's headteacher in person to persuade him to let them have two weeks off school, so Ash could support Elastica on a short tour. (The head made him wait outside his office in the corridor for half an hour.) So young that they used a half-term holiday to visit LA to bag an American record deal (Tim, sitting by the pool: 'I've just remembered I'm supposed to have done a history project by tomorrow. It's not looking likely, is it?'). So young that Tim read out his A-level results (two Bs and a C) live on Radio 1's *Evening Session*. So young that when they were asked to do photo sessions, the stylist would bring school uniforms for them to wear, as a joke.

Ash fact number 2: they were drunk. The *NME* recorded their tour manager shouting at them like a grumpy parent because they trashed their hotel rooms and their record label would have to pay for the cleaning. It also reported them pogoing on hotel beds while reading the Gideon Bible; spraying beer at all and sundry; the police being called at regular intervals to hotels because they were so out of control. At Glastonbury 1995, Rick McMurray was described as 'utterly hammered . . . gibbering about stimulants, make-up and girls'; Mark kept drinking while he was on medication. On their debut album, *1977* – so named because that was the year that Tim and Mark were born, and also the year *Star Wars* came out – the hidden track, 'Sick Party', was a recording of the band, led by Mark, being copiously sick. This epic vomit session was preceded by someone saying, 'I've got a really small knob,' also someone having a noisy wee.

Young and drunk. These two facts were repeated, over and over, in every article; because they were true, but also because the British music press had decided that there wasn't much else to discuss when it came to Ash. Every music journalist sent to cover the band ended up writing a feature in which the band got colossally, monumentally, continuously mortalled and the journalist joined in with enthusiasm. Then, after a couple of all-day-all-nighters, the journo would be forced to retire earlyish, say around 2 a.m., as they were in their twenties and therefore ancient and unable to continue, and, afterwards, would slink back home, utterly ruined. Ash? Well, they'd continue.

After a short while, the young and drunk tag started to get on the band's nerves. Why were writers so obsessed with their drinking? Everyone their age was doing the same. 'Downpatrick is the sort of place where there's nothing to do except get out of your head with drink, which most people start doing at thirteen or fourteen,' said Rick. 'People drink and fight. Or they take drugs and fight.'

And they felt that them being teenagers meant that they weren't taken seriously. 'Because we're young, people don't realise there's loads of thought going into our music,' said Tim. 'We're intelligent people, talented musicians and good songwriters. No one understands us, nobody gets us, they're always missing the point. People just think we're this wacky wee band, a happy, bouncy-castle Nirvana. We deserve to be given recognition for being a lot deeper than that. It makes sense to kids like us. They understand, but older people don't get it.'

Fair enough. Actually, Tim was a precocious songwriting talent, dreaming up songs that seemed far beyond his years, tracks packed with hooky melodies that hid themselves under the band's fuzzy guitars. And Ash fans knew it: they were mostly youngsters like them, attracted to the tunes as well as their particularly nutty teenage energy. (My friend, who's a few years younger than Ash, absolutely loved them in the '90s, because 'they were just so cool. Brilliant songs and brilliant-looking. Tim's hair was fantastic.') Ash were so fizzy, so in the moment, such an intense live proposition, with that quiet–LOUD, stop-then-JUMP-UP-AND-DOWN grunge dynamic that it was easy to miss how Tim could pull out a big chorus as readily as he could make himself sick. His talent was remarkable.

Today, if you look at the early press coverage of Ash, you might find yourself agreeing with their questioning of the young and drunk label, but for different reasons. How was it that youthful over-indulgence was the only press hook for these Downpatrick lads? How did a Northern Irish band slip imperceptibly sideways into the red-white-and-blue of Britpop? How were Ash co-opted into that idea without anyone getting upset? Did nobody notice?

Though the notion of Britpop, its caricature, often felt southern and English, the music didn't only catch on in London, or even just in English cities. But calling anything 'Brit' will always carry a different meaning in the north of Ireland. Mostly, the British music press didn't seem to realise this (apart from Northern Irish journalists like Sean O'Hagan, Stuart Bailie, Gavin Martin). Ash, by avoiding politics, by celebrating what they liked (*Star Wars*, space, girls, partying) as opposed to what they grew up with, were embracing a jolly modernity that was utterly ordinary, and so, revolutionary.

The story of Ash being young and drunk might have been limited, but in its own way, it was a privilege. The silliness of 'teenagers on the rampage', that daft neutral everyman rock 'n' roll appeal. For 1990s Northern Ireland, Ash were progress.

Ash came from Downpatrick, County Down, a small, up-the-main-street, down-the-same-street town south of Belfast. Middle-class children of professional parents, they all went to the same school, Down High, and Tim and Mark started writing songs together when they were around twelve. They worked quickly through a heavy-metal phase, a punk phase, a Nirvana phase and, at least when it came to Tim, a flirtation with ABBA phase, before deciding they were going to combine the last two into tuneful, noisy guitar pop. Rick, a couple of years above them, joined as drummer and they formed Genuine Real Teenagers, because that's what they were. A tape sent to Nirvana's London PR agency got them a manager, who then landed them a record deal with the well-respected indie label Infectious. It was that easy. Tim was fifteen.

They released a mini-album of punky songs, and then, in 1995, they started working with Owen Morris, of Oasis and Verve notoriety, who was in Loco Studios in Wales working on The Verve's *A Northern Soul*. Owen gave up his Christmas holiday at the end of 1994 to work with Ash, because that was the only time they had off school. Wanting to create some pop singles, they banged out 'Kung Fu' (which Tim wrote in three minutes), 'Girl from Mars' (which he'd written ages before, but held back from releasing because it was clearly a hit, and his parents wanted him to finish his A levels) and 'Angel Interceptor'. They released them one by one in 1995. 'Girl from Mars' went in at Number 11 and got them on *Top of the Pops* in August, the week before Blur and Oasis played 'Country House' and 'Roll With It'. Ash had to play it live, as that was the deal at that time. It's a song that drops straight into its chorus, no intro to warm up into Tim's voice, but they played it perfectly, insouciantly, with Tim singing straight down the camera-barrel, as Mark chucked himself around behind him, long limbs a-flail, and Rick hammered away on drums, looking approximately thirteen.

Their performance is a delight, to be honest, and you'd have to be the grumpiest of grumpy gits not to succumb to the stop-start joy of 'Girl From Mars': a young man's dancefloor riot tribute to the ultimate manic pixie dream girl, a cute alien that stayed up late with him playing cards and smoking cigars, but never told him her name.

In early 1996, Ash went to Rockfield Studios, also in Wales, and started working on *1977*, again with Owen Morris. Owen was in full drink-and-drugs mode – 'for him, that was part of the whole recording process,' Tim said later – and introduced the band to his approach. 'The nights got really long,' said Tim. 'He was a real maniac. He thought it'd be funny for us to go to a charity shop in this provincial town in Wales wearing eyeliner to buy women's dresses.' They wore the dresses to record. They had one track in the studio kept specifically for vibes; Owen would open up the microphone and all three of Ash would stare at it, thinking good-vibey thoughts.

Tim and Mark were only recently out of sixth form, and the previous eighteen months had been intense: recording, touring, releasing singles, doing A levels, touring. Tim had a couple of songs already written but needed to create a few in the studio. Owen picked up on a track which Tim had thought too weird, and it turned into 'Goldfinger', a Britpop-scrap-with-Nirvana-until-Teenage-Fanclub-come-in-and-knock-everyone-out anthem that got to Number Five. When *1977* was released, in May 1996, it went straight to Number One. Even now, you could probably play it from start to finish – minus, perhaps, the puking – and everyone in any teenage indie disco anywhere in the world would completely lose their minds.

Things went a little off-kilter after *1977* for Ash. With their clear grunge influence, they seemed designed for an American audience, but found, along with many other British and Irish bands, that their all-the-medals approach to drinking was not quite so celebrated in the US. MTV was the way to break through, and the band and their record label had spent a significant amount making an American video for 'Girl from Mars', their second US single after 'Kung Fu'. To ensure a top billing on MTV, Tim was scheduled to have dinner with the channel's head programmer, but got smashed and turned up late, still mullered. The MTV guy wasn't impressed. The next day, Tim was lined up to do a big interview for the channel. But he woke up 'curled up in my own vomit', missed the slot by several hours and, when he actually got to the studios, chucked up in the green room. 'I think I could have handled that better,' he said later. 'Things might have taken off in the States if I had.'

Still, they were busy. They created the hit title song for Danny Boyle's follow-up to *Trainspotting*, *A Life Less Ordinary*; they played at a *Star Wars* wrap party; they recruited Charlotte Hathaway from Night Nurse as an extra guitarist, thereby freeing Tim up to occasionally sing without guitar; they headlined Glastonbury. But their sudden success in the UK had begun to freak them out. They were uncomfortable with being on the cover of *Smash Hits*, worried that their record label wanted them to be 'some kind of boy band'. They would compare themselves with Nirvana, and get harrumphy: 'Well, Nirvana wouldn't have been marketed with individual postcards of each band member, would they?'

And so, inevitably, they made a swerve away from pop with their second album, *Nu-Clear Sounds*. It had a darker, more American feel, and the video for the first single, 'Jesus Says', which came out in October 1998, featured Tim in shades and a black sleeveless T-shirt emblazoned with JAILBAIT JUNGLE. The clip for 'Numbskull', the album's third single, went further. Based around the idea of Tim having a lost weekend in a New York hotel, it featured oodles of drugs, some self-harm and energetic romps with a sex worker. It was banned (and still isn't available online today). A few years after its release, the video was used by MTV to demonstrate to record companies what wasn't allowed in pop promos; it was also the inspiration behind the T-shirts Ash wore at Glastonbury that read REAL DRUGS REAL BLOOD REAL SEX. They were hoping to be taken seriously; to shed their teen-girl fans. And they succeeded, partly. *Nu-Clear Sounds* went in at Number Seven. 'Numbskull' didn't chart.

Ah . . . yes. The story of a band stepping back from what people liked about them is familiar, and not, if we're honest, all that interesting. Still, in 1998, Ash were involved in something more era-defining, something utterly memorable. Somehow, the teenage puke-along-a-song-thrashers played a small but vital part in the Good Friday Agreement.

Let's look at 1977 from a different angle.

'If you were a band from Northern Ireland in the '70s,' says Eamonn Forde, music-business author and 'actual real life Northern Irish person', 'you could go one of two ways. You could be like Stiff Little Fingers, and make songs about politics. Or you could look for the elements of joy and youthfulness outside that, like The Undertones. Both of those bands were around in 1977. Stiff Little Fingers got together in 1977.'

1977: in the thick of the Troubles, five years on from Bloody Sunday. A tense time when the differences between the two dominant communities of Northern Ireland were stark and embittered, violently enforced, and the British were a poisonous, much resented military presence. A time when, as soon as you went into shops, you opened your bag to be searched. When soldiers at checkpoints went through your car, when guns were trained on you as you walked along the street. When ordinary people were murdered by paramilitaries because of their religion. In 1977, 111 people were killed as a result of the Troubles; forty-nine of them were civilians.

For decades, the Protestant unionists and the Catholic nationalists had been almost completely divided, their two very conflicting histories continually banging up against each other. Twenty years after the '70s, the '90s were different in some ways, not so much in others. People were still being searched, roadblocks would still delay you getting home, sectarian killings were still taking place. In 1998, fifty-four people were killed as a result of the Troubles; forty-six of them were civilians.

'There was no consensus between the communities,' says Eamonn. 'You couldn't be neutral, you had to have an opinion one way or the other. David Butler [writer of *The Trouble with Reporting Northern Ireland*] asked this question. He said, "How can the TV news cover the 12th July parades with balance?" The answer is, it can't. The only way of covering the parades is to balance the news out, so you run a piece on the parades and also one on, for instance, GAA football. You end up with what Butler called "balanced sectarianism".

Balanced, because you've covered the loyalist parades and you've covered Gaelic football, a nationalist sport, so you've ensured that both communities have had TV air-time. Sectarian, because the activity you've covered exists completely separately from the other community and sometimes represents active discrimination against it. But balanced sectarianism was as good as it got in Northern Ireland at the time. No wonder that Ash decided to go for the Undertones approach: creating purely escapist, brilliant teenage pop music that ignored the surrounding politics. Young people were frustrated with the division and rancour, with the entrenched thinking on both sides. They wanted something else.

Ash came hard on the heels of two other big musical successes: Therapy? from Larne, and Belfast-born David 'Holmer' Holmes and Iain McReady's club-night, Sugar Sweet. Therapy?'s grunge-and-grebo-friendly thrash meant they were beloved by both indie and metal festival audiences; they toured constantly, and lead singer Andy Cairns was a music-press fixture. A mixed religion band, Therapy? released the album *Pleasure Death* in 1992. Its last track is 'Potato Junkie', which expresses frustration with Northern Ireland's entrenched histories, both cultural and political, through the winning assertion that you could be bitter and twisted because 'James Joyce is fucking my sister . . . How can I remember 1690? I was born in 1965.'

Holmer and McReady's Sugar Sweet, a rave party in Belfast, was equally apolitical, bringing together young people from all communities in a one-love acid-house atmosphere. 'The Troubles manifests itself in your psyche in ways that you cannot even understand,' said Holmer later, 'so when you're on that dancefloor and religion isn't a barrier any more – the atmosphere was just beautiful. There was all this energy released. These communities fucking hated each other but among them you had groups of people whose religion was music.'

Ash, a few years younger, followed closely on. They understood, without thinking about it, the desire among teenagers to ignore the differences of their parents' generation, to be allowed to live a life outside old boundaries. So for them to be adopted by the British music press in the same way as any other band, judged simply by their songs, their looks, their quotes, their age, their drinking habits, was a big step forward. Still, they had to go to London for it to happen: because of the Troubles, there was no real music infrastructure in Belfast, other than Terry Hooley's Good Vibrations record label during punk, which filed for bankruptcy in 1982. It wasn't like, say, Manchester or Glasgow (both cities which Belfast resembles), which had an indie music infrastructure that meant that great local bands didn't have to leave if they didn't want to. Manchester had Factory, Glasgow had Chemikal Underground; both cities boasted several clubs and venues, a thriving underground scene; both were on the map when it came to touring. Belfast, before the end of the '90s, had none of this. Bands from outside Northern Ireland rarely played, partly because they were scared (the best-known fact about Belfast was that it boasted the most bombed hotel in Europe, the Europa), and partly because the gigs were hard to insure.

So Ash left for London, and, whoosh, there they were, touring with Elastica and Garbage and Cast and Kenickie and Suede. Bands with a youthful exuberance that Ash could match and enhance; bands that were booting out the old guard, barging past the previous stars, noisily taking over. Britpop was a sort of soft power-struggle in Britain, as independent music businesses and outsider bands bustled to the centre and grabbed the spotlight, thumbed their noses at the major labels. But that wasn't happening in Northern Ireland. And neither was another consequence of the new Britpop excitement: the deliberate, but somehow casual, reclamation of the Union flag. There it was, inserted behind Brett on the front of *Select*, plastered over Noel's guitar, worn as a saucy frock by Geri Halliwell; an attempt to wrestle Britishness away from fascists. That was not happening in Northern Ireland. Not at all.

'You can't reclaim the Union flag in Northern Ireland,' says Eamonn. 'It's a flag of division. A loaded, toxic thing. Noel Gallagher wouldn't be able to play a Union flag guitar in Northern Ireland. In 1994 I was in London and it was very weird to see the flag being celebrated as something positive. I mean, back home it showed you where not to go, as a Catholic. If a pub was flying the Union flag, it would be like going into the Slaughtered Lamb in *An American Werewolf In London*, except everyone would be in a bowler hat and a sash.'

Of course, Ash knew this. They could never truly be Britpop; though, to be fair, why would they want to be? No band desired that label anyway. And Ash weren't bringing Britpop to Northern Ireland; they were bringing the new Northern Ireland to Britpop. Young, secular, not caught up in the past, they were a successful export at a time of cautious optimism. Ash embodied, through their music and in themselves, a spirited hopefulness, a disregard for the bigotries of the past.

In 1994, when the band were starting out, the IRA agreed to a ceasefire; the first real glimmer of hope for peace. In early 1998, through the hard work and dedication of many people but especially the SDLP's leader John Hume and New Labour's Mo Mowlam, the Good Friday Agreement was drawn up. It used power-sharing to restore self-government to Northern Ireland; it recognised civil rights; it meant that paramilitaries would disarm and – most controversially – political prisoners would be released. It took years of painstaking negotiation for it to be realised, and it was to be put to the vote in a referendum on 22 May. Its supporters knew that it needed to be passed by a large majority for it to have legitimacy. If 'Yes' got 60 per cent of the vote, that wasn't enough. They needed a banging win.

Someone got on the phone to Jim Sheridan, the film director, who got on the phone to Paul McGuinness, U2's manager, who got on the phone to Bono. John Hume called Bono, too. Bono did not want U2 to be involved in a 'partisan Yes campaign' but said to Hume that 'we would help if he and [David] Trimble [head of the Ulster Unionists] shared the stage with us', and also demanded that the two politicians shake hands with each other and, crucially, not speak on stage. They agreed. Bono got on the phone to Ash.

A gig was arranged at Belfast's Waterfront Hall, MC'd by the *NME*'s Stuart Bailie, with Ash and U2 playing. Ash were described in the media as 'a Protestant rock group from Downpatrick', U2 as 'the mixed religion Irish rock band' (balanced sectarianism). Sean O'Hagan from the *NME* was also there, having flown over from London with U2.

In front of 2,000 Catholic and Protestant sixth-formers, Ash zipped through a short, hit-packed set. Then U2 came on and played The Beatles' 'Don't Let Me Down'. Bono made a quick speech and then, in a perfect photo opportunity, grabbed both Hume and Trimble's hands and lifted them into the air (a move he admits he stole from Bob Marley, who did the same in 1978 with rival Jamaican politicians Michael Manley and Edward Sega). The crowd went bananas. The cameras flashed.

'John Hume looks ecstatic as well as dazed,' wrote Sean, 'brimming over with emotion. He manages a big thumbs up to the screaming girls crushed against the safety barriers. Trimble has a big smile plastered across his face. Everyone – the audience, the hangers-on, the musicians on stage – is clapping and cheering and grinning, swept up in the symbolism of the moment. Then the rock stars and the politicians bow their heads and everybody falls silent in memory of Northern Ireland's dead.'

U2 played 'One', and merged it into 'Give Peace a Chance'. Ash joined them to play Ben E. King's 'Stand By Me'. Tim didn't know all the words. Why would he? He was twenty-one.

'We were like an extension of the youth in the audience,' said Tim later. 'The moment was pretty clear to us. It was a no-brainer to drop everything and do the gig. It was the first chance we had to try to help change things. We were born right in the middle of the Troubles. Sometimes as a band we felt, in the years leading up to 1998, that we were doing more than politicians were doing in bringing people together.'

The gig was three days before the referendum. The symbolism of the politicians with Bono was strong; the sight of all the young people going mad to Ash was too.

Eamonn points out that Catholics always voted anyway. 'It was drummed into you from an early age,' he says, 'because of the civil rights movement.' The civil rights campaign was for 'one person one vote' which (and nobody can quite believe this when they hear it) wasn't established in Northern Ireland until 1969. Before then, it was one vote per household, no matter how many adults lived there; and businesses were allowed multiple votes.

The Good Friday Agreement vote was passed. The 'Yes' votes came in at 71.12 per cent, on a turnout of over 80 per cent of voters (just under one million people); young people voted almost exclusively Yes. 'Like the opposite of Brexit,' remarks Eamonn. 'Brexit happened because all the old people voted for it. The peace deal happened because all the young people voted for it.'

If you go to Belfast these days, as a tourist, for a stag night, as a student, as a business person, you might find yourself wandering around the Cathedral Quarter. This was an area of Belfast that nobody went to in the '90s; it was rough, almost derelict, dangerous. Now, it welcomes visitors of all kinds. It's the centre of Belfast's healthy cultural scene; a welcome-all-comers arts bulwark against a return to political divisions.

And if you do wander around the Cathedral Quarter, you might come across the Oh Yeah centre. Set up by Stuart Bailie and Gary Lightbody of Snow Patrol, among others, it's a vast former whiskey warehouse that's now a non-profit music centre that supports young bands and musicians from Northern Ireland. The Oh Yeah provides equipment and rehearsal facilities, it stages gigs, it has recording spaces and releases compilation LPs. It's a place for musicians to hang out with other musicians, to learn from people who already know the business, to be inspired and to make and release pop songs without having to leave Northern Ireland.

And its name? That's from Ash's fifth single from *1977*, released on 24 June 1996. 'Oh Yeah'.

England's Dreaming

CORNERSHOP
'Brimful of Asha'

At the end of 1997, the American music magazine *Spin* – at the time, a hipper, more alternative *Rolling Stone* – printed its Top 20 albums of the year. It had been a good twelve months for music, and *Spin* had a lot of great LPs to choose from. The Prodigy's *Fat of the Land* was at Number 20, just beaten by the Wu-Tang Clan's *Wu-Tang Forever* at Number 19. Belle and Sebastian made an appearance (Number 18, with *If You're Feeling Sinister*), as did Daft Punk (*Homework*, at Number 16), and Janet Jackson, Roni Size and Erykah Badu. The Top Ten featured (deeeep breath) The Chemical Brothers, Missy Elliott, Biggie Smalls, Portishead, Björk, Sleater-Kinney. At Number Two was Radiohead's *OK Computer*. And at Number One? Cornershop, with *When I Was Born for the 7th Time*.

'It was', says Cornershop's singer and songwriter, Tjinder Singh, 'the album that people had on their coffee tables in New York. That's how somebody put it.'

He and Ben Ayers (guitars, keyboards, tamboura) had had an inkling that their third album might do well. After spending the day arranging the first track they recorded for it, 'Good to Be on the Road Back Home', the engineer walked them to their car and said how much he'd enjoyed the session, 'and he seemed genuine', remembers Tjinder, sounding slightly surprised. When each track was finished, Tjinder and Ben would take it round to their record company and play it to everyone in the office. 'And every time, we got a round of applause.'

The good feeling around the album wasn't just in the UK, but in the US too; when *When I Was Born for the 7th Time* came out, they were booked to play Lollapalooza – 'We were on a sleeper bus! Travelling in ease every day, for six weeks!' – and Cornershop went down brilliantly with the audience at the gigs, everyone singing along. 'With that album', said Tjinder, 'we won people round who had not liked us at all in the past.'

People hadn't liked them in the past because, initially, like many artists, Cornershop's ambition had exceeded their ability. Though they always made their records the same way – using samples, odd sounds, mixing Indian instruments with guitars, peppering their lyrics with politics, banging everything under a proper melody – at first, they made a right racket. They had no idea you had to tune a guitar, they just made a noise. Tjinder and Ben, the band's constants, had been on a huge learning curve, from putting out their *In the Days of Ford Cortina* EP on the tiny Wiiija Records in 1993, made in Preston with music writer/musician John Robb as producer, to being signed to David Byrne's label Luaka Bop in the US, to their almost constant touring, supporting Beck, Oasis and others. They'd never taken their foot off the pedal, even when, in the mid-'90s, the initially encouraging UK music press decided to look the other way. It had taken them four years of hard work to arrive at the confident eclecticism of the double album *When I Was Born . . .* with its hip-hop feel, its splicing of genres, tempos, languages and ideas, its confident bounce between indie, Indian music, electronica, alternative, trip-hop. American country singer Paula Frazer is on 'Good to Be on the Road Back Home'; rapper Justin Warfield on 'Candyman', beat poet Allen Ginsberg on 'When the Light Appears Boy'. They covered The Beatles' 'Norwegian Wood', Tjinder singing the lyrics in Punjabi. The album is a cross-genre global delight.

When I Was Born for the 7th Time came out in September 1997, and its lead single, 'Brimful of Asha', was released the month before. A song rooted in Tjinder Singh's '70s/'80s childhood, it references, says Tjinder, everything that Cornershop is about. He has a complicated relationship to the single these days, but says that 'if there was a song to represent us, it would probably be that song'. 'Because of the record-collection element, because of the international-ness of it, because of the political elements, the technology side, the cassettes, and vinyl and all the little things that you get into as a kid, us doing that. It reflects us as a band pretty good.'

The lyrics have so much packed in, not least a celebration of the joy of Indian cinema, with its wild, romantic musical numbers, sung by playback (background) singers. Mohammed Rafi and Lata Mangeshkar are two hugely important playback singers, as is Asha Bhosle, Lata Mangeshkar's younger sister, who's the Asha in the title, the 'sadi rani' (our queen). 'Asha' also means hope in Hindi and Punjabi. 'She's the one who keeps our dream alive, in the mornings past the evening till the end of the light.' Bollywood songs soundtrack Indian people's lives, sustain them through tough times, transform their existence into something with meaning, hope, glamour and romance. Even when the hard days come: the 'government warning' about dams being built concerns India's controversial Narmada Dam, the second biggest in the world, which required thousands of people to be resettled, moved from their ancient villages, their homes.

Tjinder grew up in the West Midlands, so there are other references, too. Solid-state radio and Ferguson mono recall big-box transistor radios with an AM/FM slide, so you could tune into stations from other countries. Bande publique is French public radio (Tjinder's wife is French); All India radio, the Indian national radio station; two-in-ones, the tape decks that you used to tape tunes from the radio. Jacques Dutronc is a French ye-ye singer who also wrote songs for Françoise Hardy; the Bolan Boogie is Marc Bolan. And two record labels: Argo Records, an amazing label that offered field recordings, poetry readings and recorded Shakespeare plays; Trojan Records is, well, Trojan Records, the Willesden-based label that brought Jamaican music to the UK charts.

'Brimful of Asha' is about growing up immersed in and hopping between all these influences, the mix-and-match of your parents and your peers and your politics and what you hear on radio shows late at night and what you glean from a small stack of 7" 45 rpm singles, some yours, some your family's. In the video, you see Tjinder playing a guitar, and Ben playing a tamboura. 'It has lots of layers that people don't see,' says Tjinder. 'And it's also got the more immediate element of "45" and the word "bosom" . . . I love that, because it's not saying whether it's a male or female bosom.' The lyric tells us that Tjinder's chosen bosom-pillow is RPM, meaning music.

There's a lot going on in 'Brimful of Asha'; though, as Tjinder says, mostly people latch onto the catchy tune, the repetition of '45'. And, of course, they mostly latch onto the hugely successful Norman Cook remix of 'Brimful of Asha'. In late 1997, Cook, also known as Fatboy Slim, got in touch with Cornershop's record label and said he loved 'Brimful' and could he do a mix of it, for free? The band were on tour in the US, said yes, and thought no more about it. When they got back, Tjinder remembers playing the mix at home to his wife, in their flat off the Holloway Road. They both thought it sounded good, 'it sounded big'.

Cornershop continued their tour; in December 1997, they came back from Europe. Between landing at Dover and getting back to London, they heard the Norman Cook remix of 'Brimful of Asha' on the radio about five times. It hadn't even been released. The original single got to Number 60. The remix came out in February 1998, and went straight to Number One, knocking Celine Dion's 'My Heart Will Go On' off the top spot. Norman Cook now regards it as one of the trilogy of tracks that launched him – his remixes of 'Brimful of Asha' and Wildchild's 'Renegade Master', and his own 'The Rockafeller Skank'.

'I've only met Norman once', says Tjinder. 'He had a strong sense that people should stick with what they're good at and stay with what they're doing. He was a bit apprehensive about what he'd done. It was probably because of what happened afterwards. Because no one was expecting that.'

When Cornershop hit Number One, they were already, in their heads, moving on to their next project. So, it was a shock. Partly, it was brilliant – 'we didn't have to sell out, or do anything extraordinary or special to get there' – plus, as the album was already feted, they had the reassurance that their talent was appreciated, that the remix wasn't all they had to offer. But straightforward, smash hit, *Top of the Pops*, Saturday-morning-TV fame was difficult for them, especially Tjinder. His anxiety went haywire. 'Ben could walk into a room and no one would know who he was,' he says. 'But by sheer dint of my complexion, I'd walk into rooms, and everyone would know who I was. It's hard, it does change your life.'

Such recognition was further complicated by the fact that when Cornershop started, Tjinder had hidden being in a band from his family and community, because he knew they wouldn't have approved. He'd told his parents he was working for a record company. 'When we started out, we got death threats', he said. 'It was our own Asian community that ostracised us . . . For an Asian to have a guitar, that was sacrilege.'

Tjinder grew up in Wednesfield, near Wolverhampton. His dad, a headteacher in India, moved to the UK in 1965 and worked on the buses before training to go back into teaching; his mum came over a little later, with their oldest son, had Tjinder and his sister, and worked in a factory. He had a lovely family life, but his life outside the home wasn't always easy: 'People chasing me on motorbikes, threats from skinheads, people saying things like "You're all right but those P***s over there stink". It hurts every time . . . it feels like being punched in the face.' You can see how suddenly standing out, everyone staring, would be difficult for Tjinder.

Ben was born in Canada, but moved to Devon when he was nine. He stayed with his grandparents, learnt piano and had his mind expanded by an uncle, who played him Bob Dylan and The Beatles. 'There weren't many kids at school who were into "Ob-La-Di, Ob-La-Da" and "Old Brown Shoe", so I'd get the piss taken out of me', he said. Both Ben and Tjinder applied to Preston Poly after A levels and met each other as soon as they arrived. 'I was getting out of a car with my parents,' says Tjinder, 'and he got out of a black cab, and we agreed to go to the pub when we'd settled in. He was the first person I met.'

After college, Tjinder got a bursary to work for ICL, a computing firm, but decided an IT life wasn't for him; he stayed on at Preston Poly to be the social secretary, booking bands and comedians. But, he had 'racial resentment throughout my tenure, it was very stressful'. He was already in a band with his brother Avtar; they changed the band name to Cornershop and 'took a more political direction overnight'. Ben joined, and in 1993, they moved to London to start hanging out and working at Wiiija Records. 'A few months before that, I was sat on a toolbox in my friend's house in Leicester reading *England's Dreaming* by Jon Savage and *The Buddha of Suburbia* by Hanif Kureishi. And within three months, I was living *The Buddha of Suburbia* . . .' And releasing a single called 'England's Dreaming'.

On the same label were Huggy Bear, the shouty riot grrrl group, and they co-opted Cornershop into the same movement for a time. John Peel was a supporter – he went to a Cornershop gig at the Falcon in 1992 (Tjinder's wife was also there) – and mentioned them on his radio show that very night. It was all exciting, all DIY, all lo-fi. An awkward, homemade alternative to the increasingly slick tunes of what would become Britpop. Cornershop had an ice-cream van as their first tour bus, which they also slept in, freezing cold (of course), and so rickety you could see the road through the gear-stick casing. They toured Europe, playing squats and bars, came back to the UK and downsized so that all their equipment could fit into a car. Various members left, or were asked to leave, including Tjinder's older brother. 'Even Ben was asked to leave as well,' says Tjinder. 'I think he just said no.'

They'd seen other groups quit the label, or stop making music. They didn't want that to happen to them. So they worked hard, managed themselves, did their own mastering, learnt, made alliances. They kept creating. Tjinder and Ben started a funky electronic offshoot band called Clinton, for which Dan the Automator (of future Gorillaz fame) did a mix; he then came on to *When I Was Born* to produce 'two and a half tracks', including 'Sleep on the Left Side', about the sudden death of Tjinder's mother in 1996.

The Cornershop ethos had come from Arts and Crafts pioneer William Morris, and was, essentially, DIY and anti-corporate, anti-sell-out, 'to keep away from all the pomp and ceremony about music'. So when success hit, it spun them out: all the attention hadn't been on their wishlist, and it had arrived, at least partly, via someone else. They tried hard to keep a level head. 'We just kept everything as normal as possible,' says Tjinder. 'Maybe to the extent that people didn't like that, they thought we should rise to the challenge, be a bit more flamboyant. But we didn't.'

The band continued, but moved sideways, releasing a politics-meets-disco Clinton album, producing records for The Toes. They did a tour with Oasis, which they loved, but then stopped touring; they brought both Guigsy and Noel onto their next, excellent album, 2002's *Handcream for a Generation*. They left Luaka Bop; after the release of *Handcream*, they parted company with Wiiija. Tjinder's father died in 2001; his first child was born a few months later. It was a good time. It was also a bad time.

'I don't think I've said this before, because I've never looked back at it from now, but it did take a toll on me personally,' says Tjinder. 'It's a toll that I'm only getting over now. People used to say, "Why do musicians get paid so much?", and looking back at those twenty years, you understand why. It's taken me twenty years to make it through.'

Actually, Tjinder feels that physical and mental burn-out of artists is built into the industry model. 'It's necessary to destroy the creative,' he says, 'because if you don't, then you're not going to be able to exploit what the creators have done.' In order to make money from a success, he feels, the music industry needs the artist who made that hit single, that smash album, to stand still creatively and play the same thing over and over again, or at least make something that doesn't deviate too far. They build you up to break you, essentially; put you on tours so never-ending, so soul-sapping that you can't muster the energy for reinvention, or, indeed, for everyday life.

'It does destroy you', says Tjinder. 'Every facet of the human body is tugged at. The mental strain, the physical strain, the strain as you get older, the memories of certain things that are great, the memories that are not so good, the harder times, everything. You can't just put a pause to it. You have to live with it. And some people can't live with it, and they lose the rest of their lives because of what they've done for a few years.'

You can't understand the highlights and disasters of your twenties until you're way past that time, because up until then, you resent being categorised – fixed – as your younger self. People want you to repeat yourself, or, if you don't, to justify why you're doing something different. And they want you to do this over and over; if you succeed when you're young, you will always be asked about it, your life folded back to it, never allowed to completely move on. One foot in the past. Always re-explaining, justifying, remembering, even when you don't really remember. It changes how you feel about a time that was random and joyous, ordinary and inspired. It's only many years later that you can appreciate what you've done.

'We did enjoy it,' says Tjinder now. 'We travelled a hell of a lot. We mixed with some wonderful people. You would go to sleep thinking about music, wake up in the middle of the night to write a lyric . . . It's what you want for your children, to not have to worry, to just get on with what you want to do, and do it. And . . . it's success.'

Cornershop gave up touring in 2009. But they still make records, and their latest, *England Is a Garden*, is perhaps their best album yet, and recognised as such by critics and fans. Ben and Tjinder meet up every Tuesday and Friday lunchtime, to cook up ideas, to think about songs, to discuss politics, to continue with what they've been doing for the whole of their adult lives. Which is creating and bringing to life quirky, alternative, tuneful, multi-influenced pop songs. A British (Indian, Canadian) popular music-success story.

Choose Life

UNDERWORLD
'Born Slippy'

We've all had a night out like Underworld's 'Born Slippy' (or 'Born Slippy: Nuxx', to give it its proper title). Not just a night out dancing to it, but a night like the one the lyrics describe. Unlike many dance tracks of that era, you can't call 'Born Slippy' a journey. Instead, the words give us a series of snapshots, small moments during a bangabout out-on-the-town out-of-it adventure, the kind of shattered memories that return in sweaty, mortifying flashbacks during the daylight hours after a heavy night.

The music sounds like a sunrise, a shimmer, a beautiful awakening, and then it shifts. It starts hurtling, thumping, careering forward, and here come the snapshots . . . Here's your night out.

Girls smiling from dark doorways, inviting you into the sex clubs below. Dirty boys in the shadows, too, and lads roaming in dangerous packs, as you bump about in a drunken fuzz – chatting to randoms, bouncing between Tube and pub and tottering along the roads and into other people and then talking properly to a few outside having a cigarette. And for a while you're feeling huge and invincible – the evening's mega and so are you – until your feelings

slip a little and you slump inside your head, into your inner space . . . Only for you to smash back into real life. Another pint! On we go! You clock the stickers and cards advertising prostitutes in the phone boxes – velvet mouth, wonderful hot times – and you go in, make a phone call maybe, then stumble out again, back to The Ship and up to the bar, shouting random stuff, more lager, more shouting.

So many things to see and do. Finding your way back to the Tube with a blonde, but then she's gone, when did that happen, and, all alone, you're going back to Romford.

And the music, the kick drums and the chiming chords, sound like the train home, but also your heart pumping when you're out. There's a gallop to the beat in the middle. And somewhere, sort of hidden in the mix, there's another sound. Like the breathing you hear inside your head, a chilly tidal hum.

In 'Born Slippy', Karl Hyde is describing an early '90s night out in Soho. Though it could be anywhere, really; anywhere that lets you bump about drunk. But for him, it was Soho.

Soho was buzzy, then. Previously, it had been, not a wasteland, but a place where it was possible to walk around late on a Wednesday evening and not see anyone. The drinking places were all hidden, often not legit or accessible: either artsy drinking clubs or Paul Raymond-owned sex niteries. But in the late '80s and early '90s, small media businesses set themselves up in cheap rooms, mostly above shops. *Smash Hits* above Boy on Carnaby Street; Heavenly, Junior Boys Own, Food record labels all around the corner. Lots of film and TV companies; small clothes stores;

independent record shops like Black Market, Reckless Records, Fat Cat. And everyone who worked in those places liked to go out. The pubs filled up; the afterparties started to happen; clubs opened in places like Gossips and St Moritz. Tomato, a design agency, had its offices above Black Market Records. It was part-owned by Underworld's Rick Smith and Karl, and was their base when they came into town from Romford. When they went out, they tended to drink in The George on the corner of D'Arblay Street; or in The Ship, just nearby.

The night in 'Born Slippy' was just one of those nights, a random hammering, one of those go-to-work-then-to-the-pub-then-to-some-dive-then-home-on-the-last-train evenings that ended with Karl banging into The Ship and, for some reason, giving comedian Bill Bailey a fiver to get a round. Before Bill could do the honours, Karl turned around and scarpered. 'Karl was always one for disappearing,' a friend of his told me. 'You'd look round and he wouldn't be there any more.' But Karl would also make notes, during the evening, just little descriptions of what was happening or records of what was said. The lyrics to 'Born Slippy' were notes he took on that night. There was lager. There was shouting.

Karl Hyde and Rick Smith met in 1981, when they were both working in the kitchen of a Cardiff restaurant. Karl, from Bewdley in Worcestershire, was studying at a local art college, which had a department called The Third Area that merged art with philosophical ideas. The main one being: art is fine art, meaning visual art, but also music, sound and performance. Rick was doing an electronic and engineering degree. He dropped out when Karl

asked him to join his band, Screen Gemz. 'Screen Gemz were the biggest band in Cardiff for a month,' said Rick. 'A month later, they weren't.'

Not to worry: a few years later, Karl and Rick, along with three others, were in a band with a squiggle for a name, the squiggle usually pronounced Freur. Freur, no strangers to hair crimpers, enormo-shouldered jackets and a significant head-waggle dance, were signed by CBS and had a minor hit in 1983 with the actually-pretty-good Talk-Talk-come-Psychedelic-Furs track 'Doot Doot'. It got to Number 59. They were big in Italy. But things never really took off, and in 1987, with one member leaving and being replaced, Freur morphed into Underworld. This version of Underworld made two albums, supported the Eurythmics on a US tour and tried, really tried, to make it in the pop world. But to no avail. In 1989, they were dropped by their label and their manager; soon after, they had to file for bankruptcy. Rick sold off all his equipment and scarpered to Romford. Karl stayed in America and started playing guitar in Debbie Harry's band.

Things were bad. Rick only kept going because his wife encouraged him. He decided to stop trying to fit into the pop world and just create music he enjoyed. Which turned out to be a sort of eclectic electronica; improvised, experimental, often beautiful dance music. A friend introduced Rick to another Romford local: Darren Emerson, a nineteen-year-old City-boy-turned-acid-house-DJ. Darren joined Underworld.

When Karl returned and started making tracks with Underworld again, he was excited, though initially unsure as to where he could fit in. At that time, dance music often used samples rather than a

live singer. Where did that leave him? 'The rhythm section has always supported the singer,' he said. 'I realised I'd have to start doing the opposite, supporting the rhythm section.' Inspired by Sam Shepard's book *Motel Chronicles* and Lou Reed's *New York* album, he started to write lyrics that described little snippets of his days.

Darren introduced Rick and Karl to the dance scene, playing them house tracks from Chicago and Detroit, taking them out. And once he went to his first rave, Karl thought, 'This is it. This is the best gig I've ever been to.' Grooverider were playing. The women weren't getting hit on. No one was looking at the stage. 'The light show was fantastic, and there were fairground rides in one room and an *Alice in Wonderland* vibe in another.'

In the early 1990s, the people who'd set up outdoor raves, or clubs in disused warehouses, one-off all-nighters in empty film studios, started to bring raving indoors, inside properly designed nightclubs. Back to Basics started in Leeds in 1991, Cream started in Liverpool in 1992. Parties became so-called legal raves, though many illegal ones continued (there were still flyers for parties that required you to meet at 'Blackgrove Crossroads, near Waddesdon, Aylesbury').

Raving, for many people, was completely revolutionary. It merged many disparate tribes into one: Glastonbury 1990 felt like that. Dreadlocked travellers, odd-bod prog-heads, northern scallies (Happy Mondays were playing and a lot of people broke through the gates): everyone wanted a great night out, whether they were taking pills, or just drinking. (Karl never took drugs.) So many young people were spending their time dancing all night that the government had to both legislate against it, and provide a legal

alternative. The drinks industry lobbied for a change to the licensing laws – they were genuinely worried that no one would ever drink alcohol again – and brought out alcopops, to counter the fact that everyone was drinking water.

Acid house, rave and all their offshoots were a far bigger culture than any indie music, but because dance music didn't throw up quite as many show-off characters, it was harder for the music papers to write about; though they tried, especially *Mixmag* and *DJ* magazines. It was the tracks that mattered, and they were often made by people who deliberately stayed out of the spotlight, didn't want any attention. They didn't want to go on *Top of the Pops* anyway.

Underworld were like that. Now they'd found music they loved, everything was fun for them again. They were happy not having their photo taken; releasing music as a response to going to clubs, hearing amazing music from other artists, being excited to make their own. In 1992, they and others were given a field in Glastonbury called the Experimental Sound Field (in the same area where Lost Vagueness was eventually sited). Underworld DJ'd for seven hours the first night, and eighteen the second. 'That', said Karl later, 'became the blueprint for Underworld.'

And then *Trainspotting* happened.

Trainspotting, the film from Irvine Welsh's 1993 cult book, directed by Danny Boyle, came out in 1996. It captured a moment. Or, if not a moment – it wasn't a mid-1990s cultural documentary – a feeling.

It was about a group of friends – Renton, Spud, Sick Boy, Begbie, Tommy – people you felt you already knew. Renton (Ewan McGregor): charming, lucky, deadbeat anti-hero. Spud

(Ewen Bremner): loveable, surreal, cartoonish loser. Sick Boy (Johnny Lee Miller): out for himself and whatever he could get, mostly women and drugs. Begbie (Robert Carlyle): everyone knows a Begbie. A booze-fuelled bully, violent, unpredictable, always looking for a fight. And Tommy (Kevin McKidd): wholesome nice guy, heading for a fall. Most of the characters were heroin addicts. They were unreliable, dishonest, self-seeking, nihilistic. They were all also wildly attractive, defiant and funny. Fizzy with life even while injecting death into their veins.

'I got criticised when the book first came out for making heroin sound fun and glamorous,' says Irvine. 'I wasn't: I was making youth sound fun and glamorous. If I was sitting in a bedsit on a mattress staring at the walls with a needle in my arm, age twenty, I would trade that for being fit and solvent at sixty-something. It's the energy and the enthusiasm . . . On one level, *Trainspotting* is a terrible, miserable experience, they're fucking themselves up. But they don't care because they're young and having fun.'

Trainspotting is about youth, its rebellion and potential, its blindness to consequences, its absolutely pure belief that nothing matters, so who cares anyway. Both Danny, who was forty in 1996, and Irvine, who was two years younger, understood that youth was the story's power. 'The characters' defiance is them saying "fuck old cunts"', says Irvine. 'Old cunts aren't important. Their approval or condemnation means absolutely fuck all.'

'Born Slippy' is *Trainspotting*'s final track. It's playing as Renton walks over London's Waterloo Bridge, a bag of money slung over his shoulder, its hopeful chords and heart-attack kick drums

ringing out as he strides along, the music sounding the dawn of a new life, better than the old life, the old life that he's sloughing off, that's sliding like invisible water down his skinny back, as the silvery sun shines through the putty clouds, and the camera, which is trained on Ewan McGregor's lovely face, smudges and defocuses and warps his gradually spreading shit-eating grin into something more nightmarish. Or does it? Is that a hideous smiley face, or are we seeing things?

And as we watch, over 'Born Slippy''s hazy synths and pounding beat, in voiceover, we hear Renton say: 'The truth is that I'm a bad person. But that's going to change. I'm going to change. This is the last of that sort of thing. I'm cleaning up and I'm moving on, going straight and choosing life. I'm looking forward to it already. I'm going to be just like you . . .'

It's the flipside of the defiant mantra that he makes at the start of the film, the one that ended up on every teenager's wall, the one that reads like a prayer, as well as a curse. You know it.

'Choose Life. Choose a job. Choose a career. Choose a family. Choose a fucking big television, choose washing machines, cars, compact disc players and electrical tin openers . . . Choose DIY and wondering who the fuck you are on a Sunday morning. Choose . . . watching mind-numbing, spirit-crushing game shows, stuffing fucking junk food into your mouth. Choose . . . pishing your last in a miserable home . . . an embarrassment to the selfish, fucked-up brats you spawned to replace yourself. Choose your future. Choose life . . .'

Before *Trainspotting*, 'Born Slippy' wasn't a hit, but when it was re-released after the film, in July 1996, it went to Number Two in

the charts. 'Killing Me Softly' by The Fugees beat it to Number One; two weeks later, The Spice Girls' 'Wannabe' took over the top spot. You wonder how many more it would have sold if it had been called 'Lager and Shouting'.

'Born Slippy' is a strange track: deceptive, not straightforward. It's a few things all at once. Not quite what it seems. Underworld were surprised when Danny said he wanted it in his new film. It wasn't considered special. They'd released it on a single in 1995, but it wasn't the A-side, and the track had gone to Number 52 and then dropped out of the chart. Which brings us to the really odd thing about 'Born Slippy'. It's not 'Born Slippy'. That's the A-side of the single, but it's not the 'Born Slippy' you want. What you want is the B-side, 'Born Slippy: Nuxx'. It's often called a remix, but it's actually an entirely different track ('Nuxx') to the 'Born Slippy' that's on the A-side. There's also 'Born Slippy: Telematic', another track that's on the B-side. You don't want that one either.

This weird labelling confusion has its roots in how the UK charts (still very important in the 1990s) decided to deal with acid-house records. No one wanted *Top of the Pops* to be dominated by anonymous bods pressing keyboard buttons, so a few adjustments were made. All bands on *Top of the Pops* had to play live, for a start. And only certain record stores were allowed the counting equipment that registered which records were selling. None of the independent record shops were given it, so only dance records by artists signed to major labels got into the charts.

And then there was the palaver about CD singles. On CD singles, there was room to have as much as forty minutes of music, but

the rules were, you could only do that if the forty minutes was made up of remixes of the A-side. Underworld decided to bypass that by releasing lots of different tracks but calling them all the same name, as though they were remixes. So 'Born Slippy: Nuxx' was really just 'Nuxx'. And 'Born Slippy: Telematic' was just 'Telematic'. They were three separate tracks sold as one – 'Born Slippy' – plus two remixes.

Got it? Just to make things clearer, I'm not going to call it 'Born Slippy: Nuxx'. I'm going to call it 'Born Slippy'. (But I mean 'Born Slippy: Nuxx'.) The 'Born Slippy' we all love was just an unloved extra track released in between two Underworld albums, to tide things over, keep the fans happy. It was Danny Boyle that brought it to everyone's attention.

And here's another strange thing about 'Born Slippy'. Somehow, it's really like *Trainspotting*. It paints a picture of addiction, but it doesn't judge. *Trainspotting* doesn't promote heroin; and 'Born Slippy' doesn't promote lager and shouting. It reports, but it doesn't moralise.

The music makes it sounds like it's being positive, and for some people – the fans who jump and down, waving their cans when they hear it – it genuinely is a celebration of the joys of random yelling/sinking a few tinnies/behaving like a loon. But it wasn't written like that. It's Karl's drunken observations, notes of a man fuelled by alcohol. Which means it can be understood in many different ways. 'Born Slippy' is both celebration and commiseration, delight and subsequent regret.

Karl has said, of those times, that he'd made 'a conscious decision to use alcohol in the process of simplifying life of an evening'.

When he went out, there was so much information coming at him that he felt overwhelmed. He couldn't discern, couldn't give everything that was happening the right weight. If he'd had a drink, he felt OK, he was able to single things out, offer them up.

But eventually booze, as it can do, brought consequences, and it took over his life for a few years. He gave it up at the end of the '90s. And his feelings about 'Born Slippy' changed. He realised that he was documenting a mind going into spasm, short-circuited by alcohol. He found it hard when people saw his lyrics as a sort of football anthem, a celebration of getting hammered, when to him they were describing a nightmare. He had to get sober to live. 'The only reason we ever printed the lyrics to "Born Slippy"', he said, 'was because it became a drinking anthem, and I was so gutted because it was in fact a cry for help'. But the lyrics were only a cry for help once he knew they were. Before that, they were just reportage.

Like *Trainspotting*, 'Born Slippy' gives us a series of vivid, memorable scenes, first one, then another. They don't seem to add up to anything. To the narrator, they're just diary entries: what happened here, and then what happened there. But, over time, the scenes begin to make a story, a story that creeps into existence. There's no grand sense of a sweeping plot, no guiding God-like hand that makes everything in your life meaningful, part of a character arc, each scene building into an understandable, significant, worthy whole. It's just one thing happening after another. And after a while, that's your life.

In the film, the chords start at the end of a scene of terrible lager-fuelled Begbie violence, a silent moment full of tension, when Renton seems to make a decision. The chords are still playing

when he wakes early and creeps around the hotel room he and his friends have crashed in after their heroin deal. He gets up, has a drink of water, looks at himself in the mirror, then turns and carefully extricates the sports bag containing £16,000 from the arms of Begbie, who's cuddling it like a teddy bear. The kick drum pumps and so do our hearts. Begbie sleeps on. Renton pauses at the door, looks back. Begbie and Sick Boy are out for the count. Spud is awake. We see Spud shake his head, too upset to even look directly at Renton. Renton sees it too. But he leaves.

'Born Slippy' pushes our anti-hero out of the door, into the dawn light, through an arch to a new day. We cut back: we see Begbie smash the room up and the police arriving. Lager lager lager shouting. Sick Boy and Spud slip away. Renton's alone on the bridge. Mega mega white thing. We see Spud pick up the money Renton left him.

The whole story of the film in one sequence: messed up friendship, violence, heroin, betrayal, lack of options, and the one who faded out and got away with it. All encased, set like a perfect jewel, inside Born Slippy's clatter and chime.

Trainspotting seemed to be everywhere in 1996, partly because Ewan McGregor was everywhere in 1996. He was always about: you would see him in Soho, in everyday pubs and members-only bars, at film premières, comedians' parties, having a laugh, fully out-out. Every night was a 'Born Slippy' night for Ewan. And unlike many famous actors – possibly because he didn't yet realise he was famous – he was fun, unself-consciously himself, ordinary and remarkable all rolled into one.

Trainspotting also seemed to be everywhere because of its poster

campaign. Stylorouge, who designed the posters, were known for working with Blur, and deliberately made the campaign look more like they were selling a band, rather than a film. Bright orange blocks and plain Helvetica typeface recalled the packaging on pill bottles. The characters were separate, individualised and numbered, shot in black and white. The pictures, now, look a bit iPhoney – faces looming up at you, bodies smaller.

Polygram put £800,000 into promotion, a huge amount, especially compared to the £1.5 million Channel 4 gave to make the film. So, the posters were everywhere; the cast went on a countrywide tour with the film to talk to audiences. Irvine's book was reissued with a cover that matched the movie. There were two soundtrack albums: one featuring all the tracks used in the film, another with those that had inspired it but were taken out. Danny even shot a revamped music video for 'Lust for Life', with Iggy Pop doing his traditional topless chicken-strut dance and a few *Trainspotting* references peppered throughout.

Of course, promotion doesn't work if the film doesn't work. But it did. Danny Boyle – who'd found Irvine's book unbelievably wild – 'ferocious' – had vowed to make *Trainspotting* 'the most energetic film you've ever seen'.

And it was. I remember coming out of *Trainspotting* and feeling completely adrenalised, like a kid who'd just seen a kung fu movie. It was druggy, though not in the usual way. No bleak and grimy realism. This was exaggerated, extreme. There were real–unreal trippy sequences about losing pills in a toilet or going cold turkey; uplifting, rushy ones about clubbing and having sex. The music-video aesthetic, the fever-dream sequences, the scenes that just

banged into each other, the montages set to music. The energy. Not a sluggish, heroin-y energy. It felt like uppers, hallucinogens, ecstasy. It was a life force.

A lot of the film's spirit came from its use of music. Not just '90s music, but older tracks of the type that, pre-rave, were played in small dark clubs with a wide music policy, so: New Order, David Bowie, Lou Reed. Britpop was in there, of course: Blur, Pulp, Elastica and Sleeper, and Damon wrote a wistful hurdy-gurdy carousel piece for the final credits. (When *Trainspotting* went to Cannes, so did Damon and Justine.) But the most important tracks in the film – 'Lust for Life', 'Born Slippy' and Lou Reed's 'Perfect Day' – were not born of Britpop. Britpop hums in the background, but it's not centre stage. The dance tracks are more important. New Order's 'Temptation', which plays when Renton and Diane have sex. 'For What You Dream Of' by Bedrock ft KYO when he and Begbie go to an acid-house club for the first time: 'One thousand years from now, there won't be any guys and there won't be any girls, just wankers. Sounds all right to me.'

When *Trainspotting* opened in February 1996, it became the biggest-grossing British film of the year; and, at that time, the fourth-biggest-grossing British film ever, making around £12 million. In March it went to Cannes, and caused a sensation. In July, it opened in the USA, on just eight screens. Eventually, it was shown on 357 screens in America, still a tiny amount, and made $16.5 million.

'I remember being at Cannes and "Born Slippy" playing on a huge sound system at the end,' says Irvine. 'It was shaking the fillings from your teeth, it was really soaring. You see Renton, this

guy who's done everything wrong. He's not only been a thieving junky, he's actually ripped off his best mates. But you're still rooting for him as he's walking over that bridge. It was a moment. You could tell this was going to make Ewan a monstrous star. And a big part of that is the track.'

Dance music is more open and spacious than pop music. It allows you to insert your own mind, find your own images, put your own twist to it, more than the stories and specificities of pop. You can feel a sense of foreboding, perhaps, or a wild freedom, but that might just be you and whatever chemicals you've taken. The music does whatever you feel it does. The weird thing is, despite the sense of unity on a dancefloor, it's not the same for everyone. When you go out in your twenties, stay up late, dance all night, chat and shout, get busy, get raucous, everyone who's out with you seems the same as you. But as you get older, you realise that, for some people, that hedonism is hiding an addiction. People topple over, they fall through their rock bottom, they don't come back.

Though Karl used to hate people waving cans of lager to the lyrics to 'Born Slippy', after some years, he understood that people make the lyrics mean what they want. A mantra, a spell, a manifesto. Lager and shouting. Art and pop music made from desperation. Just some of the UK's greatest exports.

Rick has said that he thinks that part of the appeal of 'Born Slippy' is the hymn-like chords. He went to church a lot when he was young, and Welsh hymns are deep within him. And the 'interplay between dark and light', which he likes and sometimes mirrors how Underworld works. Rick has a positive world view; Karl less

so. 'It's a tune we're still doing at every concert,' said Rick to *Vice*. 'I often get asked if I'm tired of it, and it's really weird, but absolutely not. Because of this relationship that the audience have with the music, and their energy.'

Plus, there's something to do with the times it was created in, the mixed up/smashed together/something's changing era that Rick likes. 'There was energy firing off all over the place,' he said. 'Sometimes things come out of really drab places. There was beauty in debris and deconstruction and rawness. And I think that's all part of that piece.'

Karl gave up drink, and started writing an online diary every day, with photographs, which turned into a book, and into an interesting Instagram project. Since then, he and Rick have worked together and apart, collaborating with other artists over the years: Brian Eno, soundtracks for films. Experimenting with live events, working in design, making music: all elements of Karl's art-school background. Rick was the musical director for the London 2012 Olympics opening ceremony, directed by Danny Boyle.

In 2017, Danny made a sequel to *Trainspotting*: *T2 Trainspotting*, set twenty years after the first. I interviewed Ewan McGregor for it, in LA, where he lives. He was delighted to be in the film, though he'd been worried it was going to be rubbish. If he'd read the script and hated it, he would have refused, because '*Trainspotting* was the Oasis of the film world, something quite amazing.' Ewan was massively into Oasis in the '90s.

It was an emotional reconciliation for him, as after making three films with Danny – *Shallow Grave*, *Trainspotting*, *A Life Less*

Ordinary – he hadn't been cast in Danny's fourth film, *The Beach*, and Ewan had been devastated. It had taken around ten years for them to be reconciled. Aside from that, he hadn't seen Robert Carlyle since the première for *Trainspotting*, 'and I don't remember the première for *Trainspotting*, so I don't know if I saw him there or not'.

Ewan, like Karl, gave up drinking after the '90s. He'd liked it too much. 'I liked it to the point where I didn't ever want it to end,' he said, 'so I would find myself in places at seven in the morning, not knowing anybody, just because I had this hunger. An excitement about going out. A stupid teenager excitement, but in the body of an early twenties man.'

That excitement, that energy. It's not about heroin, it's about being young. Soon after he finished *T2 Trainspotting*, McGregor watched *Supersonic*, the Oasis documentary. It devastated him.

'It really slayed me,' he said. 'I can't describe it. I was so upset afterwards. Because I was such a huge Oasis fan. Like, ridiculous, a schoolboy fanaticism . . . Embarrassing. And watching that film, I really wanted to go back. Just being out there and having a great time, and being a part of what the '90s has become in my mind . . .

'I remember seeing Radiohead in Cork in a field, just after *Trainspotting* had come out, and feeling like part of it all. Anyway, I loved that documentary. I mean, I loved it and I hated it. Because it made me so sad and it made me so happy. That time is gone, it can never come again. But it changed our whole existence.'

Irvine feels differently. 'Britpop was a celebration of British culture, everything you'd seen before all rehashed again, but also

like a requiem for British culture,' he says. 'Like: all this is gonna go, from Teds to ravers and everything in between, it's all gonna be sold off to the internet to the global marketplace and sold back to us in chintzy Instagram influencers. There's gonna be a fire sale of youth culture. The party's over.'

Beat Surrender

THE CHEMICAL BROTHERS
'Setting Sun'

September 1996. Professionally jovial Radio 1 *Breakfast Show* host Chris Evans is excited about his showbiz pal Noel Gallagher's brand-new single. Noel has provided the vocals for 'Setting Sun', the new release from popular dance-music combo The Chemical Brothers, and Chris is thrilled to be able to share it with, not only his guffawing in-studio posse, but the Radio 1 *Breakfast Show* audience, also trembling with anticipation as they shovel in their Crunchy Nuts, chomp down on their toast. Noel singing! Noel, but not with Oasis! Noel in combination with a trendy dance act! What an exclusive!

Chris cues up the track. It crashes in, like a truck driving through the window of a toy shop. After around thirty seconds, he pulls it off air. 'I don't think that was a very suitable record for this time of morning, do you?' he says. He doesn't quite take out a hammer and smash up the record on air, à la Mike Reid and Frankie Goes to Hollywood's 'Relax', but he doesn't play it again, ever.

The week after, The Chemical Brothers' 'Setting Sun' goes straight in at Number One.

To be fair to Chris Evans, if we must be fair to him, 'Setting Sun' is not a breakfast record, not an ideal 'quieting the chaos of off-to-school kids' tune. Because 'Setting Sun' itself is the sound of chaos: a head-vice head-melt, a speeding car careering downhill, a too-fast rollercoaster spinning through a haunted house. Strap yourself in; once the ride starts, you're not getting off. And if that sounds like a cross between a nightmare and the biggest thrill you can have in three minutes, you're right. Emotions smash together in this record, pile on top of each other: exhilaration, horror, fun, but the Fear too.

We hear: howling, lurching sirens, the boomy funk crash of the Chems' interpretation of Ringo's drums on 'Tomorrow Never Knows', a questioning whine and a never-ending drone threat. When Noel's vocals come in, pretty soon after the noise starts, he doesn't really sound like himself. His voice has been treated, and he seems like he's shouting from far away, like he's trying to tell you something important, but your mind is too full of the sirens and the drums and the moment for you to understand. You can't focus. Everything's clamouring for your attention. You can make out a few words: 'You're the devil in me', 'You're coming on strong', 'Like a setting sun' and then the noise crashes in again.

Oddly, 'Setting Sun' isn't quite one for the dancefloor either; meaning, sure, you can play it, but what are you going to cue up before and afterwards? 'Setting Sun' is overwhelming.

Its roots are in a few places, but one of them is the Sunday Social, a club in a not-very-big room underneath a pub, The Albany in Great Portland Street. The Social was set up by independent record label/PR agency Heavenly Records, specifically so

that Tom Rowlands and Ed Simons could DJ there, after Robin Turner, Heavenly's PR, saw them play out in Manchester, as The Dust Brothers. Robin came back absolutely raving about what a brilliant night he'd had, and said to Jeff Barrett, who ran Heavenly, 'We need to set up a club.'

It was early 1994. Robin, from Newport, in Wales, had been in London for a few years. London, like any capital city, attracts people who want a life that's something more than their hometown can give them, and Robin was, mostly, living as he'd hoped: hanging out with music lovers, going to great gigs and festivals. But he hadn't found his clubbing home, quite. He'd missed Shoom, the revolutionary acid-house club, by a couple of years; also Yellow Book, a short-lived indie-dance club around in the early '90s. Now, a few clubs had moved back to having a dress code, even if it was an alternative one. 'You'd go places and it was all, "You can't come in. Three lads wearing Duffer? No, fuck off,"' he remembers. 'When I'd lived in Newport, I'd read about clubbing in London and I wanted the experience I'd read about: this community, this bond between everyone in the room, from DJs to bar staff to everyone on the floor, this sense of unity . . .'

Jeff was up for doing a club – Jeff was up for most things – but he wanted the club to be on a Sunday because then it wouldn't be too mental. Robin thought Sundays would be good, because then anyone who DJ'd alongside Tom and Ed could do their big-paying bookings on Fridays and Saturdays, and pop in to do their club on the Sunday. And also, he wanted the club to feel a bit illicit. Small and special, somewhere only certain people knew about; Sundays helped with that. At the time, the UK licensing hours

made Sunday drinking a stop-start affair: midday till 3 p.m.; then four hours off, because the pubs were shut; then 7 p.m. till 10.30 p.m. This meant that when The Albany's doors opened at 7 p.m., everyone was ready and excited. 'There was a massive sense of anticipation from the get-go,' says Robin. 'That was really important to it, there was a febrile excitement in the room.' The Social was born.

They decided to do four Sunday Socials in August, starting on the 7th. Each night had warm-up DJs, and then Tom and Ed would come on around 9 p.m. The first night's warm-up was Robin himself, as well as Paolo Hewitt, *NME* writer and renowned mod. The evening attracted about seventy people. By the second, on the 14th, where Saint Etienne were the opening DJs, 'there was a roadblock straight away, queues and it was really popular and chaotic', remembered Ed later. After that, on the 21st, the support was Gareth Sweeney, a Northern Soul DJ; and on the 28th, Kris Needs, journalist and DJ for Primal Scream. 'That was the day after the Primals headlined Reading Festival,' says Robin, 'so we all went to that and stayed up. Sunday night was like the afterparty.'

After those first four nights, The Social just rolled on. More people turned up: The Charlatans' Tim Burgess, Beth Orton, Paul Weller, Noel Gallagher, Mani from The Stone Roses, Tricky. The bouncers wouldn't let Tricky in because, they said, he was trouble. Robin went to persuade them: 'I said, "He's Tricky from Massive Attack!" They said, "We don't care, he's trouble."' Robin snuck him in anyway. Tricky DJ'd one night, but it wasn't a success: he kept putting on records at the wrong speed, then taking them off and

looking at them, letting the silence linger before putting another one on again.

I went once, or maybe twice. I remember a small set of stairs that led down into the club, straight onto the dancefloor, which was just the floor. It was really hot and sweaty, as clubs should be. And – I had forgotten this until Robin mentioned it – I remember a particular track, Jay Dee's 'Strange Funky Games and Things'. The strings, the long, long build-up.

That had come out of a particular night, after a Saint Etienne gig at the newly reopened Shepherd's Bush Empire in March 1994. A few people had gone back to Jeff's, which was round the corner, and carried on. 'And he was just putting on all these records,' says Robin, 'lots of things that none of us had heard before, because we were kids; Jeff was ten years older than us. Things like "Strange Funky Games and Things", all kinds of Barry White, Gene Page string arrangements. And that's where the germ of an idea formed, where you could have these slow-build records, just building and building. That's partly where Tom and Ed's set came from. Whatever had come before, when they came on, they started every week with "Strange Funky Games and Things". So when it started you knew where you were going and you knew it was going to build.'

The Dust Brothers had other tracks that they played every week. One was a demented acid-house record, 'Lobotomie' by Emmanuel Top, which they mixed into The Beatles' 'Tomorrow Never Knows'. It wasn't an official remix: just them playing two records together. 'Tomorrow Never Knows', the psychedelic final track of *Revolver*, is an enormous record, whether played in your earphones or in a

club. The sitar drone, the backwards voices, the *Tibetan Book of the Dead* lyrics, the huge drum riff. There were other big bangers, like Sly and Robbie's 'Boops (Here to Go)', The Specials' 'You're Wondering Now', their own remix of Bomb the Bass's 'Bug Powder Dust', and after a couple of weeks, everyone implicitly understood that Tom and Ed's set was structured a bit like a rock gig: it peaked and peaked and peaked and then went into encores. 'It was timed so there would be a final track, and the crowd would be going bananas, shouting for one more, one more, and then there were the encores,' remembers Robin. 'You would have just enough time for three, maybe four encore tracks. Like a band.'

The Social wasn't like many rave clubs, because the tracks were heavier, more distinct, the atmosphere more all-encompassing. There wasn't that insular, trancey, in-your-head feel, where everyone's dancing in their own world; instead it was a full-on communal crowd experience, people squashed up together, going mad.

'I remember people standing on tables and chairs in the small, sweaty basement of a pub,' said Saint Etienne's Sarah Cracknell later. 'Records that I'd never heard . . . it was a great time and also a real education.'

'Tom and Ed knew the power of how rock 'n' roll gigs were structured and they knew the power of riffs,' says Robin. 'It wasn't miles apart from what Oasis were doing at that point. Sonically, it's taking a different route to get there, but the effect is the same.'

Ah yes, Oasis. By summer 1994, Oasis were already big news. They'd released three singles, and the third was 'Live Forever', which came out on 8 August and everyone – *everyone* – loved. Tom and Ed played it at The Social. Later, Noel would say that

'Live Forever' was partly inspired by Manchester's acid-house scene in the late '80s/very early '90s: the Haçienda, Konspiracy, Thunderdome, plus Justin Robertson's night Most Excellent at the Wiggly Worm. He told journalist Dorian Lynskey that during those years he put down his guitar entirely and tried to write house tracks, including one called 'You Are My Dove'. *Definitely Maybe*'s 'Columbia' (one of Ed's favourites) came out of Oasis attempting to jam an acid-house track; the lyrics to 'Live Forever' are quite ravey. 'Maybe you're the same as me/We'll see things they'll never see' and then the eponymous chorus rises anthemically.

By coincidence, Tom and Ed had been students at Manchester University in the late '80s and had been at the same clubs as Noel. When Oasis first arrived on the scene, they recognised him as a face from there: 'There was a sort of familiarity in the experiences we'd shared,' said Ed. They saw Oasis play Glastonbury in June 1994 (their first ever; they went as punters) and, said Ed, 'hearing "Live Forever" for the first time in that field was something else . . .' There was a kinship. Oasis, though they certainly didn't make dance music, had a similar energy within their audience, built around the 'we', the communal experience of being together and hearing music that moved you. The arms aloft and arms around sensation of singing and dancing your heart out with everyone else. In fact, *Definitely Maybe* was reviewed in dance-music magazine *Mixmag*, by Dom Phillips, on the grounds that it was spiritually a dance record. He gave it 10 out of 10.

Tom and Ed – 'nice middle-class kids', 'spiritual brothers' – met as medieval history students at Manchester Uni in 1989. Ed came from south London, Tom from near Henley-on-Thames. In

time-honoured fashion, they recognised each other as music lovers just by how they were dressed. Ed had a selection of surfing T-shirts, as he'd spent a year in Australia; Tom 'looked like a proper raver', remembered Ed later. 'Green trousers, proper curtain bob haircut, Chevignon top.' Almost immediately, they started going to clubs together – the Haçienda, Most Excellent – and hanging out at Eastern Bloc record shop, where DJ Justin Robertson worked.

In their second year, Tom and Ed lived with others in a big house-share at 237 Dickenson Road, between Longsight and Rusholme. One of their housemates was part of a Freedom to Party rave crew and would sometimes bring back friends for an after-party; the house acquired a bit of a raving reputation, and the people who lived there were nicknamed the 237 Turbo Nutters. Its fame spread so much that, on one Saturday night, while they were watching *Blind Date*, New Order's Bernard Sumner turned up on their doorstep with a load of scally mates, looking for a party. They were excited to recognise him, but had to tell him, correctly, that there wasn't a party going on. Bernard said, 'Well, fuck off then, you wurzels,' and marched off.

Manchester is a huge student town, and was, even then: the University, plus Manchester Poly, Salford University, UMIST (science and technology), the Royal Northern College of Music, and more. Though locals always took the mickey out of students, if they were interested in music, they were seen as all right. The Haçienda DJs were from all over the place: as well as Mancunians like Mike Pickering, there was Dave Haslam, originally from Birmingham; Aberdonian Graeme Park; Greg Wilson, from

Merseyside. Some, like Dave and Justin Robertson, would come to Manchester as students and end up staying on.

Justin was from Walton-on-Thames, south-west of London. He spotted something in Tom and Ed that chimed with him, another southern boy with his own take on the Manchester scene. In 1992, he gave them a DJ slot (as 237 Turbo Nutters) at his club Naked Under Leather. After a bit, they ran out of noisy tracks to play – they liked songs with sirens in them – and started to make their own. They didn't want to make cold bleepy dance tracks, but something more wild and alive. 'We always want a human element,' said Tom, 'and we're inspired by the more experimental music that hippies produced in the '60s and '70s.' Ed: 'We want our music to be challenging, but also to get through to people. When you listen to it, you feel that something is being expressed.'

They changed their DJ name to The Dust Brothers, in homage to their favourite producers of the Beastie Boys and Beck, and made a track, 'Song to the Siren', that sampled This Mortal Coil's 'Song to the Siren'. (And yes, there was a siren on it, along with whooshing noises and a bumpy hip-hop beat.) They pressed 500 white labels and took their record around various London record shops, but no one picked it up, because it was deemed too slow (111 bpm). No one, that is, except the ultimate arbiter of dance-floor taste, Sabresonic's Andrew Weatherall. He loved 'Song to the Siren', and got Junior Boys Own to release it, so he could do a remix.

Tom and Ed moved to London. They remixed Tom's own band, Ariel, as well as others: The Charlatans, Leftfield, the Manics. Tom soon stopped Ariel and in August 1994, around the same

time as their Albany slot, he and Ed started making their first album, *Exit Planet Dust*. By October, they were fully immersed, and 'stayed up solidly for three weeks' to finish it. In early 1995, they changed their name to The Chemical Brothers, after 'Chemical Beats', their signature track: the frenzied, knobbly, squelchy round and round of it.

Exit Planet Dust came out in June 1995. Shortly before it did, in an interview with *Muzik*, Ed (slightly uncharacteristically) said he didn't think that anyone from the dance world had made an album like it, one that reflected the times. 'Why is that?' he wondered. 'Why is it left to a group like Oasis to express the way that young people want to go out and get battered every weekend? That's what The Chemical Brothers are about.'

In 1995, Tom and Ed were at Glastonbury, in a hospitality tent backstage, and bumped into Noel Gallagher. Noel immediately said he wanted to be on one of their tracks; they'd already featured Tim from The Charlatans, on 'Life Is Sweet', and Noel said, 'Why are you getting him to sing on your tracks, why aren't you asking me?' So in September, when they'd made the backing track for 'Setting Sun', they got hold of Noel's number, called him up about it and sent him round a tape of a rough version. He put it on after a long night. 'All these mad noises whooshing about for six minutes,' he remembered. 'All the girls I was with at the time were shouting, "Fucking hell, turn it off!"' Noel didn't; he kept playing it, over and over.

He did the vocals very quickly, popping into the Chemicals' studio on the way to a Manchester City match against Wycombe Wanderers. It was the first time he'd sung on a song (it was pre-'Don't Look Back in Anger'), but he didn't think about it too

long, just sang the words, some of which he'd written for an Oasis tune but never used. The lyrics are perfect; there's a slight darkness about them that recalls the heart-thumping peak of a long night out, the full juddering brain-pinch where you think, yep, it's coming on strong, I'm not sure I can handle thisssss . . . and then, the intensity somehow lessons, and you do.

After he left, Tom and Ed stayed up all night finishing the track. When it was done, they drove round to Noel's place, in Camden, intending to drop it off, but it was too early. They could have popped the tape through the letterbox, but they decided to wait until he was up. ('I suppose we just wanted to go round to Noel Gallagher's house, that felt like quite a big thing,' said Ed later.) They ended up sitting in Ed's car until they saw signs of life in the house, then rang the doorbell and Noel let them in. He gave the track the thumbs up; and that was that.

They released it without much fanfare. No special formats: just vinyl or CD. Noel didn't want to detract from the track, so didn't have his picture taken or give any interviews. The Chemicals did – they got an *NME* cover story – but in the feature, they come across as they are: not shy, but unwilling to be sold as personalities. (They call themselves 'backroom boys' and have always, from 1994 onwards, used visuals when they play live, as opposed to DJ'ing. They knew they wanted something to provide the live stimulation – whether oil-blob projections or huge reality-bending, state-of-the-art, out-into-the-audience bedazzlement – so that they didn't have to speak or perform on stage.) The Chemical Brothers weren't quite no promo, but there certainly wasn't blanket coverage of the release.

Which makes it even madder that 'Setting Sun' went in at Number One. The week before, the utterly forgettable 'Breakfast at Tiffany's' by Deep Blue (who?) had been in the top spot. The week after, it was Boyzone with 'Words'; the week after that, The Spice Girls got their second Number One with 'Say You'll Be There'. How did 'Setting Sun' do it? Hide itself among the radio-friendly fodder to pop up and take the prize? It's like the Wolf of Gysinge snuck in and won a cutest puppy competition. Even with Noel on vocals, it still seems outrageous. But it happened. Like a rip in the pop-time continuum, when the smiles and the formation dancing are torn asunder, to reveal the pulsating, snarling panic monster that was there all along.

The video for 'Setting Sun' also revealed hidden scary secrets. I remember seeing it on *Top of the Pops*, and thinking: How is that allowed? Directed by Dom and Nic, it's a full-on depiction of the peaks and troughs of an ecstasy-fuelled night. Tom and Ed only appear briefly, at the start and the end, picking up their record box, checking on a young woman, who's asleep on the ground. In between, we see her both in and out of an outdoor rave; before, during and after. At first, she's at home watching TV (it's showing protests against the Criminal Justice Bill), relaxing, though there are snap-cuts to something else, speeding through a forest, through London (is it her? did this happen?), until suddenly, there she is, her actual self, at her own front door, coming in. It's her, but she's in red, she's grinning like the devil and her pupils are enormous. Our girl has met herself coming back, and she's instantly inside her flashback, reliving the jagged memories of the night before, the strobes, the flickering, the shadows, everyone dancing,

everything fast and slow at once. Like the track, it's exhilarating. And sort of terrifying.

Big nights out have always been hectic; always gone on longer than expected; always encompassed random people met on the way; always been life-changing. But big nights out changed hugely at the end of the 1980s, when house music and – especially – ecstasy arrived in the UK. Previously, the drugs available to keep you going were booze, hash, speed, poppers, maybe acid. Only rich people had cocaine. Heroin was for druggies. Ecstasy changed that, by offering something completely new: a drug that made you want to dance for a long time and made you feel as though everyone was your friend. The nights out got longer. The vibe changed. Ecstasy swept through like wildfire. One week, you were hopping up and down to the music you liked, sitting out the tracks you didn't. A few weeks later, all the records seemed to merge seamlessly into one, and everyone in the club danced from start to finish.

And it brought together a lot of different types of people. Some came from soul, or latin, or funk, people who were already out for the dancing as well as the music; but as well as them, there was the indie crowd. A huge amount of people who grew up on The Smiths, New Order, The Jesus and Mary Chain, tried ecstasy and raving one night and thought, That's it, I'm never going back. Somehow watching The Family Cat at the Camden Falcon no longer appeals. I know many people like this.

Manchester – perhaps because it had The Haçienda – managed to adopt dance music into its indie-band culture for a little while, with Happy Mondays and, especially, The Stone Roses. In 1990, The Roses' 'Fools Gold' took over everywhere, and brought even

the indie stalwarts, the don't-look-at-me fringe-shakers, onto the dancefloor.

It would be easy to see Britpop, a few years later, as a reaction against this, as much against dance music as it was against grunge. Was it the last gasp of the 1960s ideal of white male pop bands? The final hoorah of the 'one-two-three-four', a retrospective U-turn towards a time that was passing? Yes, partly. But only partly. Because plenty of indie artists had left part of their brain somewhere in a field in Hampshire, or found themselves stumbling from a disused warehouse at 9 a.m. on a Sunday. And, even if the sound of those nights didn't translate, the dynamics and the democracy fed back in. The attitude changed. The most important aspect of acid house was the idea that everybody is and can be a star (also a punk idea). Not just swishy individuals with shoulder pads and intense rock expressions. But people you knew, people with ideas.

It worked the other way around, too. After a few years' raving, there were those who wanted the big night out, the all-together up-till-morning where-shall-we-go-next adventure, but they also wanted some personality. Some hectic, scratchy, memorable tunes, rather than perfectly mixed smooth Chicago house tracks or anonymous Italo-piano Euro versions. More bass, less treble. Or at least, more of a riff, a tune to latch onto. Something heavier. The squelch, the build, the peak, the drop.

Because everyone has other sounds stuck firm in their memories. Not just The Beatles and The Stones, not just 1980s UK post-punk alternative music, not even just disco, but also the first time you ever heard Public Enemy. The first time you ever heard

Never Mind the Bollocks, Here's the Sex Pistols, '(You Gotta) Fight for Your Right (To Party)', maybe even AC/DC's *Back in Black*. The 'waaaarrrgghhhh' in your brain that needs to come out somehow. The screaming adrenaline. The Noise.

That abandon, that release. Sometimes it seemed like The Chemical Brothers manifested the sound that looped inside your bad head, and played it out loud so you could feel better.

There were a lot of inter-friendship connections that crossed in The Social, which meant that I thought it lasted for a while: maybe eighteen months, a couple of years. But no. It was just thirteen weeks at The Albany: 7 August until 30 October 1994. It had to end, because 'it was an explosion', says Robin Turner. 'It was an incredible thing. It was hard to keep that lightning in a bottle.' After it stopped there, the club moved around; at one point it was at The Sun & 13 Cantons; at another it was at Smithfield's. Eventually, The Chemicals started a residency at Turnmills in Farringdon.

Now, of course, The Chemical Brothers don't DJ as much as they used to, though they do occasionally, at Glastonbury. But they do play live. And when they do, it's a total overwhelm, as though you go into an entirely new world and emerge, stunned, wrung out, two hours later, your brain reset. Your body is young but your mind is very old. Or, these days, the other way round.

Up With the Kids

SUPERGRASS
'Alright'

What a thing to do, to write a pop song so sunny and upbeat, so packed full of hooks and joy, that it doesn't only make people sing along and jump up and down like happy Labradors on a trampoline, it does something more. It catches a mood, and then takes that mood – which is daft optimism, blue-skied afternoons, the future unrolling out in front of you like the longest ever August bank holiday weekend – and gives it never-ending life, to fill you up, over and over. Supergrass's 'Alright' is the bubbles from a bubble gun, your head out of a car window, the long sweep down a hill on the back of someone's scooter, that time you laughed so hard from smoking weed that you flipped over the back of the blow-up sofa and somehow landed in a perfect Spider-Man crouch. It's the sun in The Kinks' 'Lazy Sunday Afternoon', the pop in M's 'Pop Musik'. Listen to that bang-along pub piano, that mickey-take Hawaiian steel guitar riff. Smoke a fag? Put it out. Keep your teeth? Nice and clean. Your kids love this song and so does your nan. Everybody loves 'Alright'.

And everybody loved Supergrass. They were The Monkees minus one (he was there, on keyboards, but he was a bit older and

didn't fit in, looks-wise. Sorry, Rob). Or maybe The Beatles minus one, especially as drummer Danny Goffey had Paul McCartney's huge dark eyes. They were, as they declared themselves, 'everyone's second favourite band'. You could draw battle lines over Blur or Oasis, wear a Fred Perry or a bucket hat as your armour, stand opposite each other singing 'Country House' and 'Roll With It' for days, and then, at the end, all play football in no man's land while *I Should Coco* booms out from start to finish. The 'Grass united everyone. They were entirely lovable.

The trio of Gaz Coombes, Mick Quinn and Danny formed from the ashes of indie-schmindie group The Jennifers and rubbish jobs in Oxford. Their neon-bright tunes smashed straight into your still-teenage heart and they looked like they loved their lives, far too young and daft and cute for adult angst. In 1994, when they had their first hit, Gaz was eighteen. He and Danny had met at Wheatley Comp: their older brothers were mates, and Rob (yes, keyboards Rob) asked fifteen-year-old Danny to keep an eye out for thirteen-year-old Gaz, who was getting picked on, mostly because he was so darn pretty that other boys called him girly. Plus, his family (mum, dad and four boys; he's the third) had moved to Oxford from San Francisco, when Gaz was eleven, so he was a bit of an outsider. Danny, tall, also girly, also a bit of an outsider (he'd moved to Oxford when he was thirteen), but armed with a group of mates, understood Gaz. They formed a band, The Jennifers, when Gaz was fifteen. I'd say that Gaz grew his sideburns in celebration, but they were already bushed to the max.

The Jennifers weren't great, though they attracted the attention of Saul Galpern's Nude Records. When they disbanded, Gaz and

Danny continued as housemates, living in a tip house on the Cowley Road with, intrepid journalists noted, fake boobs in the fireplace. Danny worked as a dinner lady (dinner laddy), and Gaz's mum made him get a job too, so he started doing kitchen shifts at the local Harvester. He'd play Jennifers' tapes over the PA system before the restaurant opened. Mick, a little older than Gaz and Danny, born of Australian parents, was also working there. He was surprised to see Gaz doing a job: in Oxford, The Jennifers were seen as a success, and every time they played locally, all the cool cats turned up. Surely such a popstar shouldn't be replenishing an all-you-can-eat salad bar? Sadly, though, The Jennifers were soon Done-ifers. Soon after, Mick popped over to the fake boob house for a jamming session, and ace new band Theodore Supergrass (Danny's name) was formed. Usefully, they got rid of the Theodore before they got famous.

As soon as Supergrass started playing together, the songs poured out of them. They spoke the same language, when it came to music: had similar references (The Beatles, David Bowie, T-Rex, Madness, Buzzcocks, even Led Zep), similar loves, told similar musical jokes. They all moved into a row of hippy houses a little outside Oxford, landed the same management as Radiohead and signed to Parlophone (like Radiohead). Then they banged out an album, and it was a belter. And then another, and likewise. And yep, once again. You might think you only know one Supergrass song, but actually, you know loads. From 1994 onwards, they released cracker-jack single after crackerjack single, each track packed with melody and loveable lines, instantly familiar without being corny, punched straight through, no messing and out. They had the pop knack.

'Alright' was the last single from their debut 1993 album *I Should Coco*, which also gave the world the tempo-changing 'Mansize Rooster', the heavy-rifferama 'Lenny' and their first single, 'Caught by the Fuzz', where Gaz adopts a silly mockney accent and tells the real-life story of him spending the night in a police cell when he was fifteen. He was a passenger in a car that was stopped by the 'fuzz', so he put his hash down his pants. Unfortunately, said hash was in a little metal tin, and when he got out of the car to talk to the police, the tin descended down his trouser leg and hit the pavement with a loud 'clink'. 'What's that, son?' wondered the policeman. Soon after, young Gaz found himself under arrest – I imagine him lifted up by the copper by his collar so his legs are running in the air – then chucked in the back of a van and taken to the police station to be banged up in a cell for the night. His mother came and got him in the morning, as the deadpan lyrics describe. 'Here comes my mum, well, she knows what I've done.'

When you write about Supergrass at this time, it's almost impossible not to make them seem like cartoons. Their life played out like a comic strip. They lived next door to each other, like *Coronation Street* characters or The Beatles in *Help!* They all matched, with dark, heavy eyebrows and madly expressive faces. They sang about the joys and trials of teenage life, but teenage life as imagined by an eight-year-old Bash Street Kid. They looked like popstars, especially Gaz, but they also looked like your little brother who came in from football and staged a raid on your wardrobe, clomped about in your stack heels and fur coats while you were out. They larked around and cheesy-grinned and did stupid formation dances in their videos, which were mostly made

by Danny's older brother Nick and his friend, collectively known as Dom and Nic.

The videos did a lot to establish Supergrass as what we might call a brand. Fast cuts, sharp editing, close-ups on shiny teeth, an eyebrow raise, eyes flicked sideways, cute what-can-you-do? expressions. You could imagine Supergrass scrumping apples and then running away from an angry gardener to the sound of a *Tom and Jerry* 'scarper' noise. They didn't only make these sorts of videos – the one for 'Lenny' is far more opium-bohemian, 'Lose It' is just a gig vid – but the ones for 'Mansize Rooster' and 'Alright' pitched them like an advert, or the opener to a madcap TV series. So much so that Steven Spielberg invited them over to LA for a meeting, because he thought they would be brilliant in a Monkees-style TV show. They went, and chatted to him about *Twilight Zone* episodes, but didn't take him up on his offer.

The canny timing of the release of 'Alright' – their record company held it back until 3 July because they knew it could be big – meant that it landed, pow, at the start of the long hot summer of 1995. The summer of 1995 was a particular time, not only in the year, but in the decade. It was a warm one; the hottest since 1976, which for anyone then in their mid-twenties had been the stuff of legends. The 1976 summer had been the 'phew what a scorcher' summer, the 'hotter than Honolulu as we hit the roaring '90s' summer', the sixteen consecutive days over thirty degrees summer. Such things might be more common now in our climate-changed world, but in the 1970s, in the UK, hot weather was a big deal. If you were a child at that time, you remembered 1976 as the greatest year ever. So almost twenty years later, in an era that

seemed to recall some of the best parts of that same childhood – the chopper bikes, the Adidas tracksuits, the T-shirts with slogans, the larks – the hot weather was also joining in with the fun. And even if you were too young to remember anything of the '70s, it was sunny, and that makes everything better.

It wasn't that everyone was exactly reliving the golden holidays of childhood – some people, like Supergrass, were only just out of those days – but there were enough little reminders for your twenties to share some of that kiddy carefree-dom. Breakfast telly was like kids TV; the Beastie Boys' 'Sabotage' was homemade 1970s cop shows; Pulp referenced *Jackie*'s photo love stories; Blur's 'Parklife' video was more 'Alright' than 'Alright'. In a couple of months, Blur's 'Country House' would tick off 'Mousetrap', Benny Hill, 'Bohemian Rhapsody' and *Carry On* . . .

One of the feelings of that summer, when Pulp headlined Glastonbury's Pyramid Stage and Blur played Mile End Stadium and Oasis played Irvine Beach, was a sort of 'blimey, we're winning' feeling. When Prodigy and Elastica and Supergrass played the Other Stage and Massive Attack, Portishead and Tricky played too, and bleached, spiky, gurning Robbie Williams, recently freed from Take That, was everywhere trying to join in, somewhere among the usual pills and thrills and bellyaches of a festival weekend, there was a feeling of a mini-takeover. Like you were watching your mates sneak into a posh do and stage a bun fight at the top table. How was this all happening? How did the offbeat outsiders become the most popular people in the land? If you took enough drugs, it could seem like a benign conspiracy.

But what had actually happened was that the bouncers had changed. Not at Glastonbury, which, as ever, was simply booking the acts that everyone wanted. Its wide-ranging music policy and physical space was large enough, even then, to accommodate the established and the up-and-coming. As well as the bolshy upstarts, there were plenty of older bands: on the Sunday night of this exciting Britpop year, the Pyramid hosted Page and Plant, Simple Minds and The Cure (who were always great at Glastonbury).

Elsewhere, though, there had been a power shift. A clear-out in the management layers above everyone's heads. In 1990, Planet 24, an independent production company owned by Bob Geldof, an old punk who knew the power of youth culture, had made a strong move into TV. First it created *The Word*, a Friday night late-night loopy explosion of a show that showcased a lot of brilliant new bands including Nirvana and Oasis (it lasted until March 1995). And then, in 1992, Geldof's company created *The Big Breakfast*. Channel 4's live daily early morning show was bright and youthful and silly and laddy and occasionally featured music guests. (In the early days, host Chris Evans interviewed Blur's Damon and Alex and called Damon first David, and then Damian.) It wasn't really anything to do with pop, but it was, you might say, a vibe.

A year later, in 1993, Matthew Bannister became controller of Radio 1 and immediately set about sacking the cheesiest of its ''ello my lovely' DJs, and replaced them with people like Mark and Lard and Zoë Ball. This caused huge ructions and resulted in the hilarious flouncing of 'Hairy Cornflake' Dave Lee Travis live on air. And in 1994, Ric Blaxhill took over as head of *Top of the Pops*

and started to include bands who were just outside the Top 40, as long as they agreed to play live. He had guest presenters, too, so the show was introduced by, variously: Jarvis, Damon, Justine, Louise Wener, Kylie Minogue, Keith Allen, Lily Savage, Vic and Bob, PJ and Duncan (aka Ant and Dec), Julian Cope, East 17. (Oh and, oops, Gary Glitter.) It wasn't just that these new bands were breaking through, it was that the new gatekeepers understood that if you want young people to watch or listen or get excited about your shows, then you need to let those young people and their idols (their friends) into the party.

Even scrappy upstart men's magazine *Loaded*, launched in 1994 and an instant success, was the result of James Brown, an *NME* writer, making a magazine with publisher Alan Lewis, also an ex-music writer who'd launched *Kerrang!*, *Sounds* and *Vox*. If Alan hadn't supported James, then his football-music-girls manifesto just wouldn't have happened. And all these background manoeuvres, none of which we considered for a minute at the time, meant that the doors to the VIP room were a little bit more ajar than they were before. If you pushed hard enough, they might open. You just needed determination, and enough of you to keep the pressure up. Like the entrance to a rave, like the fence around a festival. In 1995, 20,000 people got into Glastonbury for free. 'Me and my friends just shook the fence till it fell over and we all climbed in,' said one intrepid festival goer. A rush and a push and the land is ours.

I was once in a small car – a Fiat Panda – when my husband drove it straight into a multi-storey car park barrier (by mistake). I'd always believed that those barriers were made of metal. But

when the bantam-weight Panda hit that striped single arm, bunny-hopped into it at a speed of, ooh, 15 mph, the barrier buckled immediately, gave way like soggy cardboard, like a joke. 1995 was a time when all the pretend metal barriers gave way.

Glastonbury was pretty open then. You'd see travellers bombing about in Mad Max-ed Land Rovers, actually in the festival, driving through the crowd in front of the Pyramid Stage. If you bagged a backstage pass (pretty easy: we passed them between each other), then you could camp there too, and there was a lot of room in what was, essentially, just a big field between the Pyramid and the Other Stage. On one occasion, I remember a helicopter landing in that backstage field, bobbing down to drop off its VIP cargo (Peter Gabriel? The Levellers? Goats Don't Shave?) among all of us liggers. It was acid jazz poncho kings Galliano. I often think that can't be right: but I remember it.

And, in 1995, Supergrass arrived at Glastonbury in a helicopter, landing not backstage, but in a field towards the back, to be greeted by Jo Whiley and a Channel 4 crew. Channel 4 was covering the festival for the second year ever with presenters Mark Kermode, Mark Lamarr, Jo Whiley and Marijne from Salad haphazardly talking to musicians, stall-holders from the Green Fields, and many willing but bewildered punters. 'There's just so many people,' the punters kept saying, as they trudged in to find somewhere to camp. Jo Whiley tried her best with Supergrass but what was there for these new young heroes to say, other than, 'Hi, we're here'?

Supergrass were playing on Friday afternoon on the *NME* stage, a perfect spot. Partly because the crowd is still fairly un-raddled and up for a good time, but also because, after they've played, they

could mooch around the festival all weekend. They came on wearing paper masks of The Stone Roses – 'We made it in the end!' shouted Danny/John Squire – and then launched into an early version of 'Going Out', a track not even on *I Should Coco*. Its psychedelic punch sprung them into their *Coco* set which they banged through – 'Alright' sitting pretty in the middle – plus a couple of cover versions. *Select* magazine gave their performance 9 out of 10. The next week, *I Should Coco* went from Number Three to Number One.

Channel 4's Glastonbury coverage is hilarious, if you look at it now. Katie Puckrik struggling to get sense out of Saint Etienne's Pete Wiggs in a caravan, Mark Lamarr rude to pretty much everyone, Jo Whiley a bit too shy to get to grips with the more macho interviewees. The gap between TV Glastonbury and actual Glastonbury is vast these days (no red button can bring you the mania of the train-track cut-through between 1 and 2 a.m. on a Saturday night), but even then, what was shown on TV had nothing to do with what it was like being there. Still, it was great PR, both for the festival and for the bands. Supergrass got their Number One; Orbital and Prodigy were recognised as amazing live acts; Jarvis became everyone's favourite and 'Common People' a national anthem.

But cameras will always bland out real life. They suck the air out of an atmosphere. TV cameras do it one way, mobile phones another. How can you lose yourself in a moment when you're worried that someone might snap a picture of you looking terrible? You can't even lose your friends. You'd have to run down your battery to enjoy the best part of Glastonbury: the lost hours spent

wandering around after 2.30 a.m., talking cosmic politics with people powering generators through cycling on the spot, wondering if that actually is a flying hippo floating above the Joe Bananas stall, meeting a man with a duck, bartering for a blanket coat. Until you bump back into your friends in the Green Fields at 5 a.m., and hug them like you've not seen them for a decade, just as the dawn is breaking.

At the time, it was generally thought that the only thing Supergrass didn't have, quite, were three cartoon personalities to match their three cute video characters. But then, who could? Underneath the cheeky scamp videos was a messier, more stoner background. The little houses they all lived in were close to Gaz's parents' house, and they were less Beatles movie pads and more hippy-go-lucky squats with ex-army guys, a few dealers and a doctor (!) also living there. The doors were always open. Anyone could crash. Gaz was fifteen when he started hanging out there; his parents were a bit worried.

Once they hit success, Gaz found aspects of his new life bewildering. Though phenomenally talented and stop-the-traffic good-looking, he was naturally shy and, on occasion, quite baffled by some of the things he was required to do as part of his job. A friend of mine interviewed the band for the teen girl mag *Sugar*, and said that Gaz just couldn't get his head around the questions. (An example of a later question from *Smash Hits*: 'You're famous for looking like monkeys. Has Will Young stolen your thunder?') He didn't join in with the bitchery and competition of Britpop – none of the band did, to be fair – returning to Oxford and his long-term girlfriend between tours.

Mick was seven years older than Gaz, and he, too, would go back to Oxford quite a bit. In 1995, just as success came to swallow them up, he and his girlfriend had their first child, so he was rooted, sorted, uninclined to join parties.

Which left Danny. Danny fulfilled the cartoon remit. 'Danny from Supergrass' was here, there and everywhere, popping up at other people's gigs, retiring to a hotel room with a member of Shampoo, becoming matey with Keith Richards, just because. Happy-go-lucky and, indeed, just lucky, Danny was the type of person, as Mick said later, to fall out of a window and land on a passerby, then get up and walk off. (Mick, in contrast, fell out of a window when he was sleepwalking, smashed his vertebrae and his heel.) Attracting the A-listers simply by being himself all day and all of the night, popping up to bring the good times, seemingly without the post good times' Fear. He was more flippant and casual about the publicity aspect of the job, so he was better at it; though, of course, he was the drummer, so that made it easier.

When he was twenty-one, Danny met twenty-five-year-old Pearl Lowe, aka 'Pearl from Powder'. Pearl was the singer in Powder, a smaller Britpop-esque band that formed in 1994. He saw her backstage at a festival wearing huge sunglasses and thought she looked like 'a broken bird'; she liked his infectious carefree optimism. By early 1996, Pearl was pregnant, so in 1997, Danny moved out of the house with Gaz and in with Pearl in London. Soon 'Danny Supergrass' and 'Pearl Powder' had hopped on the Britpop party coach, travelled through *Trainspotting* picking up passengers, and parked in Primrose Hill, the centre of the more public, more paparazzi Cool Britannia era, where a lot of extremely attractive

people with money and connections all partied together, with varied addiction and tabloid consequences.

The tabloids weren't really bothered about the music aspect of Britpop, but they loved the celebrity side, the 'Primrose Hill set' of Noel Gallagher, Meg Mathews, Kate Moss, Sadie Frost, Jude Law. Danny and Pearl were part of it all – simultaneously enjoying and hating the attention – until it all became too much and they retreated into the countryside, where Pearl got sober. The strangest legacy from that time? Underneath the newspaper noise and the all-night-all-day furore, Danny and Pearl were a sweet married couple.

Still, their early lifestyle caused tensions. During the recording of Supergrass's second album, *In It For The Money*, Danny kept disappearing to play with Lodger, the band he and Pearl formed. There were interviews where it seemed as though Gaz was having a pop at Danny's lifestyle, and 'Going Out' sounds as though he might have been. But Supergrass continued, playing blistering gigs, writing Top Ten singles, taking the weird life of a successful Britpop band in their flared corduroy strides. The most admirable aspect of Supergrass is how each of them managed to have a settled family life, with kids and partners, while being in a band that took off in a way that they could never have prepared for. Most bands can't do it.

I Should Coco was a million-seller, and the fastest selling debut album on Parlophone since The Beatles' *Please Please Me*. *In It For The Money* got to Number Two, and Supergrass continued to release bangers until, in 2010, while working on their sixth album, *Release the Drones*, they found they couldn't really be in a studio

with each other any more. The easy musical understanding had gone. *Release the Drones* was never finished. 'It just sort of fizzled a bit, really,' Danny said. 'We never really fell out massively.' They all got on with other musical projects: Gaz launched a successful solo career; Mick joined various bands and is now playing with Swervedriver; Danny formed his own band, Vangoffey, as well as playing the odd gig with Babyshambles.

In 2019, Supergrass got back together for their twenty-fifth anniversary, to play some hugely successful gigs, despite multiple Covid disruptions. They're all still happily married; all still love their kids; all still play music and enjoy their lives. Our cartoon caperers, everyone's second favourite band, are Britpop survivors. And we can all be happy about that.

Raveheart

THE PRODIGY
'Firestarter'

If you ever want an insight into the pure animal energy bubbling within every toddler, the true crunk spirit that fuels their frustrated tantrums and ramps up their system-smashing desires, then just play 'Firestarter', really loud. And then louder than that. Watch the change as the track does exactly what it says it will do. It lights the fire inside. See the child's eyes widen. Witness the unnamed power hurtle through their whole body, wonder as it slams into their brain, punches into their tiny, enormous soul, winds their limbs into action and sets them free. They go nuts. They can't stop themselves. 'Firestarter' is the strongest of toddler cocaine. It's wild.

To be honest, 'Firestarter' often has the same effect on adults. It's that pendulum swing between the kick-drum crashes, whomp! in after the breakbeat, then whomp! again; it's the queasiness of the siren guitar, that weird drony whine all the way through. It's the growled and shouted lyrics. Suddenly every resentment, every disappointment, all your rage, your hurt, your shame and self-loathing . . . they're going to smash out in some physical manner,

possibly stamping your feet and gurning so you show your bottom teeth. Why has life treated you like this? Why doesn't anybody understand the extreme pain of existence? Release the headbanging Hulk inside! You could try this at the next dinner party you go to. Just change the playlist during a lull.

Maybe you're too tired to release your inner monster. So why not sit on the sofa while someone else acts it out for you? Meet Keith Flint. Keith is sporting a double mohawk and a lot of eyeliner. He's wearing a stars-and-stripes jumper, some bleached jean shorts, a chain around his throat, a strange expression in his eyes. He looks: clownish, confrontational, comical, camp. Like a brilliant comic-book villain.

The black-and-white video for 'Firestarter', filmed in the disused Aldwych Tube station, took twelve hours to film, and it's centred around our extreme anti-hero Keith. He bangs his head down with the drum kick, waggles his pierced tongue, holds his arms out and jerks his hands back, in the internationally understood sign for 'come on then, let's 'ave it'. He runs at the camera, jumps off the walls, twitches, shakes, spasms. He slaps his head as though trying to stop the churning thoughts inside. He takes an angle-grinder to the train rails. At certain points, he's suspended, flinching, on flimsy ribbons, looking like a pissed-off spider. At others, he's next to Liam, who's pacing quietly in jumper and jeans. Liam looks at him quizzically; like he's the parent and Keith is a hyped-up child. As I said, all toddlers can relate.

When Keith was small, he used to play his music – Madness or Gary Numan – really loud in his bedroom and then chuck himself around, exactly as he does in the 'Firestarter' video. His

parents would come up and tell him to stop, but he couldn't, really. Often the only way he could was to bang his head on the wall. It was what the music did to him, what it was for. It released the inchoate rage inside.

Keith's vocals for 'Firestarter' were the first time he'd ever picked up a mic and performed on a track. They came about because Liam decided that the track he was working on – which he'd thought was an instrumental – perhaps needed a voice. The track was made in Liam's usual manner: nicking and warping, turning the old into something completely new. He nabbed the 'Hey hey hey' from The Art of Noise's 'Close to the Edit'; the drums from Ten City's 'Devotion'; the guitar drone from The Breeders' 'SOS' mangled into an unsettling wail, a call to action before the beats crash in. As with so many of The Prodigy's tracks, you can hear the hip-hop inside. Keith turned up at the studio. He said: 'If I was ever going to do a vocal, this is the track I would do it on.'

The lyrics are Keith's and they *are* Keith. He wrote loads on the spot; Liam picked out the ones that worked. Liam on Keith: '"I'm the self-inflicted mind detonator", that's him. He'll build things up in his head until he's on the verge of going mad'. 'Self-inflicted' and 'I'm the bitch you hated' were the words that meant the most to Keith. Self-loathing amped up into a statement of intent that includes everyone who's listening ('*You're* the Firestarter/Twisted Firestarter'); a sad and furious zombie's 'who's with me?' war cry. A few years later, Eminem would snapshot a similar feeling, though more lightly; he said there were a million just like him 'who cuss like me, who don't give a fuck like me, who dress like me, walk, talk and act like me'. When asked what the emotion was that he

was trying to conjure with his music, Liam said: 'Just a ten-ton weight dropping.'

Keith described what it was like to finally hold the microphone, rather than just dance to Liam's music. He said: 'For six years, I've been using my body to shout. Now, I've still got the body language, but I've also got the mic, so I've got the actual ARRRGGH!' He also said: 'What you see in "Firestarter" happens inside me even if I'm on the Tube. If I'm sitting there . . . I dance without moving my body.' The fire was constantly raging inside him.

On 18 March 1996, 'Firestarter' went straight in at Number One. The Prodigy refused to perform it on *Top of the Pops*, knowing that their video would have to be shown instead. It was. There were a lot of complaints and the BBC didn't show it again. This was because it might make kids scared. I only realised this recently. For decades, I thought it was banned because it might make kids riot.

Like many people my age, I've seen The Prodigy play so many times I've lost count; from 1993 onwards, they rampaged through every festival going, whether rock, dance, alternative, pop-friendly. Glastonbury, Reading, Phoenix, T In the Park, Tribal Gathering, Roskilde. They performed live almost constantly, moving from dance clubs in 1991 quickly through to established rock venues like Brixton Academy. Between 1992 and 1997, they played 575 gigs. Only Blur, Radiohead and Garbage played more.

By the mid-'90s, their shows were honed into a guaranteed good time: banger after banger, delivered loud and scary, like a mash-up between a circus and a panto, with a full-on guts-out rock attitude that no other dance acts, no matter how popular, could deliver. The

Prodigy were as far from two anonymous blokes behind a bank of synths as Motörhead. Live, they usually had a guitarist (at a certain point this was Gizz Butt (*sic*): a blond and spiky Billy Idol lookalike who threw poses as well as wielding his guitar). Later, they added a drummer too. Liam Howlett was centre stage towards the back, behind his keyboards, dancing all the time. Maxim stalked around, staring out the crowd, delivering his vocals with *Mad Max* menace. And Keith and Leeroy Thornhill were amazing. Not back-up dancers, front-up dancers: driving everyone into a frenzy, performing Liam's music with their entire selves. Leeroy, tall, thin and bendy, loose-limbed with quick Northern Soul-style feet; Keith shorter, swift-footed too, but with a bit of a wiggle; more dramatic, arms open, and face roaring or turned upwards to the sky. Keith covered more of the stage. You couldn't take your eyes off him.

Leeroy: 'What we do is the music unleashed. This is what the music makes me feel like.'

Maxim: 'I want people to go home thinking, Fucking hell what did I see . . . this black dude on stage, he had contacts in, gold fangs and he was freaking me out.'

Liam: 'As far as I'm concerned, Keith is the best performer in Europe.'

The Prodigy always presented themselves as a band; though, actually, only Liam was signed to a record label (XL). He created all the music, and so, in '90s music-business thinking, Keith, Leeroy and Maxim were less important. Mere vibes merchants, along for the ride, sometimes accused by the music papers of being Bez times three. But that was to misunderstand how The Prodigy worked. For months before Liam got his record deal, they'd

performed as a foursome. They all had the same attitude, they all agreed about what The Prodigy was for (Liam: 'The main object is to stir people up . . . do something extreme in our field and get away with it on a big level'; Keith: 'The ethic behind it [is] to have the loudest beats, the best bass lines and the biggest sounds'). They all understood the mission: to take the hands-up-in-the-air everybody-in-the-place one-love approach of rave and combine it with the wild man constructs of rock to make something bigger, more tribal and transcendent; something of the crowd, but also full of band personality. In photos, they insisted that all four of them were pictured.

Let's take a look. There's Liam, the actual prodigy of the band's name, the teenager who started cutting and scratching in his bedroom as a kid, who won mixing competitions aged fifteen and turned that talent into making music. Keith, the long-haired, baggy-topped raver who warped himself into a neon-haired rebel ringmaster and festival crowd commander. Leeroy, the groove come to life, Keith's gangly mate from the rave days. Maxim, a reggae toaster who became a skirt-sporting, golden-toothed, cat-contact-lensed MC. Each one very different in personality and looks; each one entirely recognisable.

They looked like a band, and they were interviewed and, usually, photographed like a band. (Of the four, Keith was known for being the easiest to talk to.) Occasionally, they weren't, as with a notorious 1992 *Mixmag* cover which featured a solo picture of Liam holding a fake pistol to his own head, under the headline 'DID CHARLY KILL RAVE?' And, a few years later, in 1997, on the front of *The Face*, just Keith on his own, his mohawked head looming up from

a pink background. Both of these are now considered seminal among the small coterie of people who think very hard about 1990s magazine covers. But neither went down very well with the band.

Anyhow, those were just magazines. In real life, everyone knew The Prodigy as a band. They were treated like one on the live circuit; they looked like one in their videos. From around 1993, in Britain, they were festival gold. And in America, unlike almost every other UK band, they broke through, their 1996 'Firestarter' and *Fat of the Land* audience overlapping almost perfectly with a devil's-horn, bandana-and-complicated-boots metal crowd. The Prodigy were able to do what no other '90s British band did because they weren't arch, they weren't resentful; not grateful but not entitled either. They came, to use the parlance, to rock. There's not much difference between a Nine Inch Nails fan and a Prodigy fan, when you get to the US.

The most surprising thing about The Prodigy throughout the mid-'90s, though, was that they were still there at all. By rights, they should have disappeared around 1992, after they catapulted a series of catchy but maddening rave tracks into the Top Ten: 'Charly', 'Everybody in the Place', 'Fire' and 'Out of Space'. 'Charly', their 1991 hit which featured a talking cat from a 1970s public-service information film, didn't kill rave, but it should have killed The Prodigy. Their career path could well have been: 'Charly', then another silly track, possibly featuring Mary, Mungo and Midge, and out. Instead, 'Charly' launched a tiny sub-genre of silly children's TV rave tunes such as Shaft's 'Roobard and Custard', Urban Hype's 'A Trip to Trumpton' and Smart E's

'Sesame's Treet'. And Liam never made another track like it again. He was too talented and aware of what was going on in music to let that happen.

Still, though it demonstrated that Liam could create a brain-worm hook, 'Charly' was a daft entry into the charts, and later he said that, despite his love for acts like The Chemical Brothers, Orbital and Leftfield, he felt like they'd had an easier ride than The Prodigy, because they were never seen as naff. They were always cool. The Prodigy had to kill their old selves in order to succeed. 'Charly' had to be poisoned for them to make 'Poison'; then they burnt it all down again to get to 'Firestarter'.

Liam always knew how to hop between musical genres. From around 1986, he was part of a funky hip-hop outfit called Cut 2 Kill. He moved to London to make it, but didn't (the scene was too snobby for a cutting crew straight out of the suburbs), so, at eighteen, he returned to Braintree, Essex, where he'd grown up, and found himself slap in the centre of an absolutely bananas rave scene. He watched Adamski, N'Joi and Guru Josh play and thought, 'I could do this.' He'd already got a Roland W30 (it cost a grand; it took him a year to save the money), so he swapped making hip-hop for rave. Though, actually, hip-hop never really left him: throughout his career, no matter what genre the track, you can usually detect Liam's cutting-beats approach.

Keith and Leeroy went raving at the Barn in Braintree, and Keith would badger Liam to play tracks at after-club parties ('I'd be mangled off my head, saying, "Ah mate, play the one that goes "whoop whoop"!'). One day, Liam gave Keith a tape, with a mix on one side, and his own music on the other. Keith loved it, played

it to Leeroy, and told Liam, 'If you're going to do PAs, we're your dancers.' They roped in established reggae MC Maxim, and their first gig was at Labrynth, now demolished, a pub in east London where the owner told them he'd put a band on once before, but they'd been dragged off stage and beaten up. The Prodigy turned up at midday. They were on at 2 a.m. They smashed it.

Once they were signed, success came easily: 'Charly' went to Number Three, then 'Everybody in the Place', a track so of its time it's like a rave-doc theme tune, went to Number Two; 'Fire/Jericho' to Number 11. So far, so cheesy quaver. But the next single, 'Out of Space', which went to Five, is very different. It samples a popular Lee Perry-produced track, 'Chase the Devil', by Max Romeo and the Upsetters, and combines it with wreck-your-head techno and Liam's favourite, Kool Keith of Ultramagnetic MCs speeded up into Pinky and Perky freak-speak. 'Out of Space''s stop-start tempo, its nutty mix of genres, was unlike anything else in the charts. It's still hugely popular with fans.

The Prodigy were having hit after hit; their album, *Experience*, went to Number 12. But Liam, who was, and remains, suspicious of anything too neatly popular, decided that for him, rave was over. At a gig in 1993 in Scotland, he looked at the mashed-up kids having it with glo-sticks and thought, 'This has been and gone, I'm not into it any more.' The Prodigy made a deliberate sideways jump: they changed where they performed, moving out of suburban deely-bopper and Vicks nightclubs into the indie circuit: gig venues, universities, playing alongside guitar bands. Gradually they cultivated another audience.

In 1994 they released *Music for The Jilted Generation*, an epic

double album, featuring Pop Will Eat Itself's Clint Boon on 'Their Law', and a bunch of motorbikes on 'Speedway'. It got them nominated for the Mercury Prize the same year as Pulp (for *His 'n' Hers*), Blur (for *Parklife*) and winners M People (for an album that, in truth, we've all forgotten). It was a low-key favourite everywhere. You'd hear it pumping from the windows of builders' vans; I remember a Young British Artist telling me it was his album of the year.

In 1995, The Prodigy played the *NME* stage at Glastonbury. Pre-*Fat of the Land*, post-*Jilted Generation*, their stage show was a frenzied, frenetic triumph. Keith arrived in a blow-up see-through ball and rolled across the stage; when he emerged, we saw that his long hair had gone, replaced by a spiky pink crop and a look that was a combination of grunge and punk: check shirt, black plastic bondage trousers, eyeliner, sneer. Leeroy wore a loose silver tunic. Maxim had a long coat but mostly had his top off. They looked like characters from a fantasy film, ones with model versions that you'd find in a cornflakes packet or buy in a comic shop, position atop the plastic turrets of a clip-together gothic castle, and from there, send into epic battle. They'd be the ones leading all the anonymous plastic soldiers across the rucked-up rug. (The soldiers being us, the crowd.)

I watched their performance online recently, and they're brilliant, but it looks really strange that Keith doesn't sing at any point. He's so integral to the whole, such a champion of the vibe, it's bizarre that he wasn't even allowed to shout 'Come ONNN' into a microphone. He shouts it anyway.

That same year, Glastonbury introduced a dance tent, headlined by Massive Attack one night, Carl Cox on another, and featuring

DJs as varied as Darren Emerson and David Holmes. Now, we all know dance tents at a festival as a useful shaded place to have a nice sit down out of the sun or rain during the day, and as absolutely radio rental, taps awf, air-horn-blasting, heaving, sweating mayhem at night. But back then, to have a dance tent at all seemed exciting, even though dance music was already moving onto the main stages. Orbital had played the *NME* stage in 1994 and moved to the Pyramid in 1995. Tricky was playing the Jazz World Stage, for some reason. Though Massive Attack played a set rather than just DJ'ing, the Dance Tent wasn't about performance in the same way as the outdoor stages; it was more about the party, the crowd. The roof gave it a specific intensity that seemed almost unbearable when everything else was outside, where you felt your emotions lift off and soar into the sky.

These days, when festivals plonk Fred Again to follow Chvrches it seems strange that during the '90s it was really questioned whether people who made dance music could carry a stage. It wasn't the music – we loved the music – it was the lack of identifiable personalities. How could two anonymous men be our onstage heroes? Now, we're more open-minded. Someone as everyday as Calvin Harris can be massive; Daft Punk can build a huge career with metal helmets on their heads; Marshmello can do the same wearing a bucket with a weird smiley face on. Lynks, one of my favourite new artists, performs mad queer pop anthems in a gimp mask. I have no idea what he looks like. In the early 2000s, Damon Albarn started Gorillaz because he wanted some cartoons to take over the job of being the person that we all watched onstage. Lots of people thought: Why?

The music business was stymied by its history, by what it felt bands were meant to be. The four-white-guys-guitar-bass-maybe-a-keyboard-and-drums was still seen as the right way to go about things, unless you were black or a pop act (but you still had to be able to sing). A lot of the '90s bands fitted into the old style quite easily; some looped back and told the '60s story again. Perhaps it was the last hurrah for such bands. They're still with us, but they're not dominant any more.

Even then, we all knew that hip-hop, acid house and rave had changed everything. Anyone who was on the dancefloor, in an audience, jumping up and down in a field, didn't really care who was delivering the noise. What was that track with that weird noise in it? The one that went whomp whomp?

And yet. Music journalism, music videos and many live performances only come to real life if there's characters in there. Lighting needs someone to focus on; we all enjoy a god or goddess to stare at, to project on, to adore. In the '90s, most dance acts used lasers and cutting-edge visuals to excite, but The Prodigy – like Pulp, like Oasis, like Suede, like Blur, and more than any other dance act – understood that audiences love – need – a star.

When The Prodigy played their first gig at the rough pub in east London, the owner asked them what kind of band they were. They said they wanted to be 'like one of the greats, like The Pistols or The Clash or Pink Floyd'. They loved Nirvana, too. Their years of playing live over and over, of getting the crowd going, comes from raving, but it's also a very traditional way of learning your craft. (It's how The Beatles learnt.) Out of all the huge dance bands of the '90s, only The Prodigy brought in that rock element. And

because they combined that with Keith's almost comical look, they could break America. America likes things big and stupid. 'I have a philosophy that most of our music works on a really dumb level,' said Liam, 'which is the level most people understand.' Most UK bands of the '90s didn't want to be dumb. They wanted to be clever.

In 1997, they brought out *Fat of The Land* on Monday 30 June. It went straight to Number One. Before that, both 'Firestarter' and 'Breathe', which also features Keith on vocals, had gone to Number One. They'd moved into the big league; they'd become a national discussion point, a newspaper scandal. The *Mail on Sunday* had called on someone – who? – to 'Ban this Fire record'. Keith with a microphone was what launched them into superstardom. They needed him as a full-on rock star to really smash through. Keith grabbed the public imagination, got the tabloids frothing, became the instantly recognisable image any school kid could draw on a notebook. If you're a band with a front person that becomes a Halloween costume, you've made it.

They toured like maniacs throughout 1998, and then The Prodigy spent most of 1999 on downtime. They became part of Cool Britannia, that weird, sticky tabloidy era, the bumpy comedown after the Britpop high, when footballers and pop stars and Britpop people and supermodels and DJs all joined in taking drugs and getting smashed at the Met Bar and the Groucho and any launch of a specialist drinks brand or late-night telly show or fashion off-shoot. Out they stumbled into the flashlights of the newspaper cameras. Liam started going out with Natalie from All Saints (they are still partners and have a son), Keith dated Dawn Porter, Leeroy was engaged to Sara Cox for a while.

Back in 1997, The Prodigy played Glastonbury again, their first time as headliners on the main stage. It was three days before they brought out *The Fat of the Land*. There were a few technical problems; I remember three songs in, Dennis Pennis, the in-your-face journalist character played by Paul Kaye, had to come on stage and chat to the audience when something cut out and the band couldn't play for a little while. It was a tense situation; everyone was pissed off. He sang a Hebrew song and won the crowd over.

With friends, I'd pushed my way right into the centre of the crowd. I danced like mad to 'Smack My Bitch Up', to 'Poison' (I love 'Poison'). But around five songs in, I had a funny turn. It was a rainy Glastonbury, and I'd overdone it with the waterproofs, layering up puffa jacket with kagoule, thermals with plastic over-trousers. I'd also, to be honest, overdone it with the chemicals and underdone it with any form of solid food. Suddenly, it was imperative for me to leave. I pushed my way out through the mayhem, pulling off my outer layers as I stumbled through, and spent the second half of The Prodigy set curled up in the foetal position atop my waterproof jacket. It felt like a tiny lifeboat floating on an ocean of mud. I was lost at sea.

I wasn't enjoying myself, clearly; but I sort of was, too. The Prodigy were playing hit after hit and, outside of the intensity of the crowd, the music crashed over me, waves over the side of my anorak raft, as I sipped from a bottle of water and then curled back up again. To others, I looked like yet another Glastonbury casualty, a lightweight paying for their over-excitement by having to make themselves very small among a crowd of 80,000 – which

I was, of course – most of whom seemed to be traipsing past, trying to avoid standing on my head.

But what the barely glancing crowds didn't know was that, like Keith on the Tube, I was giving it AARRRGH within. Like Keith, I was dancing to the music, expressing all my embarrassment and self-loathing in an internal whirl of energy. Head goes thump with the kick drum, heart leaps with the breakbeat. OK, nobody could see it. But despite outside appearances, inside, yes, I was a 'Firestarter'.

Outro

We could leave my younger self there: curled up on a waterproof jacket, adrift in a muddy Somerset field, rained on, bass-battered, incapacitated. But that would be misleading, because, obviously, after a short while, I got up, and continued with my over-waterproofed raving. This isn't hard to do when you're young and your body is built for good times and there are several easily swallowed short-cuts to get to those good times. As far as I recall, I had another excellent Glastonbury. My friend Gavin Hills always used to say about festivals: it's not the drink and drugs that mess you up, it's the not eating and not sleeping. (One of the times when he said this, it was 3 a.m., we were between the *NME* and the Pyramid stages and he was dressed as a crusader, with Dairy Milk smeared on his cheeks as camouflage.) Long term, Gavin was wrong, especially if you look back at your twenties from a way away in the future, from a time when many of your friends have been through terrible addiction problems, and only some have emerged healthy. But back then, he was right, plus why argue with a friendly crusader at 3 a.m.? A timely veggie pasty and a snooze under a trestle-table sorted me right out, and off I lurched into

the night-time fun times. Let the camera zoom out. There I am, bumping about, a small person in too many layers, one among around 90,000.

Zooming out is what this book has helped me to do. When you're busy living your life, right inside what surrounds you, swimming (waving, drowning) within the water that is your environment, you can't assess it very clearly. Your time is taken up with doing: working, partying, travelling, bumping into someone who will utterly change everything and maybe having kids with them. Just keep swimming, as Dory in *Finding Nemo* has it. After all, your past was embarrassing (those bootcut trousers!) and not always happy, and like everyone else lucky enough to live into middle age and beyond, you don't want to be defined by who you used to be.

But as you get older, you feel kinder towards your younger self, and writing this book has made me feel warmer towards the 1990s, and all those who sailed in her. Before I started writing it, I had certain memories and assumptions about that time that were often a bit cynical and dismissive; a fixed attitude partly cemented by other people, some of whom were involved, some of whom weren't. There was a familiar 1990s lore that I'd absorbed and merged with my own experiences, in the manner, I imagine, that people used to do about living through the Blitz, or, you know, going to Shoom. Still, I knew that the clichéd version of that time was wrong – it was weirder than how it's usually portrayed, and more haphazard and accepting of different types of music – and one of the advantages of being a journalist is that you're actually required by your job to write everything down. I was there, and I took notes, and so did a lot of my friends.

What I discovered was that not only the long-established front-page account of that time wasn't right, but what *I'd* assumed or remembered was wrong, too. My own version of the '90s turned out to be flawed. I'd start researching and I'd come across an article of mine that I remembered absolutely nothing about, not even that I'd written it; or I'd find one that I remembered writing, but realised, after reading it, that my memory had it all confused in my head. With Radiohead, for example, I knew I'd interviewed them for some publication, but I couldn't remember where, or when, or for which magazine. It took me a while, but I found the article on a website, when a fan wrote something like, 'God, who would ask Thom such a stupid question?' and I thought, 'Hmm, that sounds like me.' With Noel Gallagher, I'd forgotten much of the detail of where we met, and who else was there, though I remembered what Liam's face was like in the hotel bar, and the furore that Noel's quote caused after the piece came out. I stumbled across an interview I'd done with Justine Frischmann that I couldn't remember anything about, not a thing, other than – suddenly, after reading it – where we'd talked and the doodle she did on a newspaper while she was speaking.

These old pieces sometimes triggered memories (the way the interviewee spoke, how they walked, what they were like when they were drunk), and sometimes they wouldn't trigger anything at all, and I'd have to take them at face value, as though they were written by somebody else. Often, they would reference small events that seemed important at the time (arguments with other bands, usually), but turned out to be trivial, forgotten or changed by time. When I talked to friends about certain bands they'd worked with

or knew personally, they'd tell me funny stories, sometimes about incidents where I was present, and I didn't always remember being there. Occasionally, I knew that I definitely wasn't there. That's why old articles are useful, the diary you never thought you needed.

·Anyway. I wrote and researched this book in a huge frenzy, over a matter of weeks, sitting on the sofa for hours as my family came in and out, typing as if my life depended on it, one cough away from a full-on tsunami of weeping. (That's my 'how to write' webinar: it's short and gives me empathy with musicians who have to explain how they came up with a song, when they just got on and did it.) At the end of this, I had a book and I also realised that there were some themes running through the mid-'90s that I'd forgotten. So here they are.

The very first is that, although we genuinely didn't think this at the time, the music industry around Britpop and other independent music really was a scene. In the way of all scenes, it was populated by people with similar interests and overlapping tastes and kindred desires, who formed little crews that mingled and separated, made other little crews, moved on. People who were flatmates or workmates, who went to the same gigs, or had the same recreational habits, or who fell in love. The bands and the music took place all around us. We were part of a scene, even though we were often at odds with each other, because we were employed by it.

We were all part of a system that was built around the assumption that artists and bands could succeed. That if their records were good, and they were interesting in interviews, then they would be showcased in the media, their music would be heard

and their music would sell – and would sell enough for them to live on. That system had a lot of room for ideas and energy, so that dynamic people could set up gigs, create pop videos, make magazines, stage club nights that worked and got attention. I'm not really talking about the major labels, though there were a few inspiring people who worked there; more the independent labels and the music mags, along with the small PR companies and live agencies, the people who kept having funny ideas and thinking, Let's do that! That was an industry; a smaller one within the grinding global corporations that were and are the music industry proper. And because the gatekeepers above us had changed, there was room, even on TV, for inventive people to let musicians play live, show off and sell themselves to an audience. So yes, it was a scene.

Interestingly, what makes that time look more like a scene are the photographs. The journalism reveals the rivalries. (All artistic scenes have competition as well as friendship within them.) I'd forgotten the extreme intensity of the 1990s conversation about music. The tribes, the stances, the arguments: not just between people who liked acid house and people who preferred indie, not even between Blur and Oasis fans, but tiny strops about a single release or a particular quote in an interview. I wasn't a follower of the inkie press, even then – I liked magazines, and pop music: I was raised by *Smash Hits* – but going through back issues of *NME* and *Melody Maker* I was astonished by just how much the writing felt like an early version of Twitter (X). It was a constant conversation, an ecosystem. So much chatter, arguments, jokes, comebacks. Pages upon pages of it. And because of that, the heat around the

weeklies was very real; both for the musicians that were written about, and for the journalists and PRs. The competition between the papers and between individual journalists was real, too.

The sheer amount of music writing was exhilarating, but its spiky jokes and hot takes could be hugely cruel. I was genuinely shocked at some of the articles: how many jokes were cracked about what people looked like, for instance, some of them by me. And, God, a great deal of the writing about women in bands made me gip. I don't think I'd understood how often women musicians were asked to justify themselves about everything (everything except their music): to have a position on sex, on feminism, on other women, on how they presented themselves, on politics, on what they read or what social class they were or what they knew about older bands. And that was just the interviews. The reviews were often savage, too. For men, a straightforward shoeing; for women, straightforward misogyny. (Such anti-women feeling could, obviously, extend towards women writers. At *Select*, we were lucky to have people – men – in charge who weren't sexist. One writer told me that *Select* saved her when she started writing there after working on the inkies.)

Anyhow, because of all these factors – the scene, the chat, the churn, the spite – there's a mutual understanding between people who were around at that time. (Not all; some personal hatreds still endure.) Especially between women. I didn't know Shirley Manson during the 1990s, or Louise Wener. We never met. But when we talked for this book, it was as though we were old friends. There was something about that time and being a young woman then that united us, as though we'd lived through something. Not a war;

a never-ending assault course, with no certificate or medal at the end. Most of it was fun, but it was relentless, and knackering.

Writing this book also helped me appreciate the toughness of being in a band. Not only did you have to do days and days of press and promotion (in real life, no Zoom), but, in order to succeed, you had to go on tour for months on end. Playing gigs and being good at them is what keeps bands going, and the connection to an audience is a huge part of what music is about. The most successful bands of the 1990s are the ones that continue to play live. But there's a lot of truth in what Cornershop's Tjinder Singh says – that the music industry set-up of album, tour, album, tour, is constructed in a way that breaks the artist. That there's something about the music industry that wants a musician to succeed, and then, repeat the same thing over and over, so that the artist ends up with no agency and their self-respect – their very sense of who they are and what they do – in complete tatters.

A couple of other things. First: I have no doubt that there are mistakes in this book, though I checked everything over and over. Actually, I have a churning feeling in my stomach that I've made at least one enormous blunder, an absolute massive howler, something along the lines of Liam and Noel not actually being related, or Britpop never being used in any article ever. What's more likely is that I've got little details wrong. Not so much chart positions, as you can check those online, but other particulars. It's just the way of things: other people were there, and they might have better memories, or know opposing facts, have cleverer insights, their own ways of looking at those times.

Also, yes, I know the list of songs could have been different. I

could have chosen 'Live Forever' or 'Animal Nitrate' or 'Car Song'. I also could have chosen different bands. I've no doubt that there are those that you would like to be there that aren't. Me too. There were bands that I wanted to include, but they didn't quite work (The Auteurs, Longpigs, Super Furry Animals). There were others that my publishers liked that I refused to write about. Here are some alternatives to the final mixtape: Bomb the Bass, 'Bug Powder Dust'; Portishead, 'Sour Times'; Massive Attack, 'Protection'; Teenage Fanclub, 'Sparky's Dream'; Lush, 'Ladykillers'; Orbital, 'Chime'; Paul Weller, 'Wild Wood'; Saint Etienne, 'Nothing Can Stop Us'; Leftfield, 'Open Up'. I'm sure you have others.

Aside from all of this, the absolutely overriding feeling that I have from writing this book is a towering admiration for every single musician in it. Their stories are all different, as is their art; but they share a resilience and bloody-mindedness, an ability to be themselves in a time when the media – not just the music papers, but also the far-scarier tabloids and telly – had a huge and belittling power that is barely imaginable now. Once you were deemed famous, you were shoved into a world that seemed to actively hate you, even as you were celebrated. But these artists continued, with their loopy desire to create, but also to be seen. To be witnessed in all their authentic weirdness, their particular beauty, designed by them, as opposed to stylists and photographers and trend-spotters. Not airbrushed or shoulder-padded or blow-dried. That had a magic then, and it still does now.

I have a theory that it was the music scene in the 1990s that ruined the specialness of pop, by banging on about how important it was. We told everyone that music was vital, an essential part

of life, and this was taken on, by brands and ad agencies, by establishment corporations, including the royal family. We didn't understand that the system was about to collapse. The 1990s music industry, major and indie, had money swirling through it, as record companies made millions from CDs, but by the end of the decade, Napster had arrived, the first person-to-person music-sharing source. We had no idea what was coming. Now, because of the internet, music is like air, or water: everyone wants access to it all the time and doesn't think they should pay for it. The assumption is that the internet has meant the devaluation of music, but I think it's the opposite. We banged on so much about music that everyone was convinced. Music is valued so highly now that it's deemed essential, a life necessity that should be on tap. You don't get water from a well any more; you don't traipse across town to get music. Music is no longer a privilege, it's a right.

And, well . . . yes. Imagine living your life without music. The river of it, how it connects to a single moment, how it spills into your future. How it tells your story, and other people's too. What a thing to create a pop song that lasts. What a talent to have. Most of us owe a vital part of our lived lives to people who make music – maybe to the people who made the music in this book – whether those people gave up completely after one album and moved on, or kept going, or stop-started, came back later. Their music continues, even when some of them couldn't carry on themselves. We should celebrate all those uncommon people that did.

Acknowledgements

Thank you to everyone who talked to me about music and the mid-'90s, especially Johnny Hopkins, Simon Price, Gillian Porter, Martin Green, John Best, Chris Floyd, Louise Wener, Shirley Manson, Gina Morris, Paul Tipler, Eamonn Forde, Tjinder Singh, Irvine Welsh,* Steven Hall, Robin Turner, Edwyn Collins, Grace Campbell. Thanks for the memories, because mine were hazy. Also: Shirley, your interview gave me the steer for the book, and Louise, yours gave everything a kick up the bum.

Special thanks to '90s queen Polly Birkbeck and her unbelievable recall: the 30TB hard-drive back-up that Britpop never knew it needed. We all think you should write a memoir, Polly.

Extra-special thanks to Andrew Harrison, steel-trap nerd mind and exemplary editor of *Select* in the mid-'90s. I wouldn't have a career without you! Thanks for reading the manuscript and pointing out mistakes without making me feel like an idiot, and

---

* Irvine wrote the novel *Trainspotting*, which included Renton's 'Choose life' rant, which Danny Boyle then put into the film and I then put it into the Underworld chapter.

thanks for still putting up with my stroppy nonsense today, as my boss at Podmasters.

Thank you to Georgina Laycock, who dragged this book out of me in four months flat with a devastating combination of unrelenting optimism and hardcore deadlines. This book would not exist without you.

Thanks also to Lauren Howard and Charlotte Hutchinson. Thanks to Caroline Westmore, for being an all-round editing don. Design supremo Sara Marafini created the perfect tape cover, thank you! The brilliant Edd Westmacott took the full-of-joy photo. Thank you to Paul Mottram, who once performed at Smashing in a former life, for the legal advice, and to Dave Watkins for impeccable copy-editing and expert grebo suggestions.

Thanks to Kirsty McLachlan, excellent agent who knows when to step in, and when to leave well alone, and who is always, always supportive and kind.

Thanks to everyone at Paper Cuts podcast, especially Liam Tait, Adam Wright and Gráinne Maguire, who were unstintingly positive about me writing this book, even when I was clearly losing my marbles. Gráinne, your pep talks on the Victoria Line kept me going for days.

Thanks to Sarah Donaldson and Jane Ferguson at the *Observer*'s *New Review*, for constant support and for building me a bridge to get over myself. Thanks to Jude Rogers for covering my column so brilliantly.

Thanks to Jax Coombes at 6 Music, superb producer of *Sound and Vision* and of a documentary I made about Britpop around ten years ago, and who knew where to find the interviews.

Acknowledgements

Thanks to Rocks Backpages for reminding me of just how vital and important the music press was in the 1990s, and special thanks to all the fantastic journalists who were writing back then, especially Sylvia Patterson, Siân Pattenden, Barbara Ellen, Mary Anne Hobbs, Caitlin Moran, Lucy O'Brien, Sheryl Garratt, Jon Savage, Sean O'Hagan, Pete Paphides, John Robb, Bob Stanley, John Harris, Andrew Harrison, David Quantick, Andrew Perry, Adam Higginbotham, Andrew Collins, Stuart Maconie, Tom Doyle, Andrew Smith, James Brown, Steve Lamacq, Clark Collis.

Thanks to Allie Dickinson, not only for transcribing my interviews, but also for encyclopaedic knowledge of the '90s music scene.

It's always good to remember the life-lighting talents who are no longer around: Keith Flint, Steve Mackey, Andy Ross, Andrew Weatherall, Gavin Hills, Dave Cavanagh, Dele Fadele, Steven Wells, Gavin Martin, Richey Edwards, Philip Hall, Mary Hansen.

Big love and thanks to Marina Gask and Chilli dog for the walks, and to Amanda Freeman, Lulu Le Vay and Louise McKinney for always being there even when I can't go out. And to Sonia Harris, for the Primavera fun times

All my love to my mum and dad, and Toby and Jonathon, who held things together when I had no weekends off. Love love love to Merrilees, to Dylan, Bhavni and Aidan, to Jasmine and Maddie.

To Paddy and Frankie, lights of my life, who don't care at all about the 1990s, I love you.

And to Smiley, who listened to me ranting on and on about music, and who will never read a word of this book, I love you.

Further Reading

There are some fantastic books out there: my particular favourites are *Just For One Day: Adventures in Britpop* by Louise Wener; *Bad Vibes* by Luke Haines; *Everything: A Book About Manic Street Preachers* by Simon Price; *All That Glitters* by Pearl Lowe; *Hell is Round the Corner* by Tricky with Andrew Perry; *This is the Noise That Keeps Me Awake* by Garbage and Jason Cohen; and Brett Anderson's excellent memoirs, *Coal Black Mornings* and *Afternoons with the Blinds Drawn*.

If you're looking for a more general Britpop book, read John Harris's classic *The Last Party* and Daniel Rachel's *Don't Look Back in Anger*.

Index

All songs by the twenty bands covered in this book are listed
under the entries for the bands.

Index

Index

Index

Index

Index